LIGHT FORCE

Also by Brother Andrew

God's Smuggler (with John and Elizabeth Sherrill)

LIGHT FORCE

THE ONLY HOPE FOR THE MIDDLE EAST

Brother Andrew

and Al Janssen

HODDER &
STOUGHTON

First published in Great Britain in 2004
This edition first published in 2005
Reprinted in 2008

The right of Brother Andrew and Al Janssen to be identified
as the Author of the Work has been asserted by them in accordance
with the Copyright, Designs and Patents Act 1988.

3

British Library Cataloguing in Publication Data
A record for this book is available from the British Library

ISBN 978 0 340 96491 0

Typeset in AGaramond by Avon DataSet Ltd,
Bidford-on-Avon, Warwickshire

Printed and bound in Great Britain by
Clays Ltd, St Ives plc

The paper and board used in this paperback are natural
recyclable products made from wood grown in sustainable forests.
The manufacturing processes conform to the environmental
regulations of the country of origin.

Hodder & Stoughton
A Division of Hachette Livre UK Ltd
338 Euston Road
London NW1 3BH
www.hodderfaith.com

CONTENTS

Part 3 West Bank and Gaza: Who Reaches the Terrorists?

Part 4 The Second Intifada: A Religious Uprising

INTRODUCTION

THE BOOK YOU ARE holding will be considered by some as controversial. That is even true within Open Doors, the ministry founded by Brother Andrew in 1955 when he travelled to Poland and saw the struggles of the Church under communism.

For those of you who are not familiar with Open Doors, we exist to strengthen and equip the Church living under or facing restriction and persecution because of their faith in Jesus Christ. To do that, we provide Bibles and other literature for persecuted Christians who otherwise could not obtain them. In 2003 we delivered nearly four million Bibles, children's Bibles, study Bibles and other scriptural books to churches in Asia, Latin America, Africa, and throughout the Muslim world. In addition, we trained twenty-two thousand pastors and church leaders in how to lead their congregations and stand strong in their faith in the midst of persecution and discrimination.

In the late 1960s, when the visibility of Brother Andrew's best-selling book *God's Smuggler* prevented him from personally returning to the Soviet Union and Eastern Europe, one of the places he felt led to visit was the Middle East. What he saw troubled him. More and more he began to speak out about the region and particularly about the rise of Muslim fanaticism, which has had a dramatic impact on the Church in the region. He felt it was critical to do whatever he could to help strengthen the Church so it could be a light in the midst of the unending conflict.

More radically, Brother Andrew also set out to reach Israel's enemies with the gospel of Jesus Christ. Sometimes he did this with words, sometimes by showing Christian love and compassion. In the process, he challenged the thinking of the local Church.

When I was appointed president of Open Doors in 1995, it freed Brother Andrew to concentrate on this region. This book describes his pilgrimage. It does not seek to be political or take sides, even though a lot of attention is given to the suffering of the dwindling community of Christians among the Palestinian population.

It is important to note that committed Christians disagree on many theological issues, such as speaking in tongues or eternal security or prophecy. The issues of Israel and the land can be among the most divisive. We've wrestled with this within Open Doors, and we have staff members who stand on both sides of the issues. Still, we love each other and work together because we share a higher call to the Church of Jesus Christ.

It is my prayer that this book will stir the body of Christ around the world to more compassion and prayer for this difficult part of the world. The closer we come to the return of Jesus Christ the more we need to stand united. Both Jewish believers in the Messiah and their Arab and Palestinian brothers and sisters living in the land need our prayers and support. May this book show the way to what I believe is the only hope for peace in the Middle East – shining the light of Jesus Christ into the darkness of this terrible conflict.

Johan Companjen, President of Open Doors

STRENGTHEN
WHAT REMAINS

A TWISTED, BLACKENED SKELETON OF steel smoulders in the middle of a Jerusalem street. Sirens scream. Onlookers weep. The announcer reports that a suicide bomber has struck again in a crowded bus.

How many times have we seen such images of terror? Have we become immune to such news? It has been going on for years, and yet we know it's not over. There will be retaliation. People will die. There will be another attack. More people will die.

Will this cycle of violence never end?

And what does this mean for us?

THE HORROR

Jerusalem, 4 September 1997

Karen Alan had finished her errands and was returning to work at the second-floor office of a building on Ben Yehuda Street. The pedestrian mall was lined with cafes and shops. Local Jerusalem residents and tourists strolled along the cobblestone street and sat at outdoor tables enjoying coffee and the people show. For foreign visitors this was a favourite destination after seeing the Old City, less than a mile east on Jaffa Road. Here tourists shopped for menorahs, mezuzahs, and embroidered yarmulkes or, for more discerning tastes, original Jewish jewellery, art, and pottery.

Within this vibrant section of West Jerusalem sat King of Kings College.[1] Just one month before, Karen had started working there as an editor and translator. She hurried up the stairs after lunch, eager to get back to work.

As Karen entered the office and set her purse on her desk, an explosion nearly knocked her off her feet. She grabbed her desk to steady herself. Almost instantly there was a second explosion, then a third even more powerful blast rocked the building.

For a moment Karen's ears rang. She braced herself for another blast. Then she heard office mates yelling. *Oh, my God, this can't be happening,* she thought. She turned and hurried with several others into an office with a window overlooking the street. As she peered out to see what had happened, she could hear shouts and screams rising from the pavement. The sight was horrifying. Bodies, both conscious and unconscious, every one covered with blood, lay in the street and on the sidewalks. One of the victims struggled to his feet and staggered blindly, blood flowing over his eyes from a gash in his head. A few witnesses stood frozen. Others were running frantically.

Karen's mind could barely process all the sensory information. Her eyes moved towards one spot where she could see the bloody legs of one of the bombers. His torso had been blown apart in the blast. She became aware of sounds. Car and store alarms screamed. A mobile phone rang, unanswered. Ambulance and police sirens announced their arrival. Dust along with the smell of explosives and burned flesh chafed her nasal passages and caused her eyes to water. The first paramedics did triage until additional help arrived. Orders were shouted. Police began corralling the crowd.

Suddenly, Karen remembered her friend Shiri, who should have been returning to her office next door. Where was she? She walked back to her desk and dialled her friend's mobile number, but there was no answer. Impulsively she hurried down the stairs and moved through horrified spectators in the lobby to the main entrance, but a policeman stopped her. A body lay right outside the door. 'No one can leave,' said the officer.

In a daze Karen climbed back up the stairs to her office. Again she dialled her friend's number, but there was no answer. Fear nearly choked her as she tried to think. All she could manage was a prayer, asking for her friend's safety. *Lord, may Shiri not be one of those bodies lying in the street.*

Everyone in the office had congregated at the windows to watch the macabre scene. Several right-wing activists had arrived from somewhere and were just outside the police line chanting, 'Death to the Arabs!' She noticed that all of the windows surrounding the mall were shattered, except for those in her office. *How many people,* she wondered, *had been hurt by flying glass?*

Karen became aware that she was shivering. Obviously she couldn't work, but she needed to do something. Every few minutes she called her friend's mobile number. Each time there was no answer. *Where are the nearest hospitals?* She grabbed a phone book and started calling hospitals. None of them had a record of her friend having been admitted. Looking again out the window, she began thinking the worst: *What will I do if one of those scorched bodies is hers? Am I ready for the worst kind of news? No way!* She felt panic rising within her. With all her will, she pushed it down.

Harderwijk, The Netherlands

After watching the evening news, I paced my office, praying for the victims of yet another terrorist attack in Israel. I reminded myself that for every person who died, there were parents, siblings, and friends in mourning. For every injured person, there was a family gathered around a hospital bed weeping and praying. For the witnesses, there were nightmares and the fear that never seems to go away. The people of Israel were reeling from the horrors that have struck them over the last several years.

For years I'd been travelling to the Middle East, visiting churches in Lebanon, Israel, West Bank, and Gaza. Whenever I heard about another attack, I wondered if any believers were caught in it. Christians are not immune from such horrors, of course. The Church cannot avoid the dangers of the society in which it exists, but I wondered how Christians were coping with the physical and emotional trauma.

I recalled another terrifying incident in August 1968, when Czechoslovakia was invaded by the Soviet army. I wondered how the invasion would affect the Church, so I loaded my Citroen station wagon with Russian Bibles and Christian literature and drove all day from Holland to the Czech border. There I met a long stream of cars leaving the country. Thousands of people were fleeing the Soviet army. I was the only person going into Czechoslovakia. Even though I didn't have a visa, the border guard admitted me into the country, and that next Sunday I preached in Prague.[2]

I was about to turn seventy years old. People were suggesting that I should retire. Travelling into combat zones was for young people. But how could I retire when my brothers and sisters were hurting and there was a chance that I could help? Many wanted to run away from the conflict in Israel. I wanted to run *to* it.

Jerusalem

It was after dark when Karen reached home and buried herself in her parents' arms. Television news was on in the living room. For a few minutes she watched the reports, unable to believe that she had been there and had narrowly escaped with her life. The facts hammered themselves into her consciousness. Three bombs had exploded in the crowded pedestrian mall in West Jerusalem. At least 7 people were dead and 192 injured, mostly due to thousands of nails packed in the explosives. Reporters agreed that this had been a particularly vicious attack.

A few minutes later the phone rang. Her father answered, then handed her the receiver. 'It's Shiri!'

'Thank God!' was all Karen could say for a moment. Through her tears, she finally said, 'I was so afraid you were out there . . .'

'I was at the post office, just a few hundred yards away,' Shiri explained. 'I didn't try to go back to the office; I just came home.'

It was a short conversation. What a relief and joy to know that her friend was safe! But then Karen felt weak. She turned off the television and slumped into an overstuffed chair. *How can I rejoice when so many others are mourning?* The initial shock of the horror was wearing off, and now the feelings and questions began to erupt. She spoke some of her thoughts aloud to her parents: 'How could these men be driven by such hate? And why?' She looked into her mother's eyes. 'Just two minutes earlier and I would have been in that mall. Why did God spare me?'

She barely slept that night. Trying to force the horrible images from her mind, she made herself focus on any Bible verses she could recall. From Ephesians 6:12, she recited, 'For our struggle is not against flesh and blood.' Today she had seen real flesh-and-blood casualties in the seemingly never-ending war between Palestinians and Israelis. With real bodies lying on the stone pavement, it was hard to think that this was foremost a spiritual battle. But her faith told her this was a war she couldn't fight physically. She had to allow God to fight it. Her part was to pray and love and embrace everyone, just as God did her. Did she believe that?

Karen thought about how much she loved her country. Born and raised in Jerusalem, she felt privileged to live in Israel and completely at home within Jewish society. What made her different from most citizens was that her family was Christian. Most people around her were culturally Jewish and religiously secular.

Her parents had taught her to be accepting of everyone, and though she lived in Israel, she had often crossed into Bethlehem and interacted with Palestinians. That had motivated her to take Arabic courses in high school, followed by a year studying the language in Jordan. Then about six months ago, she had participated in a desert encounter designed to build bridges between Messianic believers[3] and Palestinian Christians. It was sponsored by Musalaha, an organisation that promotes biblical reconciliation. Karen had enjoyed the opportunity to use her Arabic and develop new relationships with Palestinians. Clearly, not all of them were filled with hate; her Arab friends were compassionate and open to the 'other side'. Today's events could not be allowed to undermine her faith or her relationships. She would not allow it!

Again she asked, 'Why, Lord, did You spare me?' She tried to still her mind, but the prayer continued: 'Would it not have been better for You to take me in place of someone who did not know You?' In the early morning hours, tears flowed freely. Karen knew there were no answers to her questions. 'Lord, please allow me to see this situation with Your eyes.' Somehow she and the Christians around her at church and the Bible College had to be living examples of God's grace towards humankind. That wouldn't be easy, but, really, was there any other choice?

Harderwijk, The Netherlands

One question particularly troubled me after each suicide bombing, one I'd been asking for years: *Did anyone present Jesus to that young person who blew himself up?* Who was going to the terrorists? Was anyone prepared to confront them and give them a reason to live that was greater than their motivation to die? How can they know about the Prince of Peace if no one goes and tells them?

But are Muslim fundamentalists who are committed to the destruction of Israel really willing to listen to the gospel?

How can we know if we don't go, if we don't try?

NOT A MINDLESS
TERRORIST

Gaza, 9 June 2001

Gaza City was a dreary place. In every direction, one could see grey cinder block buildings, most without any architectural embellishments. Half a million people were crammed into apartments, and the only way for most families to expand was to build up, by adding another floor. But extreme poverty, caused by nearly 70 per cent unemployment, showed in the skeletons of unfinished floors atop many homes.

Apart from the main thoroughfares, many of the streets consisted of packed dirt. Donkey carts and speeding taxis kicked up a film of dust that covered people's shoes wherever they walked. There were virtually no parks, few trees, and no playgrounds. Kids, barefoot or wearing worn-out trainers, played in the streets. Occasionally there was a small, rusty Ferris wheel on a side road. Usually an older brother or uncle turned it by hand as two and sometimes more children filled each of the three wooden seats on the rickety structure.

For years, many residents have called the Gaza Strip the world's largest prison. Since the start of the second intifada[1] in September 2000, virtually no one has been allowed to leave.

The Marna House, an old stately mansion, provided a refreshing retreat from the ubiquitous dust, as well as from the poverty and bitterness of the population. A gentle evening breeze blew off the Mediterranean Sea, just a few blocks to the west, rustling the branches of palm trees inside the walled compound. Narrow dirt paths wound through a garden filled with blooming flowers. A woodpecker tapped loudly near the top of one of the trees, then flew over us with a nut in its mouth. Besides our little team, there was only one other group staying at the stately hotel – a crew from the BBC. Their armour-plated jeep, painted in blue and white and clearly identifying itself as belonging to the press, was parked in the driveway.

A huge, ancient locust tree provided shade over the patio where we waited to meet with Abdul, a representative of Islamic Jihad. He arrived precisely at 7.00 and walked briskly up the brick walkway, wearing a plain white caftan and sandals with no socks. His grey hair was thinning on top. Much of his bristly beard was white. Deep wrinkles framed his dark eyes. As we shook hands, those eyes stared intently into mine as though trying to peer into my soul. I introduced him to my friends – Al, a writer from America, and a pastor from Bethlehem, who served as our interpreter.

'Thank you for coming,' I said as we sat on the plastic patio chairs. Abdul nodded to indicate I should quickly state my intentions. 'I want to arrange a meeting with your boss,' I said, referring to Sheikh Abdullah Shami, the leader of Islamic Jihad in Gaza. I mentioned a mutual friend who had connections with Hamas. 'I have got to know several of the leaders of Hamas, and we have talked openly about Islam and Christianity. I was hoping that I might establish a similar dialogue with Islamic Jihad.'

'Who do you know in Hamas?' Abdul asked.

'I have met with Sheikh Yassin [the founder and spiritual leader of Hamas], Dr Abdulaziz Rantisi, Mahmoud Zahar, and many others.'

'What do you wish to discuss?' His piercing gaze was unrelenting.

'I represent Christians in Holland and the West. I want to have an exchange of perspectives on faith – Islam and Christianity. I would also like to know his thoughts about the Palestinian situation and about the future for peace.'

Abdul thought for a moment, then reached into his caftan and pulled out a mobile phone. He speed dialled a number and talked for a couple of minutes.

While we waited, I thought about the risks involved in meeting with Sheikh al-Shami. I realised that Islamic Jihad, like Hamas, was a sworn enemy of Israel. I was well aware of the terrible acts for which they claimed responsibility. More than once I'd been accused of being anti-Israel because I had befriended her terrorist enemies. My defence was simple: 'The best way I can help Israel is by leading her enemies to Jesus Christ.' My purpose was to introduce them to the Prince of Peace, the only One who could cure the rage in their hearts.

How could they possibly meet Jesus Christ if someone in whom He dwells didn't go to them? Perhaps through my actions I could, in some small way, bridge the gaping chasm between Israel and the Palestinians and between Christians and Muslims.

So would the leader of Islamic Jihad meet with me? Abdul flipped his phone shut and announced, 'He will see you tomorrow afternoon. I will pick you up at 3.00.'

'Thank you. May my two friends come as well?'

'Of course.' Abdul seemed to relax, his official duties fulfilled. He leaned back, pulled out a pack of cigarettes, removed one, and tapped it on the table between us as he said, 'Now I would like to ask you some questions.'

'What sort of questions?' I asked.

'About Christianity and the Bible,' he replied. 'I have spent nineteen years in prison. I was first arrested in 1971. I was freed in 1985 as part of a prisoner exchange. I was arrested again in 1988 and several more times since. When you spend that much time in prison, you have a lot of time to think.'

I wondered if Abdul had been imprisoned for terrorist activities. Or was he kept in administrative detention, as I knew thousands of Palestinians were? Regardless, prisoners had little physical activity, which, unless they determined to use their time productively, provided opportunity for their hatred to fester and grow.

Abdul leaned forward to say, 'You talk about the future of peace. The solution is Islam! I reached that conclusion in prison.'

He leaned back, lit his cigarette, and added, 'I read the Bible in prison. I also read the Quran and that's when I decided to become a Muslim.'

'You were not a Muslim already?'

'Culturally, I was a Muslim. Not intellectually. However, I have questions about the Bible and Christianity, and maybe you can answer them.'

I opened my hands on the table, inviting him to ask whatever he wished.

He didn't ask anything at first but rather launched into a passionate speech. 'Most people don't understand Islamic Jihad. We're not at all how the media represent us. What we're dealing with is a lot like what Jesus faced.' I must have registered surprise because he quickly added. 'That's right. We revere Jesus. He was a great prophet. But the Jews didn't listen to Him. Jesus symbolised for us our struggles. When I read the *Injil*,[2] I identified with Jesus. My problem is with the Old Testament. For example, in the book of Joshua, how could God order the Jews to go into Jericho and kill every living person, including women and children and all the animals? And yet we are condemned if one of our people, fighting for our land that was *taken* from us, kills a few civilians. Can you explain to me the difference?'

My friends and I were surprised by the intensity of Abdul's words. More calmly than I felt, I tried to answer his question. 'You have to understand the context,' I explained, choosing my words carefully. 'The people living in the land then were idol worshippers who practised child sacrifice among their many wicked acts. God gave them four hundred years to change their ways. When they didn't, being God, He had the right to wipe them out and replace them with the people of His choosing.'

'But that is not the situation today,' Abdul said. 'We are not pagans.'

'You are correct that this is not the same situation. The orders God gave Joshua were unique.'

Abdul crushed the remainder of his cigarette and lit another. 'Maybe you can explain this to me. Why do the Christian Zionists support Israel so strongly? I would like to understand.'

'You ask me hard questions!' I laughed and for the first time Abdul smiled for an instant. 'Let me first say that not all Christians are Zionists. There are two factors at work for many Christians. One is guilt.' Here I briefly explained how, for the most part, the Church in the West didn't rise up and protest the killing of Jews during the Holocaust. 'After the war, many Christians believed that it was necessary to give the Jews a place of their own so that they would no longer be at the mercy of a ruthless tyrant like Hitler.

'The second factor concerns theology. There are many Christians who believe that God is preparing the world for the end times and that the nation of Israel is the fulfilment of many prophecies. They conclude that if they don't support Israel, they are resisting God's plans.'

'I have heard that in the book of Zechariah the last two chapters are being fulfilled today. Do you believe that?'

Obviously Abdul had read the Minor Prophets. 'Now you ask me to explain one of the toughest passages in the Bible. Those chapters are indeed about the last days. We believe that Jesus will rule over all the earth, as it says in Zechariah 14:9. I don't need to remind you that Muslims believe this as well. But whether the present state of Israel is referenced in these verses, well, Christians do not agree on that.'

Abdul considered my words. For a moment, I almost felt that I was in a Bible study with an eager and serious university student. This man's interest in the Bible seemed genuine. Finally, he said, 'I do not believe the prophet is talking about *this* Israel.' Then he added a twist. 'If I believed the Old Testament, then I'd be a settler.' I was surprised by the passion of his statement – similar to the fervour I found in many Jewish settlers in West Bank and Gaza. Abdul stood, preparing to leave. 'You know all we want is peace!'

I stood with him and asked, 'Do you really believe the ways of Islamic Jihad will produce peace?'

Abdul shrugged. '*Inshallah*. With help from Allah.' It was a typical Arab response, invoking the name of God when he didn't really want to answer the question.

I let it pass, saying, 'I have a gift for you.' I pulled a book out of my satchel. 'I do believe there is hope for real peace, but it is not found in terrorist methods. Real peace is found through the person of Jesus whom you so admire. I'd like you to have this book.' I handed him a copy of my book *God's Smuggler* in Arabic, saying, 'This will tell you more about me and what I do. It may also help you better understand Christianity.'

He accepted the book with a curt nod, saying, 'I will read it.' Then he quickly walked away.

Al and the Palestinian pastor sat in stunned silence. Finally, Al commented that he was amazed at the man's openness.

'Why?' I asked.

'He's a thinker. He seems to be genuinely searching.'

'You are surprised that he is a human being like you and me? Perhaps it is easier to think of him as a mindless terrorist. That will do nothing to help solve the problems of the Middle East.'[3]

Later as I lay on my bed, a ceiling fan trying listlessly to move the hot, humid air in my stuffy room, I thought about how Al's response was typical of many Western Christians. The news media rarely put a face on Islamic fundamentalist groups in Gaza and West Bank. Therefore few people stopped to think that these men, like people everywhere, had families, dreams, and fears. Abdul was married, and he'd told us that he had seven young children. I could imagine him at home, sitting on his sofa with a toddler snuggled up to him on each side. This wasn't how most of us chose to think of a senior member of Islamic Jihad. I wondered how many of his colleagues were also struggling to figure out the meaning of life. For many, their only source of enlightenment was Islam.

I thought about my calling in life, how God had reached out and touched me as an angry, frustrated young soldier laid up in a hospital. How had I reached this point of interacting with some of the most feared Islamic organisations in the world? It certainly had been a strange and unexpected journey. Unable to sleep, my mind drifted back more than thirty years to my first trip to the Holy Land.

WHERE WAS THE CHURCH?

Jerusalem, 1968

This was supposed to be a vacation. During the past twelve months I had been busy promoting my first book, *God's Smuggler*, which surprised me by becoming a best-seller. The book told about my work taking Bibles behind the Iron Curtain. The message and high profile of that book prevented me from returning to Eastern Europe and the Soviet Union because I could not risk endangering my friends there. However, the Open Doors teams kept busy packing vans and trucks, transporting Bibles and other desperately needed resources to Czechoslovakia, Poland, Romania, and the Soviet Union. Because of my book, the ministry had dramatically increased, leaving me exhausted. Family and friends urged me to get away for a rest. I chose as my destination Israel, where my Lord was born and lived and died for me.

Thus far the trip had invigorated my spirit. I had driven up and down the country, staying at kibbutzim,[1] walking the beach along the Mediterranean, and enjoying the rugged beauty and silence of the Negev desert. Occasionally I saw burned-out trucks, evidence of the war a year earlier when Syria, Jordan, and Egypt attacked Israel. Briefly I had considered volunteering for the Israeli army to help defend this land – in a non-combatant role, such as a driver – but the war had ended in just six remarkable days. When the

17

dust had settled, Israel had conquered the Golan Heights, West Bank, East Jerusalem, and Gaza. I was fascinated by the resourcefulness and resilience of this twenty-year-old nation. Truly its existence was a miracle.

Now, with my trip nearing its conclusion, I visited Yad Vashem, the Holocaust museum in Jerusalem. Strolling through the dark halls, I studied artefacts and large black-and-white photographs documenting the systematic destruction of six million Jews. The images were haunting, particularly those of children. One showed a boy, about eight years old, in the Warsaw ghetto. He was wearing shorts, overcoat, and a snap-brim cap, and he had his hands raised because a Nazi soldier behind him was pointing a gun at him. Another image showed half a dozen children, including a little girl wringing her hands, her sad eyes glancing away from the camera. The caption reported they were being transported to the gas chambers at Auschwitz.

I fought back tears. We *had* to remember. We *had* to learn the lessons of history. In the late fifties I had seen Auschwitz, Buchenwald, and Dachau, where many Dutch Jews and resisters were sent. I had visited Auschwitz with my friend and mentor Sidney Wilson – he'd been imprisoned for five long years in a nearby detention camp with other foreign missionaries who had served in Western Europe until the outbreak of war. As we were leaving Auschwitz, we were asked to sign a guest book. Sidney wrote in it, 'This shows how far man can go if he lives without God in this world.'

Had we learned that crucial lesson of the twentieth century, that life without God leads only to unspeakable evil?

As I left the museum, I stopped at the Hall of Remembrance, a cavernous stone room where, imbedded in the floor, were the names of twenty-two concentration camps. An eternal flame cast an eerie light over the names. 'So that we may never forget', said the words on the wall above the flame. I couldn't help but think of another declaration: 'The light shines in the darkness, but the darkness has not understood it' (John 1:5).

My mind churned as I walked from the darkness of the museum into the bright sunshine. I strolled towards a grove of olive trees that made up the Avenue of the Righteous among the Nations. At the base of every tree was a small plaque bearing the name of a

Gentile who saved Jews, often at the cost of his or her own life. I found the tree dedicated to Corrie ten Boom – planted earlier that year – and breathed a prayer of thanks for my dear friend, who with her family had hidden many Jews in their four-storey home in Haarlem. Her father had died in prison shortly after they were arrested. Corrie and her sister, Betsie, were sent to Ravensbruck, where they boldly comforted their fellow inmates with words from a Bible they managed to smuggle past the guards. Betsie died in the camp, but Corrie survived and was telling her story around the world. The ten Boom family had certainly been a light in the midst of the darkness.

But the ten Booms' light seemed so little! There were too few candles for so great a darkness. I found a bench and sat to reflect. These trees represented many Christians, but they were only a few hundred among the millions of Christians throughout Germany and Europe. *Why didn't the Church rise up in protest? Didn't it know what was happening?*

Of course it knew! I thought of Pastor Paul Schneider. In 1938 he'd been arrested and sent to Buchenwald, where he caused a constant disturbance with his bold preaching and verbal attacks against the Nazi regime. He was placed in an isolation/torture cell because he wouldn't keep quiet. On Easter Sunday, his mighty voice thundered through his cell bars, 'Thus speaks the Lord: I am the resurrection and the life!' Thousands of people standing outdoors in long rows thought they had heard a voice from another world, like that of the prophet John the Baptist. The voice was silenced when S.S. guards stormed into his cell and beat him to death. When they carried his body out, there was not a bone unbroken. One Communist prisoner commented, 'We wouldn't need socialism and we wouldn't need communism if we had more people like Paul Schneider.'

Hundreds of pastors attended Schneider's funeral.[2] The story of his boldness was a shout throughout the Church. But clearly it had not been enough to rouse many Christians – not enough of them protested what was happening to the Jews; not enough Jews were saved. During these years, darkness overwhelmed the light.

Or did it? Can darkness ever defeat light? The light can grow dim and even be snuffed out but never by darkness. Light *always* conquers darkness. But if there is no light . . . That was the struggle I sensed in my spirit. All over the world there were conflicts, and in their midst churches existed – some were barely surviving, but others were trying to light candles to conquer the darkness around them.

I thought of the dramatic day in Warsaw when thousands of young Communists had marched past the park where I sat. I opened my Bible to the same passage that had captured my heart in 1955, Revelation 3:2: 'Wake up! Strengthen what remains and is about to die.' In Poland I knew that God was speaking to me, but I had no money and no idea about how to proceed. Miraculously, soon after that experience, I made another trip, this time to Czechoslovakia. Living by faith for all of my resources, I spent the next twelve years visiting churches in the Communist world. In most Communist countries, the Church was oppressed because it was perceived as a threat to the evil powers that dominated those countries. I learned the Church's needs and did whatever I could to help strengthen her members so that the Church could be what God intended her to be – a light in the midst of the Communist darkness.

I had assumed this part of the world would be where I would work for the rest of my life, but now in 1968 the door was closed for me to return to those countries. So what should I do? I looked again at the passage in Revelation. It was Christ's message to the church in Sardis, one of seven messages to seven churches in chapters 2 and 3.

I read through all seven messages. Two points jumped out at me – they were in all seven of God's messages to the churches. The first was 'He who has an ear, let him hear what the Spirit says to the churches.' Did God have our ears, or was it easier to give only our hearts to Jesus? This was important. God had a message for each of the seven churches in Asia Minor. Did He also have a message for churches today? If so, what was He saying to the Church in Israel and the Middle East?

The second statement sent a shiver down my spine. 'To him who overcomes . . .' I couldn't help wondering, *What about the church that* doesn't *overcome?* Clearly the implication was that individual churches could die. In fact most of the seven churches addressed in Revelation no longer existed.

So what was God saying to me? There was work for me to do here, but what was that work? I was excited about Israel, her miraculous existence, her dramatic victory in the Six Day War. But her enemies remained; her security was not assured. And in her midst, there was a Church – the body of Christ, whom He called His Bride. What was her condition? What role was she to play in this young nation?

During this vacation, I'd seen numerous old churches built over locations where Jesus supposedly was born, lived, died, and rose again. Tourists flocked to these historic sites – these ancient buildings built of stone. But my concern was with the living stones. Was there a vibrant Christian community in Israel? What about the rest of the Middle East? I knew then that my mission was to seek out the living Church in the Middle East, learn about her condition and needs, and do whatever I could to strengthen her.

Gaza, 10 June 2001

It was past midnight. The ceiling fan turned lazily above me, throwing soft patterns on the stone walls from the light coming through my window. Thirty-three years had passed since that day at Yad Vashem, and today the conflict in the Middle East seemed more intense than ever. The unending conflict sickened me, but what hurt even more was knowing that my brothers and sisters were caught in the midst of the fighting. Believers in Jesus Christ lived in Israel, the West Bank, and Gaza. They were Messianic Jews, Arab-Israeli citizens, and Palestinians, and most of them had strong thoughts about the conflict. Besides political opinions, there were theological differences. Many Jewish believers in Yeshua felt all of the land was rightfully theirs. Palestinian Christians, particularly those from whom Zionist settlers had taken land, often complained about injustices. Many Jews felt that they were God's chosen people with special privileges available to no other group. Many Palestinians felt they were second-class citizens in Israel; and worse, with no rights at all in the West Bank and Gaza.

My call was to strengthen the Church in the Middle East. Could I do it without getting caught in the crossfire of deeply held convictions? Was it possible for believers to rise above their differences and experience unity to stand against the evil darkness? This wasn't an insignificant issue. Like most Christians, I had read the book of Revelation. I knew all about the various interpretations and end-times theories, most of them involving this piece of land. There had been many books on prophecy, most recently the best-selling *Left Behind* series. Many people wanted to interpret news events from the Middle East in light of the prophecies of the Bible.

I did my best to stay out of these controversies, because there was one very important point that was often missed about the last book of the Bible. This book was written to a Church in conflict about a Church caught in conflict. There were martyrs in heaven crying out to God, 'How long?' (Rev. 6:9–10). There couldn't be martyrs without a Church. There was a description of those who overcame by the blood of the Lamb (12:11). That was the Church! There was the woman drunk with the blood of the saints – and saints make up the Church (17:6). And the angel told John that there would be one final war against the Lamb. This war would be against the Church, the body of Christ (v. 14).

While God set the time of His Son's return, I was convinced that the prophecies of Revelation could never be fulfilled without a Church in the Middle East. That was why I worked so hard here. There was a Church, but it was weak and at the point of death.

I didn't feel it was my responsibility to solve the problems in the Middle East, and besides it was ludicrous to think I could do so, but I was convinced that there was a contribution that the Christian community could make. Perhaps it was only to be light. If I could help the Church in the Middle East recognise this truth and encourage Christians to be faithful even though it was hard, that would be success. Unfortunately, many Christians, given the chance, were fleeing the area. It was hard to fault them, and yet if they all left, where would be the light in the midst of the darkness?

It had taken me many years to learn how to encourage my brothers and sisters in the Middle East. Many of these lessons were learned in Lebanon, to the north of Israel. For fifteen years the Middle East conflict was focused there, and the Church was caught in the middle. I was told that Arab newspapers wrote defiantly: 'We have killed 100,000 Christians in Lebanon and no one raised a finger; no church intervened.'

Even if few Christians tried to bring their faith to bear in Lebanon during those fifteen years of civil war, I had felt I *had* to get involved.

LEBANON: SEEKING PEACE
IN AN UNCIVIL WAR

C HRISTIANS ARE NOT IMMUNE to the impact of conflict. When
bullets fly and bombs explode, churches can be damaged or
destroyed, and believers in Jesus Christ can be injured or killed. In
this sense, the Church reflects the community in which it exists.

However, the Church is also supposed to be a light in the
darkness, but it's hard to fulfil your mission when you are fighting
for your very survival. Many Christians despair and eventually
flee to a place where it's easier to live. But those who stay, who
want to be part of the solution, fight despair. As they struggle,
they need encouragement. They need to know that their brothers
and sisters around the world are concerned for them and are
praying.

My mission has been to strengthen the Church where it
struggles for its survival. I'm not interested in simply physical
survival – that is a defeatist attitude. Instead, I want to help
Christians escape their victim mentality. I want to see them
trained, ready to advance and get on with the job of winning
people to Jesus.

But how does one go about that? I begin with the leaders. They
are the ones who must be strong for their flock, to preach the

sermons that will equip their congregations, to pray with those who are frightened, and to comfort the families as they bury those killed in the conflict. But these pastors and ministry leaders are also suffering from the trauma of living in a war zone. How can they minister to others if their own needs are not met?

That's why I went to Lebanon during the civil war that raged from 1975 to 1990 – to minister to those who minister. I went to encourage but also to listen and learn. One young man I met, Naji Abi-Hashem, trained for the pastorate as the bombs rained down on Beirut.

WEEPING FOR LEBANON

Mansouriyeh, Lebanon, 1979

Naji Abi-Hashem wept as he gazed at Beirut from the roof of the classroom building at Arab Baptist Theological Seminary in the mountain town of Mansouriyeh. From the woods behind him, he could hear and feel the rumbling concussions of cannons fired by the Syrian army. A few hundred metres below him, East Beirut was shrouded in black smoke from four days of unrelenting bombardment. The seminary was closed because of the fighting, but Naji, with a handful of stranded professors and students, was trapped, unable to travel to his parents' home in Aley or to his sister's apartment in Beirut. His nerves were frayed and he couldn't control the flow of tears as he thought of the people dying in the city below him.

The skinny twenty-six-year-old seminary student thought about how the fighting had destroyed his beloved country and altered the course of his and so many other lives. Naji had grown up in Aley, the economic centre of the Shouf, the mountains that rise majestically above Beirut and the Mediterranean. Along with Bhamdoun, Aley lay at the heart of an area where summer resorts, hotels, and restaurants attracted all sorts of tourists, including wealthy sheikhs from countries like Qatar, Saudi Arabia, and Kuwait. The wealthiest vacationers had built mansions and their own private mosque, which was open only during the summer months. Serving this 'Switzerland of the Middle East' was a population that modelled cultural integration and religious cooperation. Naji's family was devout Eastern Orthodox, but he had attended a Maronite Catholic school, where two-thirds of the students were Druze, a sect of Islam located mostly in Lebanon. His friends included Druze, Muslims, and Jews. But now those groups were fighting one another. Naji was convinced this was due to outside interference and political manipulation.

Naji had left home at the age of fifteen to attend a boarding school in Beirut, where he studied electronics. After six years of training, he'd obtained a job at the hospital of the American University in Beirut as a medical technician. That made him the major provider for his family, and his mother and several siblings had moved from Aley to live with him in an apartment in Beirut. Soon thereafter the fighting started, and their East Beirut apartment was destroyed, forcing the family to move several times. Since the hospital was in West Beirut, Naji often lived at the hospital for weeks on end because it was impossible to cross over the green line that divided the 'Christian' East from the 'Muslim' West. The green line was a no-man's zone that gained its name from the wild shrubs and trees that had overgrown the abandoned strip during the war.

As he sought to survive and pursue his dreams, Naji also wrestled with tough spiritual issues. Through the influence of his godly grandmother, six years with the Boy Scouts, and an evangelical mission in Bhamdoun, Naji had totally committed his life to Jesus Christ. Now his mind worked overtime to process many questions: *Where was God's plan in the midst of such violence? How and when would God intervene and transform these tragedies into good? Besides the physical wounds and massive property destruction, how deep were the emotional scars on the Lebanese population? What should Christians do to provide light in this darkness?* Naji wanted answers first for his tormented mind and aching soul, knowing that then he might be able to provide comfort to others. He read extensively in the Bible and many other sources but found it hard to concentrate.

He concluded that he needed to escape for a period from the war zone of Beirut and study at the seminary in Mansouriyeh, but how would he provide for his family? The question was answered providentially when he was offered the job of director of programming at a recording studio, which was situated on the seminary campus.

But for now, there were no classes at the seminary. A terrible ache coursed through Naji as he watched Beirut burn. He wondered if there would be any city left for him to minister in when he graduated from seminary. Never had he felt so helpless. In agony, he prayed, 'Lord, won't You save Lebanon? Use me in some way to help bring healing to this nation.'

P RESSURE IN LEBANON HAD built for years, but the explosion of fighting was still a shock. The problems dated back to the birth of the nation in 1943, when the French granted its independence and set up a government structure based on religious demographics. The majority Maronites, a Catholic sect that worshipped using an Eastern rite liturgy, were promised the presidency and the most seats in the legislature. In 1948 Palestinian refugees, most of them Sunni Muslims, poured into the country from Israel, upsetting the delicate balance of power. More Palestinians arrived in 1970, when Jordan expelled militants (the Palestine Liberation Organisation or PLO) following an assassination attempt on King Hussein and violent clashes between the Jordanian army and Palestinian forces during what became known as Black September. Since 1969 the Palestinians had used southern

Lebanon as their base for launching raids into Israel, which naturally led to retaliation. The Lebanese villagers, caught in the crossfire, suffered terribly but did not have the muscle power to stop the Palestinian provocations.

Meanwhile in the Palestinian refugee camps of Beirut, Yasser Arafat set up PLO headquarters, effectively forming a mini-state within Lebanon. Tensions smouldered, aggravated by the fact that some Lebanese Muslims, seeing an opportunity to grab some of the political power held by the Maronites, aligned with the Palestinians.

Open warfare erupted in 1975 between the Palestinians and a group known as the Phalangists, consisting of Maronite Christians, and quickly expanded to include other factions. At the request of Lebanon's president, Syria entered in 1976 in an attempt to end the conflict. Meanwhile, Israel threatened to invade and wipe out the PLO. The conflict was hard for a Westerner to follow, but somehow most locals seemed to know who was fighting whom.[1] What broke my heart was how the majority of ordinary people suffered. Working primarily through the Bible Society, I started going once or twice a year to visit pastors, preach in churches and evangelistic campaigns, and generally to encourage any and all believers in Christ to be strong in the midst of the conflict.

Southern Lebanon, 1980

Matousha, a small town just a few miles from the Israeli border, felt deserted. Empty houses and apartment buildings, many with gaping holes in their roofs and walls, guarded secrets of the families who had fled for their lives. Where many children should have played football in an open lot, a single boy listlessly kicked rocks. Half a dozen soldiers lounged at the central intersection, curiously eyeing me and my plastic shopping bag. I wasn't sure if they were PLO or from a mixed Lebanese militia.

'Does anyone speak English?' I asked the group, more cheerfully than I felt.

The men jabbered among themselves and laughed, almost certainly at this strange-looking Dutchman's expense. One said, 'No speak English.' Then he pointed at my bag.

I pulled out Arabic Bibles and New Testaments and started handing them to the soldiers. One of the men looked at a Bible and handed it back, 'We don't want the Israel book. We want the Jesus book.'

I put the Bible back in my bag and gave him a New Testament. 'This is *Injil*,' I said, using the Arabic word for gospel. I then handed out Arabic tracts, which the men eagerly accepted. They looked bored, ready for something to read and perhaps discuss in those early morning hours during the tense lulls in fighting when a soldier's fears about life and death ambush his consciousness.

For years Palestinians had shelled Israeli communities across the border. Naturally, Israel had responded with powerful counter-attacks, and the Lebanese people caught in the middle were the victims. Those civilians who could fled to the north.

I knew that at one time there had been an evangelical church here, and I wondered if I could find it. An old couple shuffling up the street caught my attention. The woman wore a grey wool skirt, a black sweater, and a scarf around her head. The man was dressed in a shabby brown suit and a bright red flannel shirt. With a warm greeting, I approached them. The man spoke some English, so I asked, 'Is there a church here?'

'Come. I will show you,' he said. Three blocks off the main street we stopped in front of a ruined building. 'This is the church that doesn't work anymore,' said the man.

The roof looked like Swiss cheese. Gaping holes in the walls allowed me to see through to the hill on the other side. 'What a sad building,' I said.

'Yes, sad. Tragedy,' the man agreed.

'When was this destroyed?'

The man shrugged. 'Some years ago.'

'So where do the people meet?'

'No meet. All the Christians gone.'

I looked at the couple and wondered how old they were. Every wrinkle seemed to represent an untold story of pain. 'You are still here. Shouldn't you leave? It's not safe.'

'There is no place to go,' the man said, shrugging his shoulders again. 'This is our home.'

As the man and his wife walked away, I stepped over stones and broken concrete into the sanctuary and gazed up through the roof. Limbs of trees had pushed their way through the walls. The floor was covered with rubble. The pews were gone – perhaps removed for firewood. Carefully, so as not to twist an ankle on the uneven rubble, I made my way to the remains of the platform. I wondered about the congregation. *How many had worshipped here? Where had they gone?* Perhaps some had sought refuge in Beirut. Others may have had relatives in the West, and so they had fled to safety in Europe or the Americas. I knew many families had been forced to split up and scatter in different directions. *Had any died here in the conflict? What about the pastor – where was he now? Was he preaching somewhere, or had he given up hope and abandoned the ministry?*

A deep sadness fell over me. I opened my Bible to Psalm 74. 'Turn your steps towards these everlasting ruins.' I read the words out loud to the empty building. 'All this destruction the enemy has brought on the sanctuary. Your foes roared in the place where you met with us.' I recalled how Dietrich Bonhoeffer had written beside this psalm in his Bible, 'Kristallnacht', referring to the night of terror in 1938 when the Nazis destroyed Jewish businesses and synagogues. The world hadn't responded, and the result was the Holocaust. Would the world respond any differently today to the destruction of churches in Lebanon? Did the world even know or care?

My eyes watered and I couldn't read further. Certainly, there had been a roaring in this building. The sheep in this flock were scattered. So where was the hope in this village? Sunlight shone through the holes in the roof, but the light of this church had been snuffed out. How many more lights had gone out in Lebanon? I felt an urgency in my spirit – I had to keep seeking the *living* Church.

Just 150 metres down the street from the evangelical church was a Maronite Catholic church. I found the priest there. Though his English was broken, he was able to explain that his tiny congregation of six met in a small room to the side of the sanctuary. Outside the church I looked up at the spire, topped by a cross. Above the cross flew the tattered green flag of one of the Islamic militia groups. It was a statement: Allah is greater. Translated, that meant Islam was greater than Christianity. I pointed to the flag and said to the priest, 'I long for the day when the cross rises above the Muslim flag.'

In my spirit, those words became a prayer.

Beirut, 1980

The pressure affected people in different ways. In one home where I often stayed, the husband, a pastor, couldn't keep up the facade of the gracious host. Peter wasn't home when I arrived one afternoon. His wife, Anna, and another woman were working in the kitchen. I asked for a glass of yogurt and went to take a nap. Twenty minutes later I was awakened by loud voices coming from the kitchen. When I went to investigate, I found Peter and his wife in a heated discussion. 'Why are you so excited?' I asked.

'He's nervous,' Anna answered. 'He's always nervous when there is fighting.'

While she fixed me another glass of yogurt, Peter took me to the window to show me the source of his agitation. Pointing to the house across the road, he showed me how the people were climbing down from the balcony instead of using the stairs inside. 'Why is that a problem?' I asked.

'It attracts the shooters,' he said. 'We need to stay out of sight.'

'But you were just outside . . .'

'Not on the roof, not out in the open.'

'So what can you do about it?'

'Not much,' he mumbled. Then thinking of the correct 'spiritual' answer, he added, 'I suppose I can pray.'

'Yes, let's pray. Then maybe you won't feel that you need to shout.'

Anna brought my glass of yogurt. 'He's always shouting,' she said. Then she suggested I might want to go back to my room, which I was eager to do.

We had a wonderful dinner that evening – fried potatoes and a large dish full of fried chicken. But Peter complained that it was not good. His wife rolled her eyes: 'He always complains. Even in heaven he will complain. I sincerely hope that I will get a villa far away from his when I get there.' We all laughed, even Peter.

One of their sons then asked me whether we would have our own villas in heaven. I suggested, 'Our house over there will be built from the material we sent over during our lifetime here on earth.'

Peter shook his head. 'I'm afraid the materials in my life aren't very good.'

I put my hand on his arm and assured him: 'It's not too late to start collecting the right materials. You can start now.'

Ras Beirut Baptist Church needed a young leader. The senior pastor was old and tired, so the church council approached the Arab Baptist Theological Seminary and recruited Naji Abi-Hashem, the only graduate that year. Naji respected the senior pastor and asked to work with him as an assistant. But the elderly man was weary, ready to turn over leadership to a younger man with more energy. So the elders issued a call to Naji.

The church provided the new pastor with an apartment on the lower level of the building next to the church. Given the number of missiles flying through the air, apartments on the lower floors, when surrounded by high-rises on all sides, were generally safer.

Naji's family's apartment was near the green line, and fighting there had intensified, forcing people to evacuate the area, leaving all of their belongings behind. His mother and brother had found temporary residence elsewhere, until things settled down.

Naji was preparing to move to the church building, located in West Beirut, but he and his family needed things that were left in their abandoned apartment. Early one afternoon Naji and his brother decided to risk visiting the apartment to retrieve some of their belongings. Without mentioning their plan to anyone, they set out on their dangerous errand. They had to walk through an open field to a main thoroughfare where the most prominent landmark was a Maronite cathedral. One of the militias had commandeered the building and used its steeple as a sniper's nest to control the busy street. Large earth mounds had been built in front of various buildings to protect pedestrians from the bullets.

It was quiet as Naji and his brother approached one of the mounds. 'We should be okay,' Naji said as they prepared to cross the street. But suddenly there were several shots, and they could hear bullets whistling over their heads. Hugging the dirt, they prayed and waited.

'Should we keep going or turn back?' his brother asked.

'We need the clothes from the apartment. I think we'll be okay if we go now. Let's just walk normally across the street. Then they will see we aren't a threat. Let's go.'

Naji stepped forward with more confidence than he felt, and his brother followed close behind. They strolled across the street, ducked behind another dirt pile, then made their way to the apartment building. Walking up six flights of stairs, they emerged into open air – a portion of the wall had been blown away. The apartment had obviously been looted, but fortunately most of their clothes were still there.

With arms full, they made their way back home. Their trip was uneventful, until they walked into the apartment. Then their mother began shouting hysterically: 'How could you go out in such danger? They could have killed you! They could've shot you and you die cheaply. How foolish of you! I nearly had a heart attack. Lord have mercy.'

GOD HAS
FORSAKEN LEBANON

Beirut, 1981

The crunch of broken bricks and glass mingled with my thoughts as I approached the green line in Beirut. The 'Jewel of the Mediterranean' was a shell of its former glory. I could remember how before 1975 I had enjoyed leaving the cold, rainy winters of Holland to visit my friend Father Andy, who ran a school for deaf children in Beirut. Often I'd visited the Corniche, the street along the Mediterranean where joggers ran early in the morning, city leaders conducted their business lunches, and couples strolled hand in hand as they watched the sunset. Lebanon's finest hotels and restaurants were lined up along this bright beachfront.

Now it lay in ruins. Once the economic, educational, and entertainment capital of the Middle East, Beirut now writhed from the unending combat of various militias, each staking claim to a portion of the ruins and seeking to impose its agenda. Still, some shops were open. I felt for the bag inside the pocket of my windbreaker – in it was a pretty gold pin I had just purchased for my wife's birthday, which was two days after I was scheduled to return home.

This city was a mass of contradictions. Yet I was amazed at the resiliency and survival skills of the Lebanese. One had to stand in long lines to buy bread, if it was available. But you could get the latest electronic equipment or brand-name clothing at bargain-basement prices. During a recent trip, I had bought a quality tape recorder for half of what I would have paid in Holland. After completing the sale, the shop owner had said, 'Mister Andrew, God has forsaken us. He has left Lebanon.'

This city certainly looked God-forsaken. On the side of the street where I walked stood the ghostly form of a once majestic hotel, now home to a gentle Mediterranean breeze drifting through gaping holes in its walls. Opposite it, across the street, stood a scorched apartment building. Nearby, two filthy children were playing by a fence of corrugated metal that looked like it would topple from the concussion of the next bomb blast. Perhaps the children lived in one of the apartments with a wall blasted away and were protected from the weather only by a sheet of plastic flapping in the wind.

The poverty, the filth, the undernourished children all left me depressed. A child, probably only three years old, was crying on a balcony. I smiled at him and said, 'In Jesus' name, be comforted.' For a moment he was still, but as I continued walking, he cried again. I imagined coming here and in Jesus' name laying hands on the people and seeing them healed. I wanted to cry as I continued down the busy streets.

The human population thinned dramatically as I approached the green line, which divided East, the so-called Christian sector where I was staying, from West, the predominantly Muslim area. To pass through, I had to stop at the sandbagged Christian checkpoint where a soldier examined my passport. 'Why are you going into the Muslim sector?' he asked.

'To visit friends,' I answered.

He looked at me with a mixture of suspicion and surprise. Then with a wave of annoyance, he signalled me through. At least this time I had my passport. Once I had forgotten it and had quipped at a checkpoint, 'I just came from church and all I have is my Bible.' Very sternly, the soldier had said, 'In this country you must have with you your Bible *and* your passport.' So I now carried both in a pocket of my windbreaker.

Several Lebanese people were moving in either direction through this no-man's-land. I wondered what business carried them between the two sides. I walked rapidly a couple hundred yards to the Muslim checkpoint where another guard asked, 'Why do you want to enter this sector?'

'To visit friends,' I answered, as he stared at my Dutch passport. He too waved me on.

It was only partially true that this was the Muslim sector. The division was arbitrary, created in 1975 when the Palestinians, crammed into the refugee camps, openly rebelled against the Christian group called Phalangists. One result was that Muslims and Christians generally separated into 'their sides' – Christians on the east, Muslims on the west. Supposedly it was safer that way. However, dozens of churches remained sprinkled among the many mosques on the west side. Many Christians had fled the area but not all.

West Beirut was bustling with activity. It seemed surprising to see so many cars on the streets, barely moving through a jammed intersection with a traffic signal that hadn't worked for years. A girl, seven or eight years old, wiped windshields with a dirty rag, hoping to receive a few coins. A teenage girl sat on the curb, her head resting in her hands, too tired and haggard to beg. I couldn't help but wonder if any of the combatants ever saw these victims of war and thought about their welfare.

'Want a Coca-Cola?' The voice startled me, and I looked down to see squatting on his haunches a bald, heavyset man who had set up an impromptu enterprise on the sidewalk. A row of soft drinks stood next to a cardboard box holding a one-burner stove, where the man was cooking meatballs in a bit of oil. He had one customer in a brown suit.

When I saw a small cross around the man's neck, I smiled and sat on one of the orange crates that served as the chairs for his cafe. 'Yes, Coca-Cola!' I answered.

'Where are you from?' the man asked in laboured English as he opened a warm bottle and placed it on the cardboard table in front of me.

'Holland.'

'Why do you come to Beirut?'

'I am a Christian, and I've come to visit my brothers.'

Immediately, both men crossed themselves, and the proprietor sat down on a crate opposite me, eager to talk. 'Life hard now,' he said. 'Christian and Muslim, boom, boom, boom.' He used his forefingers as guns, pointing at each other. 'What is your name?' he asked.

'Andrew.'

'And surname?'

'Brother Andrew.'

A smile grew on his face. 'Bibles to Russia and China!' Now he wanted to remove the meatballs from his burner and make me some Arabic coffee. I stood up to let him know that I had to go. It was early afternoon and I knew the fighting often started around 3.00 or 4.00. I needed to visit friends quickly so I could get back across the green line before the shelling started.

When I pulled out money to pay for my Coke, my new friend stood and put up his hands to stop me. The man in the brown suit also stood and pressed a one thousand pound note into my hand. 'For your work!' he said.

There was no way to resist their kindness and I struggled with my emotions. The value of the Lebanese pound had plummeted since 1975 and a thousand pounds was now worth only a couple of American dollars. Still, as I walked up the street from them, I recalled how often I had lived off such gifts while travelling in Communist countries. Now it seemed that I should be giving to these people who were scratching to earn a living during the few hours when guns weren't roaring.

M Y FIRST SCHEDULED stop was to visit Hannah in a small bookshop, but the doors and windows were boarded up. 'She is not home,' said the proprietor of the adjoining record shop.

'Will you please tell her that Brother Andrew stopped by to see her?' I asked.

'She will be sorry,' he answered, shaking his head. 'She needs much encouragement.'

I walked to an apartment building, pockmarked as were all the buildings by shrapnel and bullets. The lift wasn't working –

electricity was scarce and almost no lifts ran – so I walked up three floors, searched the dark hall for the right apartment, and knocked. There was no response, so I knocked again a little harder. There was the sound of metal scraping as a peephole slid open. Then the door swung wide open.

'Brother Andrew, you have come!' Philip opened his arms wide and embraced me, kissed me on both cheeks, then ushered me into his living room. His wife, Alison, peered around the corner and lit up with a smile of recognition.

The couple were in their early thirties but looked much older. The strain of living in a war zone showed in the worry lines on their faces and the premature grey in their hair. As Alison went to the kitchen to prepare coffee, I asked my friend how his church was doing. Before the civil war, four hundred people routinely attended services.

He shook his head sadly as he said, 'My congregation is only forty now.' Then he lowered his head to conceal the tears. 'Actually, last Sunday it was thirty-nine. A seventeen-year-old girl was killed . . .'

Before I could say anything, an explosion caused me to jump. The shelling from East Beirut had started early, and I could hear the thumps of nearby artillery. 'It's like this every day,' Philip said, looking up at me. 'No one goes out anymore.' He lowered his voice as he said, 'Today is my wife's birthday, and I haven't even got her a present.'

I felt my pocket where I'd put my small package. 'Philip, I have a surprise for you,' I whispered. 'But this must be our secret.'

I handed the present to my friend, who was speechless for a moment as he stared at it.

When Alison brought the tray with three tiny cups of coffee, I announced, 'I hear this is a special day,' and started to sing 'Happy Birthday'. Philip joined me in singing, as ambulance sirens accompanied us from down the street.

Then Philip gave his wife the present. Alison gasped in surprise when she unwrapped the package, then proudly attached the pin to her sweater. For the briefest moment, she glanced at me, as if to say she knew the secret but would never let on.

In just a few minutes I would have to leave. I opened my Bible and read from Hebrews 2: '[Christ] too shared in their humanity so that by his death he might destroy him who holds the power of death – that is, the devil – and free those who all their lives were held in slavery by their fear of death.' Then I said, 'I have a little acrostic for you: F-e-a-r. Fear is "false evidence appearing real".' Fear of death keeps us from being bold in this dangerous world. It's as though we're not fully convinced that we go to heaven when we die. I know, with the bombs exploding all around you, fear is a natural response, but I want to encourage you to remember that our Lord has conquered death, and so we are released from the power of fear!'

Philip nodded his head, while his wife dabbed at her tears with a handkerchief.

After a time of prayer together, their arms now around each other, Philip and Alison saw me off. As I hurried down the stairs, I thought how little it took to encourage this pastor and his wife. Just visit, sing, pray, and share God's Word. In the midst of their suffering and sorrow, we had looked at our Lord and experienced a little joy. If only I could do that with every single pastor in Beirut.

The streets were empty as I hurried towards the checkpoint. I was halfway across the green line when big guns erupted and mingled with loud machine-gun fire. As soon as I was across, I took shelter in the doorway of an abandoned office building and caught my breath. I felt no urgency about getting back on the streets. I would wait for a lull before continuing.

I thought of the shell of the church in Matousha. *How many abandoned churches were there in this country? Could anything be done to prevent further destruction of churches?*

I thought of Peter and Philip. *If leaders were fearful and frazzled, how could they help their congregations? And what about their sheep? Believers couldn't be part of the solution in Lebanon if they were huddled in fear or seeking to escape. Was there any way I could encourage them to reach out and be a light?*

Certainly I realised there were Christians participating in the fighting. For many people, Christians were just another religious group fighting to maintain or gain power. But that wasn't real Christianity! This couldn't be what Jesus Christ intended when He said, 'Blessed are the peacemakers.' Somehow this nation needed to know there was an alternative.

And then I thought of the Palestinians. They had nothing to
lose – they were without a homeland and devoid of power. I
wondered what my faith had to say to them.

THE NEED FOR
WISDOM WITH ZEAL

Beirut, spring 1982

A film crew was following me around on this trip, preparing a documentary that would air in Holland. I spoke in many churches, encouraging the Christians to stand firm. On a Sunday night, after a meeting in a packed Armenian church, a skinny young man approached me and extended his hand, saying, 'My name is Naji. I read your book in Arabic and I was impressed by it. I really liked it very much.'

'I'm glad you liked it.'

'I am the new pastor of a church in West Beirut. If you need a place to stay, I would be honoured to host you in my apartment.'

That would be perfect! I thought. I wanted to stay for a few days in West Beirut to have better access to the refugee camps there and perhaps try to make contact with the PLO leadership. 'Thank you! I am looking for a place, but I have a crew travelling with me.'

'How large?'

'Five. We're going to the Shatilla camp to film a video. The team will be with me for three more days and then they will return to Holland while I stay.'

'They are all welcome too. There are two apartments next to the church. You may stay with me as long as you wish.'

THERE WAS NO electricity at the church building. 'I can run the generator only a few hours a day,' Naji said, apologising for the inconvenience as I settled into my room. 'And we use gas bottles to heat the water. There isn't enough to provide hot showers every day.'

'Please don't worry,' I said. 'These are the conditions you live in constantly. We are here to be with you. We don't need the comforts of a hotel.'

The next day the team went with me to film at the Shatilla camp. The degradation and poverty were sickening, worse than anything I had ever seen. People were crammed into tiny shacks of corrugated metal. Children ran barefoot through narrow muddy alleyways, dodging pools of raw sewage. Clothing was hung to dry on the walls. The smell of urine and rotting food assaulted my nostrils.

The people seemed glad to see me but not the camera crew. 'Please, no camera,' said one man, emphatically placing his hand in front of the lens.

'We mean no harm,' I said naively. 'We only want to show the world how you are suffering, so you can get help.'

'No camera!' the man repeated.

Later I asked the camp commander, who spoke decent English, why the people were so afraid of the camera. 'It has a bug,' said the commander.

'A bug? What do you mean?'

'It has a bug, so Israel can guide their bombs here.'

If I hadn't known better, I would have thought maybe these people had been reading spy novels. I tried to understand their fear. Rumours were flying that Israel was about to invade Lebanon to put an end to the PLO. The people were on edge and angry.

I assumed the commandant was a member of the PLO, so I asked him, 'Would it be possible to meet one of the leaders of the PLO?' I figured he would know whom to contact.

'No problem. I will check for you.'

In one of the narrow alleys, as I handed out New Testaments, a child tugged on my sleeve and pulled me towards one of the shacks. Inside was an old couple. The man was in bed, apparently quite sick. His wife, wearing a white scarf, sat at the end of the bed. Reverently she crossed herself as I laid my hand on the man's shoulder and prayed for his healing. After she said 'Amin' to my 'Amen', I leaned over and kissed the old man on his forehead. It was a holy moment – I wanted to believe that Christ had brought a little light into this dark home.

Through an interpreter I asked the woman, 'How old are you, mother?'

'More than seventy,' she answered. She didn't know exactly.

'How long have you lived here?'

'We came here in 1948 – from Jaffa, by boat.'

'Do you have any hope that you will get out of this place?'

She shook her head. 'I want to go back to Jaffa.' There were tears in her eyes.

Outside the shack men and boys stood around. They looked bored and scared. Of one teenage boy who spoke a little English, I asked, 'Do you see any hope for the future?'

He looked at me. 'No hope,' he said, his eyes listless. 'There is no hope.'

These were just a few individuals among four hundred thousand Palestinians living in the most terrible circumstances. They had no country. They were not welcome in Lebanon, but they had no other place to go. Their hearts were in the country from which they had fled, but they had no real hope they would see their homes again. These were people for whom Jesus Christ had died. I'd passed out a few Arabic New Testaments, but much more was needed.

Almost every building in Beirut was protected by a strong, imposing iron gate, usually black. Each was like an ugly scar but was a necessary precaution, even for a church. One never knew when a militia group might attempt to enter, perhaps to steal money or intimidate occupants or hide from the fighting or sometimes take control of the building as a temporary headquarters or, even worse, as a sniper nest.

Beyond the gate at Ras Beirut Baptist Church was a small courtyard, then two more doors to pass through before reaching the church foyer.

One afternoon, the bell at the front gate rang. When Naji rose from his desk and looked out the window, he saw a group of rough looking men standing at the gate. Two men, brandishing automatic rifles, kept watch down both sides of the street. Another rang the bell again. Naji froze for a moment, but he knew he had to act. If he didn't, these men might shoot up his building. Better to find out what they wanted and try to manoeuvre the situation peacefully. With caution Naji approached the men. Without opening the gate, he said, '*Marhaba*. May I help you gentlemen?'[1]

'We are here to see Mr Andrew,' the leader answered.

Quickly Naji unlocked the gate and escorted the group into the church foyer. He didn't want anyone to see that his church was entertaining a militia group. The last thing he needed was for some rival militia to think he had chosen sides in this ruthless combat zone. The leader smiled and introduced himself. Naji missed the name but caught two important facts. This man was a major and he was an assistant to Yasser Arafat.

So this was the PLO. They were the reason for Israel's pending invasion. 'I am honoured to meet you, sir,' Naji responded while his mind raced and his heart prayed for wisdom. 'I am very sorry Brother Andrew is not here at the moment. I truly apologise.'

'He said he would meet us here at 3.00.'

'Perhaps he's held up in traffic or at a checkpoint, or the roads are closed. I will certainly tell him that you came to see him at the appointed time.'

Several of the men were nosing around the facility. Hospitality required that Naji offer them coffee, but before he could, the bell rang again. Naji ran to the glass door and peered outside. At the gate stood Brother Andrew.

I TALKED WITH THE major for more than an hour and learned more about the PLO, its goals, and its aims for the Middle East.

After the delegation departed, Naji cautiously approached me: 'Brother Andrew, I want to talk with you, please. It's very important.' My friend seemed troubled as we sat down in his living room. He leaned forward and looked intensely into my eyes. 'Brother Andrew, I want to learn from you about your interest in the PLO. What are your objectives? Could you share with me, please?'

'Of course, Naji. But you look worried. Is there something wrong?'

'This is very important to me as pastor of this church. I'm worried that those men coming here to this very building has put the church in extreme jeopardy.'

Now, I was concerned, because the last thing I wanted to do was to endanger the work of any church. 'Naji, I'm sorry. I thought this would be a safe place to meet.'

My friend shifted uncomfortably, staring at the floor. 'Promise me you won't bring anyone else here or tell them about coming to meet you here. You can meet somewhere else. I can guide you, take you to a restaurant or some public place. If you want to meet with them in their headquarters, that's fine. But not in a Christian agency.' He met my gaze and explained, 'We are trying extremely hard to remain neutral and friendly so we may resume our worship and witness to our Lord without being dragged into the awful politics of this divisive war.'

'I understand, Naji. I'm sorry.'

'You may think I don't have a strong faith or won't take risks. This is too complicated to explain. But I live here. My people live here. You're only here for a few days and then you're gone, but we will reap the consequences of one single misinterpretation for a long time. So I hope you will respect that.'

'So my meeting this afternoon, that put you in danger?'

Naji nodded. 'Here I can't affiliate with any political or militia leader because that will reflect on me and the church and we are already in a very difficult position. Most of these groups look at us as pro-Western because most of our missionaries are from the

West and from America. They see America as pro-Israel and so they look at us as pro-Israel too. We walk a fine line to prove that we are authentic Lebanese and Middle Eastern Christians, and we want to keep our message and activities purely spiritual. We pray for everyone, but we don't want to affiliate ourselves with anyone. Besides, each group may cause us much trouble, demand services, and make our lives miserable.'

'Please forgive me, Naji. I will not do that again.'

Instantly the young pastor seemed to relax. 'How about some Lebanese herb tea? I have yansoun [dried anise], my favourite.'

As we drank our tea, Naji smiled and asked, 'So, why are you going to the PLO, anyway?'

'If possible, I'd like to meet all sides. I'm curious about what they are thinking, what they want, what they are feeling. I want to know what they think the solution is for the conflict. I want to know what their spiritual faith is, if any. I'm looking for common ground so that I can tell them about my Lord and Saviour Jesus Christ.'

'You have a great deal of zeal! I hope you will put wisdom with that zeal and consult as many as possible. You don't need to consult me; I'm a younger brother. But this is crucial business, and you don't want to inadvertently cause more problems than we already have.'

'That is wise counsel,' I agreed.

Before I went to my room, we stood and exchanged a warm hug. Naji and I had developed a beautiful ritual. Sometime during the day, often first thing in the morning, we both opened our arms and sang, 'Give us today our daily hug!' It was a precious routine that we would continue every time we met in subsequent years.

M Y CONVERSATION WITH Naji was a warning to be careful about involving the local believers too quickly in some of the work I felt led to do. I believed my work was to strengthen the local church so it could be a light in the midst of darkness. But how does one go about that? I could preach, and I did several times each week. I could encourage pastors and ministry leaders.

I could visit believers who were suffering. And I could provide Bibles and other resources they needed for their work.

But just how does the Church shine its light in a war zone? That was a trickier question. I could say that the Church ought to be an agent for peace, but just what did that mean? And how could the Church do that when Christians were literally trying to stay out of the line of fire? I thought I could help the local believers answer these questions, but to do that, I needed to understand a lot more – the pressures Christians were under and the thinking of the factions fighting around them.

Naji had a keen mind, making him an excellent sounding board for questions that I had about Lebanon and the Middle East. 'So what do you think is the answer?' I asked him one evening when we were eating dinner at a local restaurant. 'If we as Christians are peacemakers, how do we fulfil our call?'

'It's complex,' Naji answered. 'The current situation in the Middle East has many dynamics and there are disputes on many levels. One thing I would encourage here in Lebanon is for the outsiders to leave us alone and let us solve our problems.'

'You mean Syria and Israel . . .'

'And the Palestinians, Libya, Iran, and the United States. There would be no war now if all the outsiders, and particularly the superpowers, would leave us alone.'

I had heard that several times. Lebanese had corrected me when I mentioned the 'civil war', for they did not want to acknowledge that the conflicts were primarily among Lebanese people. I countered: 'Naji, if you can't solve your problems, then you shouldn't be surprised that others come in and try to bring peace.'

'But they forget that we have a history of cooperation. I grew up in a community with Druze, Muslims, Jews, and Christians, and we all got along well. So why now an endless war? I believe the triggers are from outside interference. I think we can work things out if we're allowed to do so.'

'I would like to think you are right. But I don't see much cooperation right now.'

'In the Middle East, you will have periods of calm and periods of conflict. I don't know if there will ever be permanent peace.'

'Then how can you blame the West for your problems?'

Naji tried to explain what had gone wrong in this beautiful country. 'It's easy to create an ethnic, religious, or political conflict to serve the political interests of more powerful nations. Being so open and free, Lebanon attracted radical groups of all sorts from neighbouring countries, which, along with the PLO, created a consortium of militias. They want to turn Lebanon into a Palestinian-Muslim nation. They think that would eventually solve the Middle East crisis by providing an alternate home for the Palestinian people and by making Lebanon a moderately Islamic state, which could join the rest of the Arabic-Muslim world. Then every party in the Middle East would be satisfied, including the Jewish state of Israel.'

'That is quite an explanation. You are saying that this conflict can be understood only in the context of the whole Middle East crisis. But you haven't explained why the West is the problem.'

'There are many groups that are angry with the West in general and the United States government in particular. They resent the West for its cultural invasion, economic exploitation, political manipulation, military superiority and intimidation, and imperialistic greed. And they are specifically angry with the United States government for its unconditional support and overt bias towards Israel, which is poised right now to invade Lebanon, because the United States government allows it. Israel is viewed as an ambitious nation that would like to be the superpower in the Middle East, dominating its politics, resources, and affairs. These sentiments affect us and our ministry because many equate our version of Christianity with the West.'

I knew many of my friends would be offended by these words, but I needed to listen and probe so that I could understand what my brother was thinking and feeling. 'Christianity grew up right here in the Middle East,' I protested. 'You yourself grew up in an Eastern Orthodox tradition.'

'That's different from Western Christianity. Many here in the East assume that Protestants and evangelicals are following a Christianity that was imported from America. Also, community and religious leaders as well as ordinary God-fearing people resent the products, movies, magazines, lifestyles, music, advertisements, and TV shows that the West exports. They connect them to the culture of the Christian West.'

Naji spoke with passion and insight, but I wanted to know what we should do. 'I think your analysis is insightful. But is there a solution? What can the Church here in Lebanon *do*?'

My friend sighed and answered, 'Peace is such a profound and beautiful concept. In Arabic the word we use is *salaam*. We use it as a holistic greeting, a wish for well-being and health. It is more than the absence of conflict or war. It is the biblical concept of *shalom*.'

'I don't see much *salaam* or *shalom* right now.'

'No, the term *peace* has been rather abused. It's been mixed up with hidden agendas and has lost its cultural meaning and spiritual depth. Depending on who is doing the talking and who is listening, the word is so easy to utter but so difficult to define, and more importantly, so difficult to construct.'

'I agree. That's why I think we should put forward a distinctly Christian peace plan. If we remain silent, then we have no chance of making any difference at all.'

Naji gave me a sad smile. 'I suppose we should try. I don't know if we can do much, but we should try. Remember, there is a time to speak and a time to be silent. In this season those of us who are under severe pressure from all sides must hold our ground and remain faithful to God. In times like these, steadfastness is a great virtue and a great witness by itself. These days we are called to simply maintain a *presence*. We do represent Christ and carry His name in this season of deep trouble.'

As we rose to leave the restaurant, I pulled out several thousand Lebanese pounds to pay the bill. After leaving a generous tip, the dinner had still cost me slightly more than two American dollars.

'I have an idea,' I said as we stepped outside. 'Why don't you and I organise an evangelistic campaign here in West Beirut? We'll rent a large hall and open the meeting to everyone. We'll invite all those militia leaders.'

Naji remained courteous to this enthusiastic preacher as he said, 'I'm not sure about an evangelistic campaign right now. Maybe later. Let's talk about it during your next visit. Okay?'

'Okay. But soon!'

A PLAN FOR PEACE

Harderwijk, The Netherlands, 1986
Ever since hostilities had erupted in Lebanon in 1975, I had reflected a lot on the subject of peace. My talks with Naji were important for gaining insight into the country's complex problems. Like me, he had wrestled with how to help be part of the solution. He felt frustrated with how little he could actually do. Listening politely to my idea of a large evangelistic campaign, he had tried patiently to explain why that wouldn't work. Bringing all of the militias together in a large meeting was inviting an explosion. The gospel had to be spread in some other way.

With sadness and sympathy I thought about our last discussion in Lebanon in 1983 when Naji had told me about his opportunity to continue graduate studies in the United States. 'When I accepted the call to Ras Beirut Baptist Church, I expected to pastor here all of my life,' he said and then confided that some problems he was having within the congregation had caused him to re-evaluate. 'This church doesn't need me as much now. The senior pastor has rested for a while and is willing to resume more of the work, and my assistant is eager to take on more responsibilities. So it's a good time for me to phase out. Besides, I want to further my education in the areas of counselling and psychology, which are great needs for the people of Lebanon. However, I want to study these subjects from a Christian and theological perspective.'

'You are coming back to Lebanon, aren't you?' I asked.

'Of course. And while I am in the States, I will be an ambassador for the East.'

'Yes,' I smiled. 'You will be a missionary from Lebanon to the West.'

I prayed that my friend would indeed return to Lebanon after completing his doctoral studies.[1] In fact now as I considered my next trip to Beirut, I wanted to talk with him. For some time I had felt a growing need to present some sort of formal peace plan for church leaders.

As a foreigner in Lebanon, I could move easily through most of the numerous checkpoints, while many of my friends were confined to a limited area. My heart went out to the soldiers checking cars and papers. I would smile at them, crack a joke, and hand them an Arabic tract, saying, 'You should read this. It has the real solution for peace.' My friends who drove me around started referring to these encounters as 'checkpoint evangelism'. Those were light moments amid great suffering, but they weren't part of a serious peace plan.

Meanwhile tens of thousands of Christians had fled the country. Few foreign workers remained. Most people left because it was impossible to support or protect their families. Multitudes more wished they could migrate but lacked the means. How could anyone blame them? Among those who remained, some were simply cultural Christians – they'd grown up in the church and that was how they identified themselves.

However, among all the various religious denominations in Lebanon were true believers who detested the bloody conflict and endless power struggles. I knew they felt helpless. At times they were accused of not being nationalistic or patriotic. They tried to serve and be a blessing, but they were having to endure the same suffering as the rest of the population. In spite of their small number, could these people become an active, positive force for peace? I believed they could – if someone would provide them with a plan.

I took out a pad of paper and began writing.

Beirut, 1986

This had to be one of the most unusual peace conferences ever convened. There were no heads of state in attendance, no ambassadors or negotiators. We weren't haggling over the shape of the table within a luxurious mansion. Rather we were seated in folding chairs in a nondescript meeting room in the basement of a Beirut office building. Outside, various militias aimed their guns at one another. Inside, a foolish Dutch missionary met with men like Ghassan, a pastor and president of Arab Baptist Seminary, and Lucien, president of the Bible Society in Lebanon, plus a few brave missionaries and about two dozen local pastors, including Peter and Philip.

As I thought about the tragedy of Lebanon, it was easy to feel helpless. We couldn't stop the soldiers from fighting – we had no military might. We couldn't stop other countries from invading. In fact the strongest military forces in the world had not been able to change this situation. Meanwhile, militant leaders believed they could defeat the world's greatest military because their will was greater than that of the West. After all, they had driven the United States out with just a couple of well-placed bombs.

Did I really think that this small group of church leaders could make any difference in a conflict that had raged around them for more than eleven years? Powers far greater than us were determined to impose their will – did I really think we could stop them? On the other hand, how could we sit around and do nothing? For better or worse, the Church was how God chose to shine His light into the darkness.

This peace plan was carefully crafted from Scripture. I had consulted with the leadership of Open Doors, and they were in Holland praying for me right now. After one of the local pastors offered a prayer for our meeting, I launched right in. 'I would like to begin by making some observations about this unending conflict here in Lebanon. Many people expect solutions to come from the outside. They will not come. Many people wait for others to take the initiative. But *we* must take the initiative. Many others to whom I have already spoken express the desire for peace at any price. This is very dangerous and irresponsible and indicates that no one has yet seriously pursued a plan for peace.'

I spoke with passion, but inside I wasn't at all sure this was going to work. The men in the room listened, but their faces revealed no emotion. Were they simply being polite? Did they believe they could do something practical about the conflict around them?

'I would like to address three questions,' I continued. 'The first question is, What is our objective? The answer is simple: We want peace. We already know that. So we go on to the second question: What method do we choose? We must begin where we are. And as it happens, God has placed us here in Lebanon. The reason is because we see this conflict as a spiritual battle. All other definitions fail, and that's why solutions are so elusive. So we who are here must proclaim peace. First Corinthians 1:21 says God "was pleased through the foolishness of what was preached to save those who believe".' This becomes a very personal thing, because God's plan for a changing world is always to change people. No one can be part of the solution if he is still part of the problem.'

I then referred to three verses in Ephesians 2. First, *Jesus is our peace;* He has broken down the dividing wall of hostility. Second, *He made peace* by reconciling us to God through the cross, thereby bringing the hostility to an end. Third, Jesus came and *preached peace.* 'There is something creative in the very act of proclaiming, because it expresses faith, and God honours faith. To those who say that this sounds too spiritual for such a practical problem, I ask, Have we ever given Jesus a chance? Is He or is He not God?'

As the men shifted in their chairs, I took a deep breath and continued. 'This problem of peace breaks down into three parts. First, peace in our heart. God can never bring peace to the world through people who do not have peace in their own hearts. Second, peace in our own home. Through the sheer determination pledged by every individual member, we say, "We shall not fight!" That means not fighting one another in the home, not fighting our neighbour, not fighting our friends, not fighting our colleagues, fellow students, or anyone. The very basis of our life and actions is the peace that God has given, and from that peace, we act. Our homes, therefore, become homes of peace. And the number of "homes of peace" will determine how close Lebanon is to peace.

'Let me emphasise this point. We need to create a movement. Every "home of peace" should be recognisable. That implies that this is a haven where everyone is welcome to find refuge. It could be done with a sticker or a symbol on the front door or whatever we have courage for. Every "home of peace" could have some literature, which the Bible Society will produce, on the theme of peace, and Open Doors will finance that. The third part is peace in our community, in our churches, in our spheres of influence. It is said that they will know we are Christians by our love. This peace movement will demonstrate love everywhere we go.

'Finally, the third question, What are our resources? Our resources are people. That is, all those who say, 'Enough is enough,' all those who are discouraged, all those who expect God to do a miracle, all those who say there's no human solution, no political solution, no military solution. All of these people, and that includes us in this room, are our resources.

'In conclusion, I say that this is simply one method to bring about peace in Lebanon. It has not been tried yet. We must give God a chance, and it's open for all those who love Jesus Christ and who through that very fact alone have enough motivation to make sacrifices and to risk something in order to get peace. May God bless you as you prayerfully ponder this peace plan, and let me know what God is telling you.'

I sat down and waited. There was silence for a few moments. Then one pastor commented haltingly, 'Brother Andrew, I would like to think that we can do something. The conditions, as you know, are horrible. But we are so few. Look at this room. There are twenty-five, maybe thirty of us.'

'That's why I put resources last,' I said. 'If we start with resources, we will make our goals too small. But if our vision is God's heart, He can multiply our resources.'

Then Peter asked, 'Brother Andrew, could you tell us a little more about what you are thinking with the "home of peace" concept?'

I was pleased that my friend realised the importance of this. 'I am proposing that every Christian home become a home of refuge. If you talk about peace in a conference but your home is not involved, it means your heart is not involved, so you will get nowhere. This is the whole principle of any change – to catch the heart, the imagination.'

'So how do we begin?' asked Philip.

'I think we begin with our own congregations. We preach from the pulpit – we could begin with the passage in Ephesians 2 – and we encourage each family in our church to make their home a home of peace. If this is to work, it must become a movement. If enough families make their homes a home of refuge, the idea can spread.'

I offered to provide publicity. 'This is necessary, if only to help you not feel alone. The Church in the West needs to pray for this effort. We will need to raise funds, and there are a lot of Lebanese in America who are potential donors. Remember that the world sees the Lebanese as fighters and troublemakers. I want to let them know that there is a Christian peace movement that is not – and I emphasise *not* – politically motivated. This is not just one more party among many in Lebanon. Therefore all Christians around the world can identify with us.'

The discussion continued through the morning, but then the men started to rise to go to other commitments. 'We thank you for presenting this,' said one of the pastors.

'Yes,' another said. 'You have given us much to think about.'

No one said, 'Let's meet again. Let's make a commitment to follow through on this.'

The men scattered to their individual congregations.

Lord, will this effort bear any fruit? I prayed. Or was this just a naive and ultimately futile exercise?

EIGHT

IT'S JUST A MESS

Beirut, August 1989

The shooting started before sundown that evening. Lucien hustled his family downstairs to the basement. In their bunker they chose a movie to pop into the VCR. Electricity was still on, but a generator was standing by, ready for the inevitable interruption of power. 'Tonight let's watch *The Hiding Place*,' said Huguette, Lucien's wife.

'A rather apt title, given our situation,' said Martin, their son.

'Is anyone hungry?' Lucien asked. Huguette gave him instructions, and he headed upstairs to the kitchen for fruit, flat bread, hummus, and a salad she had prepared earlier that afternoon. As he opened the refrigerator, the phone rang. He crossed the marble entryway to the table that stood by a pillar at the entrance to the spacious living room, which also doubled as a meeting place for the church Lucien pastored.

'Hello.' Lucien never heard who called. He never actually heard the blast that knocked him off his feet and buried him in plaster and rubble. His wife appeared as in a silent film, checked his vital signs, then noticed something through the dust and smoke. She stepped over him, grabbed the gas heater and heaved it out the window. Only then, looking past her, did Lucien see that an artillery shell had totally destroyed their living room.

After dusting the debris off him, Huguette put a compress on his head to stop the bleeding. Lucien's sons helped him to his feet, and the three of them dragged him to the basement door and carried him down the steps to safety. There, in the dark room, the movie *The Hiding Place* was playing, but Lucien couldn't hear it. He turned to his wife and saw her lips moving. With horror, he realised that the blast had made him deaf.

Larnaca, Cyprus, September 1989

The ferryboat that usually transported me to Lebanon floated idly at the dock. There was none of the usual activity, no bright lights, no cars driving on board, no passengers milling around the deck. A sign in the ticket window indicated there would be no ferry service until further notice.

Air travel into Beirut had been extremely dangerous and unreliable for several years. The easiest way for me to get there was to fly to Larnaca on the island of Cyprus, then take an overnight ferry about one hundred miles to Lebanon. However, the ferry service presented its own risks after Israel diverted one boat to Haifa in 1984 and detained some of its passengers.[1]

I knocked on the glass of the ticket window and caught the attention of a man working in the back room. He came to the window and opened it, saying, 'There is no ferry tonight.'

I smiled. 'I understand. But do you know if there is some other way I can get to Beirut?'

He pointed behind him. 'Try over a few boats. There may be one taking some people to Jounieh.' That was a small harbour north of Beirut, in the Christian sector.

Sure enough, three piers over there was a man taking passengers onto a large speedboat. I pulled out a wad of American money and paid the captain 150 dollars before boarding. A varied group of about thirty people were seated around the cabin of the bobbing boat. There was a nervous businessman wearing slacks, polo shirt, and windbreaker, fidgeting with his briefcase. A Lebanese couple, the wife's head covered by a scarf, nervously held hands. A young man in jeans and a sweatshirt tossed his backpack into a corner of the cabin and looked east towards his next adventure.

An hour after sunset the captain started the engine and pulled out of the harbour. Behind me I could see the lights of Larnaca falling away, replaced by the looming silhouette of Cyprus. Ahead was only inky blackness. The boat cut through five-foot swells, and I felt the mist from the waves spraying over the bow. Soon the businessman hurried to the head to ease the nausea he felt.

We were about ten miles from our destination when the speedboat captain shut off the running lights, leaving only the soft green glow of his instrument panel. It was then that I saw lights flashing in the distance. 'Looks like a storm,' the business-man muttered.

'Artillery,' said the captain. 'They're really going at it tonight.'

We watched in morbid fascination as flashes of artillery lit up the Beirut skyline. The captain spoke again. 'We're going to land in Jounieh.' That was a once sleepy fishing village that, since 1975, had grown into a city, developed by Christians fleeing from the fighting in Beirut just a few miles to the south. 'Make sure you grab all of your belongings. I need to load up passengers and be away as quickly as possible.' He didn't have to add that he felt he was risking his life every time he made this trip.

The boat didn't begin to slow until the shadow of the dock was visible directly ahead. The captain cut his motor and silently drifted up against the bumpers hanging from the pier. As soon as the first rope was looped over a pile, the young man in jeans grabbed his backpack, jumped onto the pier, and headed on his way. I looked into the shadows and thought I recognised the form of my friend. I waved, and he waved back. I grabbed my suitcase and jumped off the rocking boat. Lucien stepped forward and embraced me in a big hug.

The concussion from an explosion shook us. It seemed only a few blocks away and was followed by the rapid pulse of machine-gun fire. Revving the motor, the powerboat captain yelled, and several people jumped on board before he pulled away from the pier, made a sharp U-turn, and roared into the night.

Lucien pulled on my arm, hurrying me to his car, parked at the top of the quay. His tyres screeched as we pulled onto the narrow street and headed north, away from the battle.

WE DROVE THROUGH several narrow backstreets to one of the serpentine roads that climbed Mount Lebanon. I held my breath as Lucien drove. Finally, I exhaled in a sigh of relief as we passed beneath the giant statue of the Virgin Mary in Harissa. 'We're taking the long way home,' Lucien explained in his French accent. 'We'll avoid Beirut and, hopefully, all the fighting.' I couldn't help but notice the word *hopefully*. Lucien reached over and gripped my arm. 'Don't worry. I know these roads well. We'll be fine.'

Three times we had to stop at checkpoints, but in each case, after a brief review of Lucien's papers and my passport, we were waved through. Finally, I spoke: 'I'm sure glad you came. How did you know where to find me?'

'I've ridden on that boat myself,' he explained. 'I checked earlier today and learned the ferry wasn't running, so I figured I'd find you in Jounieh.'

How many people would brave artillery and machine-gun fire to pick me up in the middle of the night? My dear friend had suffered much because of the war. His watch business had failed after his shop was destroyed in 1976. Lucien was a pastor who had supported himself with his business. He felt he had to move his wife and children to safety, so he packed up the family car and drove through Syria, Turkey, Greece, Yugoslavia, and northern Italy to Switzerland. But despite the offer of a good job and safety for his family, he and his wife, Huguette, didn't feel right about their escape. Four months later they returned to Beirut. That's when he was asked to assume leadership of the Bible Society in Lebanon.

Since the outbreak of the civil war, Lucien and his family had moved eight times. Four times they'd lost their home to bombs or refugees. These were desperate times and in some parts of Beirut if a family left their home for even half a day, refugees would occupy it, and there was nothing the owners could do. On one occasion, his landlord decided to emigrate to Australia and sold the building.

The new landlord promptly evicted all of the tenants. When Lucien refused to leave, the new owner demolished the building around his apartment.

Finally, Lucien built his current home on family property in the mountains, believing that it was outside the range of the fighting. After moving into the mountains, Lucien started a church that met in his living room. Soon the conflict expanded and surrounded the new home. Five times Lucien's house had been hit by artillery fire, the last time just a month earlier, when he had been injured.

Given all he'd been through, I was concerned about how Lucien was holding up under the strain. At the top of the mountain, just before we would have headed down into the Bekaa Valley, we turned south, passing by the canyons and gullies that divided communities on the slopes below us. The tension of our getaway had subsided, and I felt free to ask Lucien how he was recovering from the latest attack on his house. 'I couldn't hear anything for a week,' he answered. 'I thought I had lost my hearing permanently, but, thank God, that's okay now. However, it's getting wearisome.' He paused, sighed deeply, then added, 'Andrew, I don't think I can put my family through this any more.'

I sensed my friend needed to talk and I encouraged him by asking, 'Where would you go?'

'We could take that boat you were on tonight. The home office wants us to move the work to Cyprus.' He was referring to the offices of the United Bible Society in England. 'They feel Cyprus is safer. They can provide a better facility. And the Lebanese pound has collapsed so it would be better economically.'

'But you're hesitating?'

'Somehow I feel the ministry belongs here, among the people whom we're helping.'

There was more, and I prodded. 'What else is troubling you?'

My friend was quiet a few moments before saying, 'It feels like this war will never stop. It's been fourteen years. Do you know that nearly one hundred thousand Christians have been killed in this war? But the Church in the West is silent. No one seems to care! Of course, that's just an impersonal number. What's hardest is the emotional toll it takes on you as a pastor. This year I've buried two men from our congregation. One was the man who laid the marble tiles on the floor of our home. The other was vaporised in an explosion. We "buried" him in an empty coffin.'

Tears welled up in my eyes as I felt some of Lucien's pain. 'How is your congregation holding up?' I asked.

After another long sigh, he answered. 'What choice do we have? We need each other. But many, like me, wonder why they should stay. If there's no hope . . .' His voice trailed off.

'Is your church still meeting in your home?'

He shook his head. 'We can't. You'll see. It's just a mess.'

The night's combat had ceased by the time we arrived at Lucien's home. The living room was blocked off, and I couldn't view it in the dark. It was nearly 3.00 am and I'd had a very long day. Still, as I lay down in my friend's guest room, it took me a while to fall asleep. I was here specifically to help people like Lucien, men and women who ministered to others and led the Church in the midst of this conflict. They were not superheroes. They were ordinary people confronting extraordinarily difficult situations. They had families to support. It was only natural that they wearied of the unending fighting. When the opportunity came to emigrate to Europe or Australia or North America, many couldn't resist. I understood the natural desire to flee to safety, but I also believed that a vibrant Church, the living body of Christ, had to be present in the midst of strife. Jesus said He is the light of the world and that His people are the light of the world. Both statements are true. People in whom Christ dwells provide hope in the midst of conflict. But how can they be light if they lose hope? How could they be light in Lebanon if they fled, leaving only darkness behind?

BEING WITH US
IS THE GREATEST
ENCOURAGEMENT

Beirut, 1989

The morning mist was burning off over the city. I stood on Lucien's balcony but didn't touch the twisted metal railing that teetered loosely at the edge. The Mediterranean Sea wasn't yet in view, but down below I could see wisps of smoke from two buildings, destroyed in last night's fighting. Behind me yawned the opening to Lucien's home. The French doors had been blown off and a piece of plywood, which I'd pushed to the side, was in their place. The stone walls of Lucien's home and of all the surrounding buildings were scarred and pockmarked by shrapnel. Next to me stood the remains of an orange easy chair with huge chunks of stuffing carved out by shrapnel. I placed my hand on it to see if it was sturdy.

Lucien's voice startled me. 'It's safe to sit on it, if you want.'

Pointing into the house, I asked, 'Where were you standing when the bomb exploded?'

With a nod of his head he indicated that I should follow him. The living room was a mess. The worst of the rubble and dust had been cleared away, but chunks of the marble floor were missing, holes from shrapnel marked the walls, and sofas and easy chairs looked like they'd been torn apart by cats with razor-sharp claws. Damaged paintings and framed photos with cracked glass leaned against the wall. Standing by the pillar at the other side of the room, Lucien said, 'I was right behind this pillar and that is what saved my life.' Then he turned me around. 'All the glass was blown out. And see this gas space heater?' He pointed to a hole in the metal heater at my feet. 'My wife smelled gas and threw it out the window.'

'I'm amazed no one else was hurt.'

'The basement is surrounded by rock. The house is set in what used to be a quarry. So the basement is quite safe. Everyone else was downstairs, watching *The Hiding Place*.'

'So Corrie ten Boom saved another family!' Lucien smiled at the irony. I walked back towards the balcony, my shoes crunching on tiny pieces of marble and plaster, and my friend followed me. The fog had now burned off and the intense blue sky and the spectacular view of the Mediterranean Sea seemed to mock the destruction around us.

I put my arm around my friend's shoulders and said, 'May I pray for you?' He nodded. Quietly I asked God to give my friend the strength to carry on in the midst of this war. I prayed for resources to rebuild his home, for protection for his family, and for the ongoing work of the Bible Society. 'Lord, You know the only answers are in Your Word. May this ministry continue through Your faithful servant, Lucien.'

He joined me in saying 'Amen'. Then I thought of a word picture. 'Do you know the lesson of the spider and the cobweb? When the spider's web is damaged or destroyed, it immediately begins to spin a new web. Always. If anything destroys our society, our life, our work, we must begin at once to rebuild, to make it as new, as if we do not expect it to be destroyed again.' Lucien let out a gasp of surprise. 'And if it is attacked again, God will give the grace to do it again.' *And again and again and again,* I thought, preaching to myself.

'You know, when the war started, people stopped coming to see us,' Lucien said, gazing towards the horizon. 'But you have come. Your being with us is the greatest encouragement.'

T HE FIGHTING RESUMED early that afternoon. A part of me wanted to hustle down to the safety of the basement, yet I lingered, watching two big guns, belching blue smoke, fire from a camouflaged spot in the forest below us. Then a shell landed in the forest about 300 metres in front of us, and Lucien said we'd better go downstairs. As we did, he said, 'Do you know what the first minister of defence in Lebanon was called? His English was rather poor. He called himself "the Minister of Boom Boom".'

'Rather appropriate,' I sadly agreed as we heard another muffled boom of artillery fire.

Huguette was worried about their seventeen-year-old son, Martin, and his friend Matthieu who had taken the car to run some errands and had not returned. Several neighbours joined us in the basement, including an Armenian couple and their two daughters plus two sisters from Sri Lanka. We listened to the three o'clock news and learned that the previous day 20 had been killed and 130 wounded. The other item of interest was that General Aoun, one of the Maronite leaders, was offering to meet Walid Jumblatt, leader of the Druze, to discuss terms of agreement for a future Lebanon.

Whenever it was quiet for ten minutes or so, we climbed back upstairs to assess the situation. Lucien helped me distinguish the sound of outgoing and incoming fire. Of course, I was reminded that the most dangerous sound was the one you never heard – there was no warning for the missile headed directly at you.

Lucien's face brightened when Martin returned home safely. I greeted the son who'd grown an inch in the year since I'd last visited. Lucien called over the second boy and told me, 'I want you to meet Matthieu!' The young man shook my hand and then embraced Lucien like a father. 'Brother Andrew, this is also my son.'

Nearby explosions urged us back into the basement. I felt like a yo-yo, going up and down the stairs, at the mercy of the militias I couldn't see. Most of us sat on crates or chairs. Martin and Matthieu sat on the floor, leaning against the rock wall. I stared at Matthieu. He looked like a brother to Martin. He was a lanky teenager, arms folded, eyes closed as he rested. His face was hard, as though he had suffered far more than his age should permit.

Lucien observed me staring at the boy. 'We adopted him four

months ago,' he said. 'He's had no family. He was picked up off the street and forced to serve in a militia at the age of eleven.'

In my years of visiting Lebanon, I couldn't help but notice that the age of Palestinian and Lebanese combatants had dropped. It wasn't unusual to see ten-, eleven- and twelve-year-old boys, their shoulders slumping under the weight of M-16 rifles, grenades hanging from their belts, wielding authority over any elders who dared encroach on territory occupied by their particular militia. I couldn't help but wonder about the future of these kids and of their fractured nation.

'His life was unbearable,' Lucien explained, as though reading my thoughts. 'But the kids are trapped. They dare not escape once they're in the clutches of one of these militias. So when Matthieu abandoned his unit, he was arrested for desertion and imprisoned. Someone in our church learned about him, and we began to pray for him. Miraculously, he was released after a few months and we took him in.' Lucien's voice choked momentarily and I could see he was proud of this boy, as he was proud of his own flesh and blood.

By sunset the fighting had become constant, and ten of us were trapped in the quarry-turned-basement. Lucien, Martin, and Matthieu brought out guitars, and for an hour we sang choruses and hymns and prayed for Lebanon. Then Lucien asked if I would like to preach. I rarely pass up any opportunity to expound on the Scriptures. This tiny congregation, huddled together, was as precious to me as that in any cathedral or megachurch. I opened my Bible and breathed a prayer: *Lord, give me Your message for these brave people.*

I turned to John 21. 'It is the Lord!' I started, referring to verse seven of the chapter. 'It has been several weeks since the crucifixion and resurrection. The disciples are discouraged. They feel like they have lost everything. They haven't seen Jesus for many days. They have no routine in life. They don't know what to do. Jesus has told them to go into the world, but where? And what is their message? What is their mandate? They've run out of money because their treasurer committed suicide. So Peter says, "Let's go fishing." Unfortunately, the others didn't say, "No, Peter, let's pray about the future!" They all followed Peter and spent all *night* in a sea filled with fish and they caught *nothing*.

'What a tragic word! They caught *nothing*. All night. Nothing.' I noticed a smile from the two teenage boys. 'You can have all kinds of activities outside the direction of Christ. You can be a do-gooder, be busy, do a million things, but if you do your own thing instead of following Christ, your tombstone will say: "All night. Nothing."

'The turning point for the fishermen came when a supposed stranger appeared on the beach. He called to them, "Have you caught any fish?" They shouted back, "No!" They were so chagrined they couldn't even shout "No, *sir*!" They were fed up with themselves and everything.

'How grumpy we can become when things don't go our way! The stranger saw the fish the disciples couldn't see. When, at His direction, they threw their net over the other side, there was a miracle – God pushed the fish in – more than the net could hold. Then the disciple whom Jesus loved said, "It is the Lord!" '

In this informal way I spoke to my little flock as they listened intently, identifying with the circumstances and struggles of the disciples. 'The lordship of Christ. It's the call to a productive life. When the disciples arrive on land, they're cold, they're tired, they're hungry, and they're lonely. But Jesus is the Lord of their need. There is a charcoal fire and a hot breakfast waiting for them. Jesus gives them heat, rest, food, and Himself. It's touching that the almighty God got up early that morning to cook breakfast for His disgruntled friends. He was Lord of their need. This was a gentle reminder to them and to us. He is the Lord of our need. Exactly what you need, Jesus provides. The people in Lebanon have tremendous needs, but you can show them that the Lord will meet those needs.'

THE NEXT TWO days were busy. Lucien and I left early in the morning to visit pastors and encourage them. The third day dawned a glorious morning, the kind that reminded me again of why Lebanon was the jewel of the Mediterranean. I told Lucien and Huguette that I was going to take a walk. Without thinking, I grabbed my camera, hoping to get a panoramic photo of Beirut and the Mediterranean Sea. I walked up the mountain road, staying as far to the side as possible to avoid cars heading into Beirut. After about a quarter mile, I turned off onto a dirt road and continued my little hike to an opening with a marvellous vista. I lifted my camera and took a picture of Jounieh, beautifully framed by the boughs of two trees.

I turned my attention south. The coastline was crystal clear, and I could make out the Seaside Park and American University of Beirut. I raised my camera to take another photo when two soldiers suddenly descended on me. One of them grabbed the camera while the other gripped my arm and said, 'Please, come with us.' As I walked up the dirt road with them, I could make out a gun station being used by a militia. This was not good.

We went into a little hut, and they ordered me to sit on a metal chair while one of the soldiers sat opposite me at a metal desk. The other man stood guard at the door. The man at the desk glared at me as he held the camera in his hands. 'Why are you taking pictures?' he demanded.

'It is a beautiful morning. I was taking photographs of Beirut and the sea.'

'It is not permitted,' he said, and with that, opened the camera and removed the film. Then he continued to hold the camera as he said, 'What are you doing up here?'

'I'm staying with friends.'

'Who are they?'

'Lucien. He and his family live just down the road from here.'

'How long have you been there?'

'I arrived four days ago.'

'From where?'

'I live in Holland.'

The two soldiers talked for a minute in Arabic, then the one at the desk said, 'Come with me.'

We rode in a jeep down the mountain into Beirut to what appeared to be some kind of headquarters. There I was handed over to another interrogator who asked me where I was staying and what I was doing in Lebanon.

'I am visiting church leaders.'

The questioner looked confused. 'What churches?'

'I'm working with the Bible Society of Lebanon, which works with many churches.'

'Where is this Bible Society?'

I told him where it was located, and he then conferred with another associate in Arabic. I became concerned that this man might want to know all the people I'd been meeting with. I wasn't sure which side these soldiers were on. *Lord, please protect me,* I prayed. *May I be able to honestly answer every question, but may they ask only the questions that I can answer without endangering the people I work with.* It wasn't the most articulate prayer, but a sense of peace came over me.

'You have been here before?'

'Yes, I visit Lebanon twice each year.'

'Only in Beirut?'

'No, sir. I travel to other towns. I speak at churches and visit Christian workers. Anywhere there are Christians, I go to encourage them.'

'Tell me what places you have travelled to.'

I mentioned several towns I had visited on recent trips, including Hammana. When I mentioned Hammana, the interrogator looked up from his notepad and stopped writing.

'Where were you in Hammana?' he asked.

'I visited Hamlin Hospital.'

'Why?'

'There is a Dutch nurse there.' I mentioned her name, then said, 'I wanted to bring her greetings from Holland and encourage her.'

'I know her!' said the man. 'Who else do you know at the hospital?'

I mentioned a doctor.

'I know him too.' He put his pen down and sat back in the chair. 'I am from Hammana.' Then he yelled to an assistant and ordered him to bring us coffee.

As we drank the thick Arabic coffee, I breathed a sigh of relief. While I never volunteered information, I had determined never to lie when asked direct questions. This circumstance proved the wisdom of that policy. But what prompted me to mention Hammana out of all the places I'd visited? The only answer was that God was in charge!

After we finished our coffee, the interrogator stood and shook my hand and said I was free to leave. He even ordered one of the soldiers to drive me back up the mountain.

THE NEXT MORNING I sat on the balcony in the pockmarked orange chair and prayed, preparing to leave Lucien and stay with a pastor in Beirut. A mutual friend was scheduled to pick me up in about an hour. 'Andrew, you have to see this!' Lucien was standing in the doorway, waving a letter and a cheque. 'It's the most amazing thing, from a Jordanian brother. Let me read from the letter. "The Lord spoke to me that the proceeds I just received from my business need to go to my friend Lucien for his house." There's enough to repair most if not all of the damage!'

I stood and we embraced. 'This has never happened to me before,' he said as we stepped back into his home. 'The first time someone ever sends me money for my home is after you come, when I'd given up hope, and you believed God and prayed for me. He is indeed the Lord of our need!'

Lucien's family had gathered in the dining room to celebrate the answered prayer. As I looked at them, my friend had another encouraging word for me: 'My son, Matthieu. In part it's because of you that he's with us.'

I must have looked at him with a strange expression, because he laughed. 'Don't you remember? Three years ago you challenged the church leaders to create homes of peace. Well, that's what we did. Where else would this fine boy find peace and Christian love and hope for a real life?'

As I rode down the mountain into the war zone that was Beirut, I thought of all the suffering in Lebanon that had torn at my heart. After hearing the gut-wrenching stories and seeing bombed-out, abandoned church buildings, I couldn't sit by without at least making some attempt at a solution. I thought of friends like Naji, Peter, and Philip, pastors who had laboured under severe conditions. They had motivated me to try to be a catalyst for peace. Perhaps my efforts hadn't accomplished much, but today, seeing Lucien's and Matthieu's joy made me extremely grateful that I had tried.

I HAVE NO POWER

Beirut, 1989

'Lucien, what went wrong?' I asked my friend in his office at the Bible Society in Beirut. 'Has anyone besides you acted on the peace plan?'

Leaning back in his chair, he looked at me over the top of his reading glasses. 'Not many,' he admitted. 'We printed the literature, but most of it is sitting in our warehouse.'

'No one seems to really care. What is holding us back?'

Lucien removed his glasses and leaned forward, taking a sip of coffee before he spoke. 'No, people do care. But I think the problem is with us, with the Church in Lebanon. We don't have peace among ourselves, so how can we be a light for peace in the country?' He sighed deeply and continued. 'Even among our small group of evangelicals, there is division. One church teaches that a woman without a head covering isn't "born again". In another, charismatics are in conflict with non-charismatics. We struggle to hold our own congregation together because of differences in music. The old people want hymns accompanied by piano; the young people want choruses accompanied by guitars and drums. The only reason we haven't split over this is that our young people were more mature and offered to cut back on their loud music – for the good of the body.'

I understood the problem for I'd observed it many times. Shortly before presenting the peace plan, I had spoken in a Baptist church in a town north of Beirut. Two women entered the meeting without head coverings. One of the elders pointed them out to me and whispered, 'They're probably not born again.' On another occasion, I spoke to a large meeting of Maronite charismatics and brought some conservative evangelical friends along – a miracle in itself. They enjoyed the meeting but afterwards said to me sadly, 'Great service. Too bad they were not born again.' So certain Christians had taken it on themselves to judge the hearts of men and women. How could these people be agents for peace?

Then I'd met with a Nazarene pastor. He told me that his church had been destroyed and the congregation had no place to meet. 'What can we do?' he asked. I suggested, 'Why not send them to other evangelical churches?' He looked at me with a shocked expression, as though it had never occurred to him. 'You think we should do that?' I couldn't help but think, *Are the denominational walls so high that even in the most dire of circumstances we can't help one another?*

'Why can't we lay aside our theological differences for the good of the whole Church?' I asked Lucien. 'If we do nothing, then it's hopeless.'

'I agree with your plan. You know I do. I've done what I can, but there aren't too many following us.'

I closed my eyes and tried to understand what this meant. 'I struggle with this question: Can God use Christians to bring about peace without being political? I believe He can. If we deny that, it means we are defenceless in the hands of any cruel manipulator, be he religious or political.' That promoted a thought. 'Lucien, maybe we can do something to show how this works. On the boat from Larnaca, I thought about the two militias now fighting around your home. You said they are led by Christians?'

'Yes, General Aoun and Dr Geagea are both Maronites.'

'Then we ought to appeal to them, based on their mutual faith.'

Lucien chuckled. 'Andrew, what makes you think their faith is anything more than cultural?'

'I know that. But what can we *do*? The Maronite patriarch –

doesn't he have any authority? Can't he make those men stop fighting each other?'

My friend was smiling now. 'I know the patriarch. I'll schedule an appointment for us.'

T HE ROOTS OF the Maronite Church go back to the church in Antioch, where believers were first called Christians (Acts 11:26). A priest named Maron, who died in 410 AD, influenced one group of these Christians. The followers of Maron were persecuted and fled to the mountains of Lebanon. They celebrated an Eastern Orthodox liturgy, but since the time of the Crusades, they have been under the authority of the Roman Catholic Church.

With the aid of the French, Maronites had held primary political power since 1920. Under the National Pact of 1943, Maronites always filled the presidency due to their supposed population majority. But by the 1970s, Muslims outnumbered them and demanded a reform of the system. The Maronites would not hear of it, and this was one reason for the civil war. During the conflict, they had earned a reputation for brutality that gave the term *Christian* a most foul connotation. Some considered this war a case of 'the Maronites against everyone else'.[1]

Now Maronites were fighting against each other. I wondered: *Could I appeal to the leader of this church to force these two combatants to reconcile?*

The patriarchate of the Maronite Church was located at Bkerke in the foothills above Jounieh, just below the famous statue of Mary in Harissa. So far, this compound had managed to escape much damage from the fighting. There was a quiet bustle as priests and secretaries scurried around, conducting the business of the Church. His Beatitude Mar Nasrallah Boutros Sfeir greeted Lucien and me at the entrance to the great hall, a bright, gold-coloured room, with a red Middle Eastern carpet covering the floor and red-cushioned chairs along the walls. Three chandeliers lit the room, which could easily accommodate an audience of one hundred or more. It felt strange to have a small meeting in such a huge room. We sat at the far end, the patriarch on his throne, beneath a portrait of Pope John Paul II, with Lucien and me on his right. A television crew, waiting for an interview with the patriarch, followed us in to obtain some backup footage.

The patriarch was a short man, bald, with a snow-white beard. He was dressed in a black cassock with a bright red cincture around his waist. He spoke decent English, so we didn't require an interpreter, but his voice was very soft, and I had to strain to hear him.

I knew our time was limited. This man seemed friendly enough, so I plunged ahead, explaining who I was and the work that I had done over the years, first in the Communist world and then in the Middle East. After presenting him with an Arabic copy of *God's Smuggler,* I made an observation, how on recent trips I had noticed many young people on the ferry to Cyprus who told me they were leaving Lebanon for good. 'They all want to get out of Lebanon,' I said. 'I told some of them they should stay or come back, because they need to rebuild the country. I would imagine that concerns you too. I know tens of thousands from the Maronite Church have left the country.'

Patriarch Sfeir nodded his head and said, 'I am of your opinion. As a church we are encouraging our people to stay. But it is not possible to them because they have to work; they have to eat.' For the next few minutes we talked about the political situation. It was obvious that this man was politically savvy, referring to United Nations resolutions and various groups that were in conflict within Lebanon. But he repeated lines I'd heard elsewhere, that the real problem was the outsiders – Syria, Israel, various nations supplying arms to various militias. 'Cut the arms,' he said to me, 'and it will be all over. Without the arms, they will stop fighting.'

Since this wasn't the main purpose of my visit, I changed direction and said, 'I am here as a fellow Christian who is concerned that Christians are fighting one another.' The patriarch nodded his head as he listened. 'I have challenged the pastors I know to be agents for peace.' I pulled out a copy of the peace plan and gave it to him. 'I believe there can be a Christian peace plan for Lebanon. I would like for you to have this. A number of denominations, churches, and Christian organisations, like the Bible Society, want to proclaim the peace that Jesus Christ came to give. I think we must take the initiative. But my question for you is, How can anyone be part of the solution if he is still part of the problem? Specifically, how can Christians be taken seriously as peacemakers when some continue to fight each other? Let me give you one specific example: General Aoun and Dr Geagea. Both are Maronites, are they not?'

The patriarch sighed deeply and admitted, 'Yes, they are.'

'My friend here,' I pointed to Lucien, 'is caught in the middle of their fighting. Not long ago his home was hit by one of their bombs and nearly destroyed. Many, many people have suffered and died because of this war. Can't we do something to stop this?'

The man seemed genuinely grieved. 'I know. It is bad. I have considered excommunicating them both, but I don't think it would do any good.'

I decided to press my point: 'You are their bishop. Surely, you could summon them both to this room. Have them kneel right here on this red carpet. Tell them to repent of their sin and stop fighting each other. Surely you have the authority to do that!'

I stopped and waited. He said nothing, staring at the red rug. Then he sighed again and said, 'Andrew, you don't understand.' He looked at me with sad eyes, raised his palms upward off the armrests of his throne, and said, 'I have no power in this matter. There is nothing I can do.'

Lucien and I drove away from the palace with a deep sadness. How tragic that Christians could fight each other, and the leader of their denomination feel powerless to stop them. This country needed people to stick out their necks and *do* something. Well, I wasn't going to accept that there was nothing we could do. With God's help, I would demonstrate that Christians were not powerless.

ELEVEN

MEETING WITH
AN AYATOLLAH

Beirut, 1990

Sleep was rarely deep or restful for the middle-aged man lying on a mattress in a tiny basement cell. As he rolled over, he felt the tug of the chain that linked his ankle to the radiator and prevented his finding a comfortable position. He placed a hand on his forehead. It was clammy. The aches in his muscles convinced him that he was battling a fever.

Traffic sounds drifted through the walls, telling him that another day was dawning, another day of captivity, another day in which the drivers and pedestrians outside were unaware that a well-publicised hostage languished so near them.

The rattle of a key in the door jerked him out of his lethargy. He lunged for his blindfold and quickly wrapped it around his eyes. Over and over his captors had reminded him: 'You must cover your eyes when we come in. Otherwise we must kill you.' He could see the shoes of the jailer approaching him. 'Are you hungry?' a voice asked. Without waiting for an answer, a plate and cup were placed next to the mattress. Breakfast was a cup of lukewarm tea and a piece of day-old pita bread stuffed with a chunk of cheese.

As the jailer left the room and locked the door, the prisoner wondered, *How long have I endured this routine?* He'd lost count of the days and weeks. Judging by the seasons, it had been three years. And there was no end in sight. Out of habit, he bowed his head and prayed. 'Lord, I thank You for this bread and cheese and tea.' He stopped. Did he really mean that? Was he truly thankful for his daily bread? How cavalierly he had said grace over the years when he had an abundance. Now, he could only rely on the pity of his captors. And lean on the grace of his God.

Hope had vanished months ago. Still he prayed. There were no other options; if he didn't pray, he would go mad.[1]

FOR A LONG time it had been dangerous to travel to Beirut. In the late eighties, however, the warnings from my friends before each trip increased: 'It's not safe for Westerners. You could be the next hostage. You should wait until things calm down.' But things hadn't calmed down for years. I ignored the advice and travelled again and again to Lebanon. It wasn't that I had a death wish. I believed God had called me to help my brothers and sisters living in the midst of war, and one of the best ways to help was to *be* there with them.

The first hostages were taken in 1984. Most of the abductions had occurred in West Beirut. The usual scenario was for several armed men to ambush a single foreigner near his home. The captures were often in broad daylight, for no one dared to interfere with the kidnappers. The identity of the groups that captured dozens of Americans, British, and French citizens was usually murky. Often cited was a group called Islamic Jihad, but no one seemed to know who they really were. They took academics, journalists, businessmen, and clergy.

Though no Dutchman had yet been captured, it was naive to

think I couldn't be a target. I took care not to walk alone in certain areas of the city. Usually my hosts drove me to my various appointments and speaking engagements.

Certainly I wished to avoid capture, but I was concerned about what was happening and wondered about the motives of the captors. What did they expect to obtain for these hostages? Money? Political advantage? An exchange of prisoners? Many of the hostages had been confined for years, but no one knew where they were kept. If that wasn't troubling enough, there was the fact that even more Lebanese had suffered the same fate. Shi'ite Muslims were being held prisoner by Israel in southern Lebanon, but the media rarely reported on them. They were simply considered casualties of the unending civil war.

I began to wonder if I should do something. But what could I do? I didn't know any hostages personally, but I knew people who knew them and it hurt to see their anguish. One person told me he prayed constantly for a friend who had been a captive for more than three years. 'We get very little news,' he said. 'But I hear he is not well. I don't want him to die in that cellar or wherever it is that they hold him.'

Local church leaders in Beirut felt helpless. If they tried to intervene, they risked their lives and, more important, the safety of their congregations. But I wondered if it might be different for me. I wasn't local. I wasn't American or British. Maybe I could shine a light on the situation. My friend's report about the suffering of an actual hostage triggered an idea. Perhaps I could arrange for an exchange. My children were grown, and my affairs were in order, so I was willing to take someone's place. It wouldn't solve the plight of all the hostages, but it might be a start. But to whom would I take this idea?

The mosque in the southern suburb of Beirut was packed for Friday prayers. It was mostly young men, many wearing white turbans, who sat cross-legged on the rugs. A few black-veiled women observed from a balcony. From another small balcony facing the crowd stood a distinguished man in a black turban, a silver robe, and a black cape. A neatly groomed silver beard, at least six inches long, framed his oval face. He spoke into a microphone, quietly but with an authority that commanded the full attention of his audience. Below the speaker, half a dozen black-bearded security men, dressed in long-sleeved shirts and Western-style jeans or slacks, stood respectfully at attention. With their backs to the speaker, their eyes constantly searched the crowd to make sure there was no one intending to hurt their beloved imam. All remembered the attack a few years earlier when gunmen had sprayed the imam's car with bullets. While he'd escaped unharmed, one bullet had lodged in his turban.

For many in the crowd, this service was the highlight of their week. For the last several years, Ayatollah Sayyid Muhammad Husayn Fadlallah[2] had preached a message of revolutionary Islam. Tapes of his sermons were sold by the tens of thousands on the streets of Beirut. He articulated the longing of Shi'ites, who for years had lagged politically behind the Maronites and Sunnis. In expressing his frustrations, Sheikh Fadlallah provided the inspiration for a new political and military force in Lebanon, the Hezbollah or 'party of God'.

This powerful cleric was born in Najaf, the most holy Shi'ite city in Iraq, where Muhammad's cousin and son-in-law Ali is buried. From Ali had emerged the branch of Islam known as Shi'ism, and Fadlallah had thrived in this centre of Shi'ite learning.[3] After completing his education, he chose for his place of ministry one of the poorest Palestinian refugee camps in Beirut. Over the years his influence had grown through a combination of social work – clinics, youth clubs, and a school of Islamic studies – and his powerful oratorical skills. He captured the imagination of young, frustrated men and filled them with a vision for Islam – a faith that transcended Arab nationalism and repositioned the Palestinian conflict with Israel as a war with worldwide implications. For Fadlallah and his thousands of followers, the conflict in which they were involved was a war between Islam and infidels.

Fadlallah's vision for Lebanon was a country free of foreign influence, with all religious groups living in harmony under the dominance of Islam. It was time for Islam to rise and regain the greatness it enjoyed centuries before. The poor and disenfranchised that made up most of the Shi'ite population feasted on his words. In the mosque the audience heard his call to a deep personal faith lived in dedication to the cause: 'It is the individual who will grasp the gun, who will fly the plane. Tell me, by God, how will the individual advance this fateful cause, unless he possesses profound faith and moral fortitude, so that he will not yield to temptation?'[4]

Tapping my toe nervously, I sat in the lobby of the Garden Hotel in West Beirut. Resting on my lap, wrapped in plain paper, was a large, gilded Arabic Bible, which I'd acquired from my friends at the Bible Society. I had probed into the source of the hostage-taking and discovered that behind the murky group called Islamic Jihad was the well-organised movement Hezbollah, inspired by the charismatic Islamic preacher Ayatollah Fadlallah. I had asked to meet with him, and the man who arranged this meeting, ironically named Jihad, was also my interpreter.

What would stop Hezbollah from adding me to their collection of hostages? I had thought and prayed about that and concluded that I wasn't afraid of joining their captives, but I preferred to do so on my own terms.

Suddenly several men walked into the lobby. The clerk behind the front desk watched us intently, and the other loiterers in the lobby left quickly. I stood up as the man in charge, after glancing around the room, approached me. 'Are you Andrew?'

'Yes, I am Brother Andrew.'

'Do you have a car?'

'Yes, it's parked out front.'

'Then follow us.' One of the men held open the door and four men surrounded me as we left the hotel. Right in front was a van that had been converted into a crude armoured personnel carrier. I could see gun barrels pointing out the windows. Some curious onlookers watched from across the street and wondered if this were another kidnapping.

Jihad and I climbed into his car and started to follow the van. In front of it was a car with lights and sirens blaring. Another car, filled with tough-looking men, followed us. The convoy quickly sped up over sixty miles per hour. The lead car raced ahead to make sure intersections were cleared. Since no one dared to challenge us, we drove through every stoplight (many of which didn't work) unhindered. I couldn't help but laugh at the absurdity of the sight as tyres squealed through several narrow streets, and then we moved onto the main road towards the airport. I felt as if I were in a chase scene from a James Bond movie.

The 'chase' lasted about thirty minutes. Then we passed through a heavily protected checkpoint and stopped in a parking lot. A cordon of well-armed soldiers ringed the parking area. One of them grabbed my package, peered under the wrapping, and felt around the edges to make sure it was really a book and not a bomb. I smiled at the men and quipped, 'This is a lot of protection for an unarmed Dutchman!' A couple of the men smiled and nodded, probably not understanding a word I said.

Quickly I was escorted to a small reception room where a man with a closely cropped black beard, wearing a white dress shirt and slacks but no tie, welcomed me. 'The sheikh is expecting you and will see you in a few minutes. Would you like some coffee?' Apart from the soldiers standing idly around, this could be any Western office. Phones were ringing. A young man was using a photocopier. The only aberration was that no women worked here. A soldier, a rifle slung over his shoulder, served me a tiny cup of delicious coffee.

As I sipped my coffee, I prayed: *Lord, give me exactly the words to say to this man. You gave Yourself up for me on the cross. I am now willing to give myself up for one of my brothers. May this be a light in the darkness.*

The phone rang and the receptionist answered, then nodded to me, 'The sheikh will now see you.' Two soldiers escorted me through a small cobblestone courtyard, into another building, and up a flight of stairs. We entered a large reception area, where chairs lined the walls.

One of the sheikh's assistants met me, shook my hand and held up a tape recorder. 'I hope you don't mind if we record this conversation. The sheikh wants us to record all of his meetings.'

'Of course I don't mind,' I answered.

'Then we are ready.' A set of double doors opened into another room, also with chairs lining the walls. Standing in front of his seat against the far wall was Muhammad Husayn Fadlallah, dressed in a long grey caftan, covered by a black cape-like robe, and wearing a black turban on his head.

I introduced myself, and we shook hands. 'I have brought you a gift,' I said, while unwrapping the Bible and presenting it to him with both hands.

I heard a camera click as he received the large book and softly answered, *'Shukran.'* [5] Then he indicated that I should sit to his left. Jihad sat to my left and two of Fadlallah's assistants sat opposite me.

A fine, grey-patterned wallpaper covered the walls of the room; grey curtains that matched the sheikh's caftan draped the large window to Fadlallah's right. The rest of the chairs in the room were empty, but I could imagine that often this room was filled with Muslim clerics and political leaders. The only art of any kind was a framed photo of Ayatollah Khomeini gazing sternly down on us. The Iranian cleric and ruler, though he had died the year before, remained the spiritual and political inspiration for the radical Islamic movement throughout the Arab world. From my perspective, Sheikh Fadlallah was thus declaring his roots.

'I appreciate your willingness to see me,' I said, and immediately Jihad translated into Arabic. 'I have been coming to Lebanon for many years. I am a Christian and I am here representing Jesus Christ, attempting to do whatever I can to help bring peace to this country.'

The sheikh nodded. His right hand played with his black robe; in his left hand he fingered a string of prayer beads.

'That is why I want you to have a copy of the Bible. I don't know what the Quran says about hostage-taking, but I know what the Bible says, and God is against it. That is why I hope you will read this book. This is my present to you.'

He smiled and answered as an assistant came in and offered each of us a cup of strong coffee. 'We are friends with Christians. Christians are our brothers. If both Muslims and Christians would read their holy books, they would understand each other better.'

I took a sip of coffee then launched into my main reason for coming to meet him. 'In that spirit of cooperation, I believe that God wants you to release the hostages. All of them.'

He didn't respond immediately, and I held my breath. Then with his soft, baritone voice, he said, 'I don't see how I can help you.'

'You are the head of Hezbollah. Surely you can order the hostages released.'

A wry smile crossed his face. 'You can meet with Hezbollah leaders, but I do not represent Hezbollah.'

I'm sure my face registered a look of surprise. 'I was told that you were the man I needed to talk to if I wanted to make contact with Hezbollah.'

'The claim that I am the leader of Hezbollah is untrue. I'm not the leader of any organisation or party.'

'So who represents Hezbollah?'

'Hezbollah has its leaders. You can meet with them and talk with them.'

The English of my translator was awkward and I wasn't sure I was being understood. But I was sure of this – Sheikh Fadlallah was the spiritual inspiration behind the movement of Hezbollah. He might not run the organisation on a day-to-day basis, but he certainly wielded a great deal of influence over it. If there was a message they needed to hear, certainly Fadlallah could deliver it.

So what was my message? There was one man, a devout Christian, among the hostages. He'd been captured three years ago, and I'd heard that he wasn't well. 'I have come fully prepared to stay here and take the place of this man,' I said, naming the hostage.

This produced the first real reaction from the ayatollah. He turned towards me with a look of shock on his face – a look that implied *Are you mad?*

'This man has suffered enough,' I continued. 'Let him go back to his wife and children. I have put my house in order. I will take his place. Chain me to the radiator. Put me in the dark cellar. But let him go.'

For a moment, there was no response. I stared at him, trying to read his face and body language. But like a champion poker player, he revealed nothing. Then he said quietly, 'How can you say that?'

'This is the spirit of Jesus,' I answered, having prepared my defence. 'He died on the cross to let us go free. He died so we could live. Now I'm ready to give myself up so my friend can go free. That is what Christianity is all about.'

'I have never heard about this kind of Christianity,' Fadlallah said. So that is what we talked about. I told him that my role as an evangelist was to preach the gospel, the good news that God has paid the price for our sins by the death of Jesus on the cross. I knew that Muslims didn't believe Jesus had died, but that Judas took His place on the cross and Jesus was taken up into heaven. But the consequence of that belief was that the Muslims knew nothing about freedom. Ayatollahs Fadlallah and Khomeini knew all about law, but nothing about grace. This message was news to my host.

Quickly our hour passed. One of the assistants stood to remind the sheikh that another group was waiting to see him in the anteroom. Fadlallah stood, and a photographer snapped some photos of us. As the double doors opened, he turned to me and said, 'Thank you for coming. I am sorry that I cannot accept your offer. But please, come back and see me any time you are in Lebanon.'

Did I really expect that Sheikh Fadlallah would broker a trade, me for another hostage? It was a sincere offer, and I think he knew that I was genuine. But I now realised that he had intentionally distanced himself from the rank and file of Hezbollah that were fighting and taking Westerners hostage. Surely he could have communicated my offer and influenced their decision. But then maybe the purpose of this meeting wasn't for the hostages. Maybe it was for the soul of the ayatollah himself.

SEE THE SON OF
RIGHTEOUSNESS RISE

Mansouriyeh, Lebanon, 1990

A cool breeze from the west swept over the courtyard, where seven hundred chairs were set up in front of a stage, and through the open window of the Arab Baptist Seminary library, where I was relaxing before I spoke at the final night of a four-night evangelistic outreach. More than three hundred had attended the first night, and the crowd had increased by another hundred each subsequent night. I was encouraged by the response. Many churches were represented, and people had brought friends and neighbours.

I looked over the courtyard and prayed for the people who would soon start filling those seats. Then I turned back into the room. How many times I had visited this school! It was important because it was one of the very few Arabic-speaking seminaries in the region and students attended from many countries. To strengthen the Church in the Middle East, I believed that solid training of pastors and leaders was imperative. So I supported the school in any way I could, and Open Doors contributed financially. Unfortunately, the civil war had prevented many students from travelling here, but my friend and the school's president, Ghassan Khalaf, had worked tirelessly to keep the school open, so that when the fighting ended, it would be ready to receive students from several Arab countries.

Some popping sounds interrupted my thoughts. The breeze brought more than refreshing air; it also bore the sounds of shooting from the city of Beirut. I thought of every person pulling a trigger, letting go of his frustration and hatred. Then I thought of the bullets hitting a target, exploding, bringing fear, pain, wounds, and death. I imagined the people screaming and running, ambulances racing with sirens wailing. Will there ever be an end to this?

My eyes glanced over a wall of books, looking for a particular volume. I didn't find it, but I didn't have to, for years before, this little book had challenged me as I prepared to speak to the seminary students at a chapel service. The title was *What If This Was Your Last Sermon?* It was a question that every pastor should ask, and it had haunted me. What if this evangelistic service were the final message I would ever deliver? Would I change what I was planning to say? What would I pray if I knew this was my last prayer? Where would I go if I knew it was my last journey?

I raised my hands towards heaven and thanked God for the privilege of serving Him here in Lebanon. 'Lord, may I have Your message tonight for this large gathering,' I prayed out loud.

A praise band began playing as people streamed into the courtyard. Young people dominated the audience, and the music was more lively than what was heard in many churches – much more to their liking. Though it was more than an hour until I spoke, I made my way to the assembly, soaking up the enthusiastic singing. I didn't know the words they sang, but I could sense their hearts of love for the Lord they praised.

I picked a seat a few rows from the front and looked around. My eyes were drawn to a young man in his mid-twenties. His name was George and two nights ago he stood up when I issued a challenge and rededicated his life to Christ. Bullets had wounded him badly during the war, and his left side was partly paralysed. He turned and smiled at me. As I gazed into his eyes, I tried to remember which one was his good eye. As the next praise song began, I noticed the young man's shoes – high-top basketball trainers, with blue stripes and green blocks, and in big letters on the heel, the word *JUMP*. How ironic! George would never jump again.

During a break between songs, George hobbled over to me and gave me a big hug. 'Brother Andrew, I have missed you.'

'But it's only been one day since I saw you!' I answered with a laugh. 'But you know I missed you too!'

On this night my message was based on the short book of Jonah. It was a story everyone loved, and it gave me a means to make several points. 'Jonah's problem was that he was unwilling to do the will of God. Nineveh's problem was that they were lost – totally lost. And only Jonah knew the way out. God also had a problem. He had no other messengers. Unfortunately, Jonah spent God's money on a Mediterranean cruise. Jonah ran in the wrong direction. He hid. He slept. He snored!' My interpreter didn't have to translate my loud snore into the mike. The crowd laughed with surprise.

They were enjoying the story, but my point wasn't to entertain. I told how Jonah volunteered to die to save the sailors in the storm and how God provided a fish to rescue Jonah.

'God still loved Nineveh,' I said. 'After a submarine trip, Jonah arrived, proclaimed God's message, and saw the greatest revival ever. Think of it – the *entire* city, including the king, repented. But was Jonah happy? He didn't love the city that God loved. Jonah saw them as the enemy instead of people who were lost. He wanted their damnation, while God wanted their salvation.'

I turned and pointed to the city below us. 'I know many of you probably feel like Jonah. You see and hear the fighting day after day and you want to run away. You feel that it's hopeless, that this city can never be reached for Christ. If you feel that way, remember that Jonah failed his Lord the first time, but God gave him a second chance. At times we all have let the Lord down. We get depressed and maybe even deny Him, but God gives us a second chance. "The word of the LORD came to Jonah a *second time*: 'Go to the great city of Nineveh and proclaim to it the message I give you.' " God didn't say, "Jonah, you are a useless man." He told Jonah to get up and start again.'

As I had each evening, I gave the opportunity for people to meet Jesus Christ, and several in the audience stood. But I also had a challenge for believers. There was a city God loved right below us. Who would bring the good news to Beirut? More people started to stand, many with tears streaming down their cheeks. Soon nearly the entire congregation was on their feet, dedicated to being God's personal agents for peace in a city that desperately needed hope.

I reminded them that Jonah sat on the east of Nineveh. 'Why east? Because then he could see the sun go down on Nineveh. Here we are in the mountains on the east side of Beirut, the Christian side. The west is the Muslim part of the city. Do we want to see those people destroyed? Wouldn't it be better to sit west of the city and watch the sun rise? I say that because the Son of Righteousness will rise over the heathen, over the world, over the nations. So let's not sit on the east side to watch the downfall of the city. Let's change positions. Move to the west side and see God's Son of Righteousness rise. Don't give up! Don't give in to pessimism.'

Yes, these people could make a difference, if they would allow God to use them, if they refused to behave like Jonah, who turned and ran. I thought of my friend Naji and how I had begged him to help me conduct an evangelistic campaign in West Beirut. That had not been possible, and I realised now that I probably would never see that dream fulfilled. But in another respect, these men and women in front of me could do more with their lives than I ever could in a single campaign. They were the Light Force commissioned to proclaim hope and peace to Beirut and Lebanon.

GHASSAN KHALAF WAS one of those faithful servants of God who had stayed put during the war, keeping his academic ambitions on hold – for ten years he had done little work on his PhD dissertation – to pastor a church and provide stability to the Arab Baptist Seminary nestled in the hills above Beirut. At the conclusion of the final night of the outreach, he invited me to dinner. He seemed pleased with the results of the campaign, with approximately six hundred attending the final meeting. But there was also a weary look in his face. Fifteen years of living and ministering within what he called 'an open hell' had aged him.

The seminary was barely surviving. To illustrate, Ghassan placed a book on the edge of the table where we were eating. 'I'm living all the time like this. As you can see, the book is about to topple to the floor. If I put the least pressure on it, it will fall. I first met you in 1979, and Open Doors was supporting the seminary even before that. You can see why every dollar your ministry provides to the school is much appreciated. It's keeping us alive. We're not falling. Ask me, "Ghassan, how is your faith?" I say, "God is faithful!" My faith has grown over these years.'

I asked him to tell me how his church congregation was managing. He closed his eyes for a moment, then told me about one incident where he went to visit a young woman who had lost her husband in a recent skirmish, leaving her with three little children. 'There were several friends there, trying to comfort her. When she saw me, she shouted, "I don't believe in God! Don't speak to me about Him! He doesn't care for us! He is just watching us and letting us die!" Andrew, I felt a wave of compassion for her. She only said what thousands in Lebanon are feeling.'

'So what do you say to these people?' I asked.

'After she calmed down, I said, "Dear lady, what you have said about God would all be true if He had not become flesh and died on the cross to redeem us. That proves that God does care. God in Christ was involved in our situation. Because He has passed through suffering, He is able to help those who suffer. Do you believe that?" She nodded. I know she believes that, but it is so hard.'

'You have to minister to people like this woman, but you are suffering as well.'

My friend agreed. 'I remember one black period when day after day the sky rained mortar shells and rockets. No place was spared from shrapnel. Everyone was in danger of having his house burned or losing his money, his car, his possessions, or even his life. Those were anxious days. I remember days of confusion, and I asked God for victory over the feelings of anxiety.'

'And did He give you peace?'

He smiled as he answered. 'One night, I dreamed that my car was stolen. Feelings of resentment attacked me. A struggle began in my soul between complaint and contentment. After a cruel struggle I completely surrendered and accepted the loss. Then I woke up. I was happy it was only a dream. But then I thought: *It is beautiful to be victorious in a dream, but it is more glorious to be victorious over anxiety in real life, while I am awake.*'

'When God gives you that peace, then you are able to pass it on to others.'

'There have been some people – we call them "the war rich" – who have profited from the war. But for God's children, this has been an opportunity to prove the genuineness of our faith. We have become "war rich" on a spiritual plane.'

I was deeply touched by this man's humble testimony of God's faithfulness. Then he soberly added, 'You know, over the years almost all foreign missionaries and missionary agencies have left the country. They've gone to Cyprus, Athens, Istanbul, Amman. What remains here are the local churches and the nationals. We feel forsaken. We feel cut off from our bigger family. No evangelical leader from the West came here to ask, "How are you? What are you feeling? What do you need?" '

He started laughing. 'Then you came! Do you know what it means when Brother Andrew comes to Lebanon and lives with us among the shelling and bombing and difficulties? That is the value of your visits. Every time you come, there is a spirit of revival in my heart.'

Harderwijk, October 1991

The war was over. There had been promises before, but this time the peace seemed to be holding. In October of 1989 the Lebanese National Assembly had hammered out an agreement in Taif, Saudi Arabia, that divided power equally between Muslims and Maronite Christians and called for disbanding of militias. General Aoun had rejected the accord, but most of the other leaders, perhaps weary of war, had signed on. Changes had been slow, but gradually, fighting ground to a halt.

After listening to a BBC news report on the Taif Accord, I turned off the television and reflected on what was accomplished during fifteen bloody years of civil war. The PLO was driven out by the Israelis. The Syrians had invaded and still claimed a presence in the country – there was no evidence they planned to leave soon. Israel maintained a buffer zone for security in the southern part of Lebanon. A new fundamentalist Muslim power had emerged under the name of Hezbollah, the party of God. And the political structure remained basically unchanged, though supposedly more representative of the population. Only time would reveal if this was a real peace that would last.

What about the Church in Lebanon? There was no doubt that thousands of Christians of all denominations had died. Many more had fled and likely would never return to their native land. And, to my reckoning, the Church had almost no impact on the peace process. The Church had simply survived, and I wasn't sure if it was stronger or weaker. There were certainly a number of God's faithful servants who persevered and were His instruments during the conflict. Plus there were evangelistic meetings where people, hungry for peace in their troubled souls, came to know the Prince of Peace. God's presence remained in Lebanon, but was the Church all it should be?

And what about my personal contribution? I had averaged two trips per year into Lebanon for the past fifteen years, trying to encourage Church leaders. I had handed out thousands of tracts and Bibles. I had preached everywhere I was invited. I had tried to challenge the Church, especially urging it to be proactive in the peace process. I had also forged ahead, trying to do what perhaps the local Christians could not do by speaking with political, military, and religious leaders – to PLO, Druze, Hezbollah, Maronites, and more. There were many things I could point to that I had done. But to what end?

I looked at a handwritten letter I had received from my friend and translator Jihad, after our meeting with Ayatollah Fadlallah: 'Dear Brother Andrew. I will never forget when the man with grey hair and blue eyes came from the Free West to this complicated Middle East in order to secure the release of his brothers and our brothers at the same time who are in captivity by presenting himself as the sacrifice. I will never forget you, Brother Andrew. Sincerely yours, Jihad.'

So here was one Muslim man whom my life had touched. That was good. But my primary work was with the local Christian community. Was the Church better off because of my efforts? Was it prepared to be God's tool in a new Lebanon? I couldn't really answer those questions. I knew only that I could see little in the way of results. 'Lord, is there a better way?' I said aloud in the late-night quiet of my office. 'I've been working in the Middle East now for more than twenty years. I can point to many people I've met and activities I've done. But were they the right people, the right activities? I want to do those things that are significant.'

About one thing I was absolutely sure. There *must* be a vibrant Church in the Middle East. If we allow the Church to disappear, then we're getting rid of the Christians just as effectively as any Muslim fundamentalists might hope to accomplish. Then what would be the hope for the region? There would be no end to the fighting. Perhaps Christians couldn't end the warfare, but certainly they could be a light in the darkness.

My thoughts drifted south, to a land I loved, the country of Israel. I had visited there several times since my first trip in 1968. As in Lebanon, I visited with Church leaders. Lately the conflict between Palestinians and Israelis had increased, and that was causing problems for the Christians. It might be quiet in Lebanon, but there was an intifada in the Holy Land. I sensed it was time to give more attention to that region. 'Lord, show me what to do next,' I prayed.

WEST BANK AND GAZA:
WHO REACHES THE
TERRORISTS?

Jerusalem, late 1970s

I had always enjoyed preaching in Israel. The congregations responded enthusiastically to stories of the work of Open Doors in the Soviet Union and Eastern Europe. Some of the churches consisted of foreign workers, allowing me to preach in English without an interpreter. Occasionally I preached to one of the half dozen congregations of Messianic believers and thoroughly enjoyed their Jewish style of worship. However, most of my time was spent learning and listening. I travelled all over the country, visiting missions and kibbutzim and encouraging evangelistic outreaches, such as one on the beaches in Eilat (populated heavily by drug addicts).

Several times over the years I visited Narkis Street Baptist Church in Jerusalem. The senior pastor, Robert L. Lindsey, a renowned Bible scholar, had invited me to preach and tell my stories of the suffering Church in the Soviet Union. After one of those services, an intense young woman came forward to greet me. She would not release my hand as she stared into my eyes and said, 'I'm glad you are talking about the suffering Church in

Eastern Europe. But there is also a suffering Church right here!'

'I don't understand,' I said, trying to release myself from her firm grip. 'Narkis Street Church is a suffering church?'

'No, not this particular church.'

'You mean the Messianic congregations?' I knew there were a few Jewish churches in the country, and they occasionally faced harassment from Orthodox Jews.

'No! I'm a Palestinian,' she announced. 'I love the Lord Jesus Christ. And I'm not the only one. There are thousands of us, and we are struggling for our survival.' Now that she had my attention, she released my hand.

'Please explain,' I said, encouraging her to go on.

'In 1948 maybe 15 per cent of Palestinians were Christians. But a lot of them fled when Israel conquered many of our towns and villages.[1] Many more have left because it is so hard to survive here, to make a decent living, and to practise our faith. Now we are only 3 per cent Christians, maybe less.'

'Please tell me where I can find these Christians.'

'There is a small Baptist church in Gaza,' she explained. 'There are Christians in Nazareth. There are congregations scattered throughout Israel and the West Bank. The biggest churches are in Bethlehem and the two towns on either side – Beit Jala and Beit Sahour.'

For several years I'd been seeking to understand the burden I had first felt at Yad Vashem. While I had preached in churches and met with rabbis and other religious leaders, I still had no clear understanding of what I should be doing. This woman's intense words seemed to point me in the direction I needed to look. I had not seriously thought about all parts of the Church in the Holy Land. My work was to seek my brothers and sisters. If there was a Church among Palestinians, I needed to learn about her, learn about her condition, and see if I could help her.

How would I begin? First, I needed to find out where these churches were. Why had I not heard about these Christians? I knew about all the tourist sites, the buildings – the dead stones. I thought about the Christian tour groups that visit with great interest Jerusalem and other locations in the Holy Land, but on Sundays they usually hold private worship services in their hotels. They rarely attend a local Messianic congregation, let alone an

Arab church. It was time for me to launch out and seriously look for my brothers and sisters – the living stones of the Holy Land.[2]

One man in particular would become my mentor. His story begins during the first war between Israel and the Arab nations, just after Israel declared its statehood in 1948.

THIRTEEN

A WELL-AIMED STONE

Jerusalem, May 1948

Fighting had been non-stop for nearly a week. Sometimes you could hear it in the distance; other days it swirled around the neighbourhood. Today the guns were on their street.

The nine-year-old boy crouched in the corner, away from the window of the living room, and flinched every time he heard bursts of gunfire. His four-month-old sister was crying in the next room. Shouts could be heard from neighbouring apartments. Although the sun was setting, experience told him that darkness would bring no relief from the terrifying sounds. The constant confusion was more than Bishara Awad and his six brothers and sisters could stand.

Suddenly a piercing scream filled the house. Bishara's mother, Huda, hand over her mouth, ran through the room and out the front door, followed by Bishara's older brother Nicola. 'Get back inside!' the mother shouted as she reached her husband's body in the street. She grabbed his arms and dragged him into the house. As soon as she was inside the door, Nicola and Bishara helped pull the body to the dining room. Together they lifted it onto the table. Bishara looked at the face of his father and knew instantly that he was dead. A large red spot on his forehead was the single mark left by a bullet. Elias Nicola Awad, caught in the crossfire between the Jordanian army and soldiers of the Haganah (Israeli paramilitary force prior to the formation of the nation of Israel in 1948), was the latest casualty of the Arab-Israeli war.

The next morning, when shooting temporarily subsided, neighbours gathered in the small apartment. Several men from the neighbourhood came and consulted with Bishara's mother. No priests or pastors were able to reach them, so the men dug a grave in the courtyard behind the apartment building. Huda Awad read words of comfort from the Bible. Together, tears streaming down their faces, the children joined their mother in reciting the Lord's Prayer. Then the men carried the body to the makeshift grave.

Fierce fighting resumed that afternoon but ended before dark. At midnight there was an ominous knock on the door. It was a Jordanian soldier, who ordered the family to evacuate. 'Go quickly. We expect the Israeli army to return at any moment. We will let you know when it is safe to return.'

Ellen, Bishara's seven-year-old sister, put on six dresses over her nightgown. The rest of the family, without even a suitcase, left in whatever clothes they wore and joined the procession towards the old city of Jerusalem. Huda carried the baby, Diana, trying to keep her calm as they walked through the Damascus Gate. Just inside the ancient wall, a Muslim family took them in, provided blankets and food, and allowed the eight refugees to sleep in a storage room containing cans of kerosene.

The Awad family never saw their home again.

Beit Jala, spring 1974

Bishara Awad slipped out of bed so as not to awaken his wife and went to his office. There, agitated by the frustration that had been building for weeks, he paced the floor. As the principal of the Hope School, Bishara loved his work, but he needed to see results. There were nearly one hundred boys under his care, and every time he looked at them, it was like seeing himself in a mirror. Their stories were similar to his own story.

Often Bishara thought about his youth. After the Awad family had lost their home in 1948, the family remained in the ancient walled city of Jerusalem. Bishara's mother found a job as a nurse for twenty-five dollars a month, but it wasn't enough to feed and provide for seven children. To ensure that her children would have an education, she placed all but the oldest, Nicola, in orphanages. The girls were enrolled in Dar Al-Tifl school. Bishara, Alex, and Mubarak were placed in the Dar Al-Awlad school and orphanage a few blocks outside the old city. It was a miserable existence. Many nights the boys went to sleep hungry. Once the brothers instigated a protest because of the lack of food. As a result, the principal agreed to add one egg per month to each student's meals, but that promise was kept for only two months.

The boys were allowed to visit home once a month. For Bishara, times with his mother were precious. It was her faith that influenced him and each of his siblings. 'Always show the Lord to everybody,' she would say. 'It is never right to take revenge.' He never forgot that, even after going to the United States to study. His mother, of course, couldn't afford to send him to college, but she had prayed and, miraculously, he'd obtained a full scholarship to attend Dakota Wesleyan University in Mitchell, South Dakota.

While pursuing a master's degree in education, war disrupted his life again. The Six Day War of 1967 allowed Israel to gain control of Gaza, the West Bank, the Golan Heights, and East Jerusalem. By decree, those Palestinians who were not physically home during the conquest were prohibited from returning to their land. Thus Bishara was separated from his family and the land of his birth. The only way he could return was to become an American citizen.

Finally, with US passport in hand, Bishara returned to the Holy Land under the auspices of the Mennonite Central Committee, as principal of Hope Secondary School for boys, located in Beit Jala, a town adjacent to Bethlehem.[1]

He and his mother tried to visit his boyhood home, but the building had been destroyed and a road built, so they couldn't even find the exact location. 'After the 1967 war, I wrote to the Mayor of Jerusalem,' Huda told her son. 'I asked him if we could move your father's bones, but he refused me permission.' So there wasn't even a gravestone to commemorate his father's existence.

One thing was not lost, however. His father and his mother had provided a strong Christian influence, which Bishara wanted to impart to his students. What he saw among the boys at Hope School disturbed him deeply. The conflict between Israelis and Palestinians was leaving scars on these children. Many had lost one or both parents. Others had been separated from their parents during the confusion of the '67 war and didn't even know if they were dead or alive. Many of the teenagers wet their beds at night. Both the boarders and day students displayed anger and violent behaviour.

As principal, Bishara tried to impart to these troubled kids the messages his mother had often preached – to love God, love your neighbours, and love your enemies. But these boys weren't responding. They would sit in chapel sessions and listen to Bishara's messages, but none had turned their own hearts to God. He could see their hatred on the playground as they role-played revenge against Jewish soldiers. 'Why, Lord?' Bishara prayed out loud. 'Why are there no results? Why would You bring me back to my homeland and not use me?'

The silence seemed to accuse him.

He walked the halls, past the room where the boys

slept. Many of them tossed and turned fitfully, groaning or talking in their sleep. He wondered about their dreams, which no doubt reflected their private pains. Each of them had experienced harassment from Israeli soldiers. It wasn't unusual for the kids to be ordered to empty their schoolbags, have their books thrown on the ground, and then be ordered to pick them up. Feeling humiliated and powerless to do anything effectively, many students had thrown stones at the soldiers and carried their defiance of authority over to the teachers at the school.

Bishara walked out the back door of the school building and stood under the night sky. A near-full moon illuminated Elah Valley below. This was the location where, according to many Bible experts, David had fought and defeated Goliath. In his mind Bishara could almost see the armies – the Philistines camped on the western hill, the Israelites on the east – and the nine-foot giant advancing to taunt the troops under King Saul's command. And he could see little David boldly confronting him.

Unfortunately, Bishara realised he was on the wrong side. As he 'heard' the taunts of the giant, he recognised his own voice. The Philistine verbalised the emotions he'd repressed for so long. Hatred welled up in him as Goliath cursed the Jews. Bishara blamed the Israelis for the death of his father and the loss of his home in 1948. He blamed them for the twelve years he'd lived in an orphanage, separated from his mother. He blamed them for the years of exile in the United States. For so long the hatred had festered, mostly below his conscious-ness. Now he recognised that same hatred in the boys under his care. It was destroying them, and he was powerless to help them unless he, their principal, conquered his own anger and bitterness.

Tears welled up in his eyes. How could he, a man who had given his life to Jesus Christ a dozen years before, who was committed to be an instrument of God in the Holy Land, help these angry young boys? There was only one answer. His voice broke the silence of the night: 'Lord, I beg You. Forgive me for hating the Jews and for allowing that hatred to control my life.'

With every ounce of his being, Bishara meant that prayer. Looking again over the valley, he could imagine the brave shepherd David charging Goliath, swinging the slingshot, and toppling the giant with a single, well-aimed stone. Bishara's prayer was an equally well-placed stone. It almost seemed too easy as he felt the giant of hatred fall before him. He sensed God's presence enveloping him, and the frustration, hopelessness, and hatred were washed away, replaced with love.

I WANT TO SEE
LIVING STONES

Beit Jala, 1981

We met after a church meeting in Jerusalem. Bishara Awad had a
kind face and a warm smile that invited trust. He told me a little
about his work at the Hope School for boys, and, thinking of the
challenge from the Palestinian lady, I blurted out, 'I would like to
visit you.'

Two days later Bishara's car pulled up in front of the small
YMCA in East Jerusalem where I was staying. It was a short
trip from Jerusalem to the outskirts of Beit Jala, where the
school was located. The main building was built of stone. It
had a curved entry, capped by a crude cross, formed by two
sticks, on the roof above a sign with a drawing of praying
hands and the words 'Hope School' in both Arabic and English.
To one side was a small, dusty soccer field. Beyond that was
a farm building. 'We raise chickens,' Bishara explained as we
began the tour. 'There are about a thousand hens that provide
eggs for the children, and the extras we sell to help support the
school.'

'How else is the school funded?' I asked.

'The Mennonite Church in America provides some funding.

105

And individuals can adopt a child and pay for his care and education.'

'How much does it cost to support one boy for a year?'

'One thousand dollars per year. That supporter also establishes a relationship with the child.'

'Then I want to support a child. Do you have any Muslim boys who need support?'

'Oh, yes, several.' He thought a minute, then mentioned Sharaf. 'He's an orphan, so he lives here as a boarder.'

'I will look forward to supporting Sharaf and praying for him.'

After a tour of classrooms, dormitories, and the dining room, Bishara invited me into his apartment for coffee. He had a gentle voice that I imagined would be calming to hyperactive boys. And it inspired confidence in me. I felt this was someone I could trust.

'Please tell me why you are coming to Palestine,' he said.

'I seek my brethren!' I answered. 'It bothers me that millions of Christian tourists come every year from Western Europe and from America to see dead stones. I want to see the *living* stones.'

As Bishara poured coffee for both of us and added cream and sugar for me, he asked, 'And what do you do when you find these living stones?'

'I ask questions. I listen. I learn. I visit places where it is difficult for the Church. I want to know how Christians are struggling and if they are suffering. I want to know their needs. And where I can, I help. In the Soviet Union and Eastern Europe, that means delivering Bibles, because it is extremely difficult for the Church to obtain Bibles legally.'

'So what do you know about the Palestinian Church?'

'A couple of years ago, a woman told me that there is a suffering Church here among the Palestinians. Shortly afterwards I was travelling with Victor Hashweh.'

Bishara nodded; he knew the evangelist from Jordan.

'We were discussing the Palestinian refugees, and I asked him why Arab governments had urged them to leave in 1948 until the war was over and it was safe to return.'

My new friend winced, and I quickly added, 'That is what many Christians in the West believe. Victor started to cry. He said, "Andrew, I was there. My family was there. We were *driven* out at gunpoint." '

'Have you heard of Deir Yassin?' Bishara asked quietly.

'I've heard some vague references to it,' I said. 'But I really don't know much.'

'In 1948 an entire village, Deir Yassin, was destroyed.' He pointed towards Jerusalem and said, 'Just over there, where the suburb of Har Nof is now, two hundred and fifty men, women, children, babies were slaughtered by the Irgun.' He was referring to the Israeli paramilitary in 1948. 'This was just three years after the Holocaust. A few men were left alive and driven around to other villages to tell the story; then those men were killed too. The result was a panic. That is why so many Palestinians fled. Entire villages were emptied, which is exactly what the Israelis wanted. They just took over those people's homes.'[1]

Bishara sat quietly while I pondered this horrible tale. I could imagine a little of what the Palestinians felt. I still remembered how the Germans destroyed the Dutch city of Rotterdam during World War II, just to intimidate us and force us to yield to their authority. Though only a young teenager, I had felt nothing but contempt for and rebellion against the German occupation of Holland. 'Honestly, between you and Victor, that is the first I've heard about refugees from the Palestinian perspective.'

Softly Bishara said, 'So you have started to discover the truth.'

I shifted uneasily in my chair, not at all sure that I knew the truth about this horrible, decades-long conflict. I knew I loved the Jews. How could I not love God's chosen people! But I also loved the Church of Jesus Christ, wherever I found her. What was I to do with this information? 'I'm trying to under-stand the situation,' I told Bishara. 'I know there is a huge chasm between Jews and Palestinians, but I'm particularly concerned about how those differences affect the Church. I want to meet the Palestinian believers, to see how they live, to hear their concerns, to find out how they minister and what they dream about for the future of the Church. Obviously you are well acquainted with the Palestinian Church. I would love it if you could teach me.'

I was surprised how quickly I had stated my goals, but I sensed it was time for action, and I needed someone to guide me.

Bishara rose, and I assumed he intended to take me back to Jerusalem, but instead he invited me to follow him to a room near the front of the school. It looked like another classroom, though in it there were biblical maps, Hebrew and Greek alphabets, and posters of the Holy Land. 'Perhaps the best way to begin is by telling you about my vision,' he said. 'This room is the home of Bethlehem Bible College.'

'Wonderful!' I said. 'I want to hear all about it.'

'Let's take a ride.' We got in Bishara's car and drove through Beit Jala, past the Greek Orthodox, Catholic, and Lutheran churches, each an impressive building. Bishara talked as he drove: 'You ask about the condition of the Church. The number one need is leadership. You will see beautiful church buildings here, but buildings are not enough. The Church is dying because there are fewer and fewer shepherds.'

We moved from Beit Jala into Bethlehem, crossed over the Jerusalem-Hebron Road, and wound our way to Manger Square and the Church of the Nativity. Though it was late in the afternoon, swarms of tourists were still bending down to enter the Door of Humility, less than five feet high and the only entrance to the church.

'Christians here need a vision,' Bishara said as we observed the scene. 'You spoke of dead stones and living stones. This is believed to be the oldest church building in the world, built over the place where Jesus was supposedly born. Hundreds of thousands of tourists come every year, especially around Christmastime.' Then he turned me around. 'Now look across this mall and tell me what you see.'

Directly opposite the Church of the Nativity, on the other side of Manger Square, was a mosque with a tall minaret, topped with a crescent.

'A mosque,' I answered.

'When builders constructed that mosque, they carefully measured it to make sure that it would be several inches taller than the bell towers of the Church of the Nativity. Brother Andrew, there is a spiritual battle going on here for the hearts and souls of people, and these two buildings symbolise it. Now, please follow me.'

I hesitated. Something about this sight spoke deeply to me, something I had suspected but had hardly dared to express.

I hurried to catch up to Bishara. We descended ancient, well-worn stone stairs to Shepherd Street, turned left, and walked to

Manger Street, just a block away. Everything about this area was old. The cobblestone streets seemed to want to tell stories of centuries of history they had known.

Bishara continued to instruct me: 'Approximately two-thirds of all Palestinian Christians live in this area of Bethlehem, Beit Jala, and Beit Sahour. This area used to be nearly all Christian, but after the war of 1948, many Christians started to emigrate. Many like me went abroad to study, but most have never returned. Others have closed up their businesses and moved. In their place came refugees – we have several refugee camps in the area. Bethlehem is now about 60 per cent Muslim and 40 per cent Christian, but the number of Christians continues to drop.'

Two blocks farther on we stopped in front of a three-storey, white stone building. 'This building is available for rent. Here is where I would like to move Bethlehem Bible College.' He turned and confronted me as he said, 'It is my dream to see the Church grow. To do that, we must begin to train leaders. And to do that, we must have a Bible school. We need pastors, youth workers, and ministry leaders. We need teachers who know the Bible well to train them, and we need classes taught in Arabic not English. It is my dream to see dozens of Palestinians of every denomination coming here to study the Bible.'

'This is fantastic!' I said. 'Have you shared your dream with church leaders here? What do they think?'

'I presented this vision to fourteen church leaders, pastors, and priests, and they all encouraged me to move ahead.' Then he chuckled. 'One of them, a Nazarene pastor, gave me twenty dollars. That was the seed money for the college!'

'You're going to need a lot more than twenty dollars! Tell me, what will it cost to move into this building? How can Open Doors help?'

We returned to Hope School and talked late into the evening over a chicken dinner that Bishara's wife, Salwa, fixed for us. Bishara presented to me his budget for moving the fledgling college and operating it for the next year.

On that day a special friendship began. During my subsequent visits, Bishara opened my eyes to a whole new side of the conflict between Israel and the Palestinians. Until then I had mostly heard only one side of the story. I admired and supported Israel because

I believed they were God's chosen people, but I had not stopped to consider that God's chosen people were not perfect and that I could still love them while critiquing what they did.

Even Bishara said to me, 'I really do not hate Israel, but I do believe they have lost their soul. And we must help them find it.' Bishara seemed genuinely sorrowful.

Later I meditated on his words. Had Israel really lost its soul? Did he mean that politically? Or did he mean that God had withdrawn from the country? Regardless, Bishara wasn't condemning but offering healing. What was particularly troubling was that there were far more Christians among the Palestinians than among the Israelis. So the burden to make a difference was greater on the Palestinian side, and they needed more encouragement in the effort. But this was a challenge. Most, perhaps all, Arab/Palestinian Christians had roots in the land that went back centuries. Many, like Bishara, had lost their homes in the war of 1948. They were angry, hurting, and struggling to understand the meaning of their lives. They heard the claim that the Jews were God's chosen people, but Palestinian Christians had a hard time loving the Jews when so many had lost their homes to the Israelis and had their orchards razed so Jewish settlements could be built on their land.

Bishara took me for a walk near Hope School and pointed out buildings going up on the opposite hill. 'That's Gilo,' he said. 'Israel has annexed it. They say it is part of Jerusalem.' Then he pointed to the town of Beit Jala, spread out below us. 'But these people used to raise olives and graze their sheep where Gilo is now. The land was simply taken, with no consideration that my neighbours had owned that land for centuries.'

'They didn't buy the land?'

'As far as I know there was no payment whatsoever, though there are rumours that a few Palestinians did sell. But if that's true, they would never admit it; they would be considered traitors and would be killed.'

Harderwijk, late 1981

For the first time I had a real sense of why Palestinians were angry and hurt. Daily they felt the impact of Zionism, and it deeply disturbed the Christians in the West Bank. While I didn't minimise this perspective, something even bigger captured my attention. As

I tried to understand why I was drawn to Bishara's dream for a college, I thought about the mosque and church on opposite sides of Manger Square. There was a greater issue that made this a crucial project for Open Doors to support.

My leadership team wasn't so quick to embrace my conclusions. Sitting in my office, they challenged me with the practical realities of our ministry. 'We have our hands full in the Communist world,' said Johan Companjen, the tall, blond Dutchman who was my personal assistant. Johan and his wife, Anneke, had been missionaries in Vietnam but had to escape when the country fell in 1975. Since then, Johan had accompanied me on many of my travels and had provided critical leadership to our work. He had just reported on the remaining costs from Project Pearl, a huge undertaking that earlier in the year delivered one million Bibles to China in a single night.

Another leader's report told about how an Open Doors team had taken a printing press into Eastern Europe. 'We are now starting to equip our brethren so they have the ability to print their own materials.'

I was thrilled with that news. 'We should work ourselves out of a job!' I said. 'We should equip them so they can do their own work without being so dependent on us.'

'I agree,' said Johan. 'But if we're going to move into a new area of work, my question is how this college in Bethlehem fits into our mission. We exist to strengthen the Church in places where it is persecuted, but that isn't the case in the Middle East. Sure the Church has many challenges there, but what is the source of this urgency?'

I realised Johan was focusing on the Church in the midst of communism, but I was convinced there was a much bigger battle looming. 'Communism is dying,' I stated. Several of the men in the room seemed puzzled by my assertion. 'It is time. Communism is a toothless tiger, and it will surely fall. It *must* fall.'

'How can you say that?' protested one of the men. 'You are talking about one of the two superpowers.'

'Because, at the core, communism is a bankrupt worldview. It says there is no God and that you can change people by changing their environment. As Christians, we know that is nonsense. What is our worldview?'

Johan answered: 'The Bible says man must change, and then he can change his environment.'

'Exactly! That is why communism cannot succeed. It has lasted sixty years. I don't believe it will last to one hundred years. It's already crumbling.' For the first time I was going to express my observations to the ministry leadership. 'There is another threat that we need to take very seriously. It's existed far longer than communism, and it will challenge the Church. Some of you may remember when I travelled to Central Asia a few years ago. You know what I saw? Empty mosques and empty schools that Muslims call madrasas. Islam has suffered as much as Christianity under the Soviets, but the structure is there. Islam can lie dormant for decades, even for centuries, but it will not go away. It's a sleeping giant, and it started to awaken two years ago in Iran under Ayatollah Khomeini. I think the fundamentalist form of Islam that Khomeini preaches is going to grow and become very powerful in the next few years. The Church needs to be prepared for this challenge.'

'How will the Islam challenge be different from communism?' asked one of the leaders.

'Communism made a statement: "There is no God!" Islam challenges us with a question: "Who is God?" They have an answer, and they believe it so passionately that they are willing to take it to the world and to die for it if need be.'

My team was listening intently. I leaned forward to give three reasons why I believed Islam was on the rise. 'First, they have a well-developed eschatology. They believe in the end they will conquer and rule the world. Second, something happened in 1973 that we must not forget.'

'The oil embargo?' someone asked.

'Correct! That is when Muslims began to realise they had real power. They believe Allah put all of that oil under their dirty sand for a reason – to give them immense wealth that could be used to spread Islam around the world.'

'What's the third reason?' asked Johan.

'The collapse of morals in the West. Muslims see it as a failure of Christianity. When communism also collapses, they will declare to the world, "Islam is the answer!" With that, I believe, they will go farther than the Church has ever gone with the Great

Commission. We go out to win souls here and there. They will confront the whole world with a total system, and they will pay whatever price it takes, even with their lives.'

My team had seen me passionate before, and sometimes they challenged me about my prophetic views. Now one of them raised his voice: 'You may be right, but what does this have to do with Israel? Isn't that a conflict between Palestinians and Jews?'

'That's only part of the trouble. There is another conflict. Jerusalem is a critical issue for Muslims. Islam believes that any land that it once ruled always belongs to Islam and thus must be recaptured. That's why they will never give up their conviction that all of the Holy Land must be under Islam. *That* is the challenge facing the Church.'

The room was quiet for a moment. Finally, Johan said, 'So what shall we do?'

'Strengthen what remains, which is at the point of being overpowered. The Church is dying in the Holy Land. It is at the point of being overpowered on several fronts. Zionism, yes, is a factor, but so is the economic pressure, caused by the refugee problem and immigration of Jews from around the world. However, the biggest factor will be the rise of Muslim fundamentalism, which I believe is going to rise up and rebel against Israel. That is why we *must* support Bethlehem Bible College. It will train the leaders so desperately needed for a spiritual resistance movement.'

We talked for a few minutes about practical matters. There was little we could do financially right then. We were still paying the bills for Project Pearl, plus we had many other commitments to fulfil. But we could donate some books for their library. We could encourage Bishara and promote his work. And in time – it would take a few years – we could begin to reallocate more of our resources from the Communist world to this arena.

As our meeting was about to break up, I concluded with this statement: 'Islam is where the primary conflict will be for the next one hundred years. And the outcome will decide what this world will look like for the next one thousand years.'

'Unless the Lord returns!' said one of the men.

Almost automatically I straightened my back. How deeply this fatalistic streak has permeated the thinking and theology of many

Christians! We forget that most of the prophecies relating to future events are connected to conditions. 'Yes, sure,' I replied rather impatiently. 'Until the Lord returns. But He said that first the gospel must be preached to all nations, and *then* the end would come. Giving up without a fight really means that Jesus will never come back. Therefore, let's be faithful. We must be on tiptoes, alert and active!'

WHAT ARE WE
SUPPOSED TO DO?

Gaza, 1987

The young man, barely out of his teenage years, was agitated. 'We must forgive our oppressors. That's the message of Christianity.'

'Where are you getting these crazy ideas?' asked his equally agitated father.

'From the Bible . . .'

'You mean from that Baptist church you go to. What is wrong with our church? You go around acting like some kind of super Christian.'

Hanna Massad and his father had fought over Hanna's church for several years. For generations the Massad family had belonged to the Greek Orthodox Church, but Hanna had struggled with the traditional faith of his parents. As a teenager, he had started attending Gaza Baptist Church, the only evangelical church in Gaza. His father put up with the rebellion until Hanna announced that he was being baptised. That was considered an act of betrayal and a humiliation. It was hard enough to live as a tiny minority among a million

Muslims, but then your own son rejects your faith.

'I'm not rejecting the faith!' Hanna protested. 'I'm simply responding to the teachings of the Bible. Your church only practises a ritual, but it doesn't preach the gospel. I left the church because there was emptiness in my life. I want the reality of Christ, and I found it in the Baptist church.' Hanna knew he was provoking his father, but he couldn't stop now. 'I think we need to take the words of Jesus seriously, to love our enemies, to turn the other cheek, to bless those who persecute us.'

The older man seethed as he listened to his son. 'Have you gone mad? Have you forgotten where we come from? Your mother was driven from her home in Jaffa in 1948. Her family came here to Gaza with nothing but the clothes they were wearing. They lost everything.'

Hanna had heard all this before. But this time, his father wanted to drive the point home. 'Come with me!' The son followed as his father led him to a secret hiding place. The man pulled out a box, unlocked it, and pulled out a sheaf of papers and some keys. 'Look at this!' he demanded. 'This is a deed for one hundred dunams of land.[1] It belongs to me and your uncle and aunt. And these are keys to the home that the Israelis took from us. Those Jews that you want to forgive stole our property. They stole *your* inheritance!'

VIOLENCE ERUPTED IN early December 1987. On 6 December an Israeli was stabbed to death in Gaza. The next day four Palestinians from the Jabalya refugee camp were killed in a traffic accident and rumours quickly spread that it really wasn't an accident, that the four were actually killed by Israelis as revenge for the stabbing death. That provided the spark for mass protests and rioting by Palestinians in Jerusalem, Gaza, and the West Bank. The rebellion or intifada was officially under way.[2]

This conflict was of a very different nature from what I'd observed before – not a few rogues working alone but a sustained uprising that would not die. Thousands of boys, many not yet in their teens, took to the streets day after day and threw stones at the Israeli soldiers. At first the professional soldiers didn't know how to respond, and the Palestinians believed they had gained the upper hand with media pictures that showed numerous little Davids fighting the heavily armed Goliath of the Israeli Defence Force (IDF). But the anger was expressed in other ways as well. There were general strikes. Businesses were shut down. Workers refused to go to work at Israeli businesses. Palestinians refused to purchase Israeli products. And in Beit Sahour, the residents refused to pay taxes to Israel.

The explosion had been building for years. While economic conditions had improved in West Bank and in Gaza under Israeli control, they still remained far below those in Israel proper. The Gaza Strip was one of the most densely populated pieces of land in the world. By 1987, 2,500 settlers occupied 28 per cent of the seven-by-thirty-mile strip, while nearly 1,000,000 people were crammed in the remaining 72 per cent, in refugee camps and cities along the Mediterranean Sea.[3] In the West Bank, it was reported that Jewish settlers were allowed to use twelve times more water than were the Palestinians.[4]

But the primary force behind the intifada, according to my Palestinian friends, was a pervasive feeling of humiliation. Year after year residents of West Bank and Gaza had lived under restriction, experiencing curfews for sometimes days at a time, sealing (and sometimes destruction) of homes of suspected resisters, midnight searches that ransacked homes, detention of thousands of young men without charge, not to mention the endless identity checks, body searches, and restriction of movement within West Bank and Gaza and between the territories and Israel. The Palestinians generally felt they had no rights whatsoever, and after years of humiliation, there was a deep thirst among many for change or for escape.

Israel, of course, had strong counter-arguments for their methods, usually related to their need for security and their right to exist. The sealing and destruction of homes was intended to deter resisters who might reconsider their actions if they knew they would hurt their families. Potential terrorists had to be caught, and a Palestinian in jail was someone who couldn't hurt Israel. I understood these motivations, but at times I wondered if Israel's methods made them *less* secure as a people. The West Bank and Gaza seemed like a breeding ground for resistance.

In the midst of the uprising were Palestinian Christians. How were they responding?

Beit Sahour, 1988

On the dinner table Nawal Qumsieh laid out hummus, two salads, a main dish of chicken and rice, and fresh bread for her family. After her husband had asked the Lord's blessing on their meal and everyone started to eat, she inquired about her children's day. The two high school students were quiet, and her mother's instincts told her something was very wrong. 'Tell me. What is happening?'

The older boy finally admitted, 'Our friends want us to throw stones at the soldiers.'

The younger brother then jumped in. 'They said we're cowards . . .'

'Traitors,' added the older brother.

'What are we supposed to do? We don't think we should go and throw stones. But they push us and beat us up if we don't go.'

Nawal said, 'We can make our views known peacefully. That is the Christian way.' She said it with conviction.

'We know, Mum,' said the younger son. 'But many of the boys don't agree. What are we supposed to do?'

The older son was scheduled to complete his secondary education that spring. 'I've decided I have to leave,' he announced. 'I will go to university in the United States or Canada. And I don't expect to return. This is no place to live. There are no good jobs. I want to get married and raise a family, but what future is there here for my children?'

Nawal sighed. She knew what her son said was true. After dinner she slipped outside to a quiet spot where she often sat and prayed. She couldn't help but reflect with sadness on the situation. Her family had lived in the area for at least four hundred years. They'd lived in caves at first while caring for their sheep. Eventually they'd built homes and planted orchards. Their present house had been in the family for more than one hundred years.

Many of the more than one thousand members of the extended Qumsieh family had scattered. The exodus had started with the war of 1948. More had left as a result of the wars of 1956 and 1967, when Israel conquered the West Bank region.[5] Some had settled in the United States, others in Canada. It was those relatives who gave her sons options. The boys didn't have to stay in Beit Sahour, and what could she possibly do to convince them otherwise? In North America they would obtain an excellent education. There the future was bright. Here in the West Bank, no one knew how long the intifada would rage. Those boys throwing rocks were being maimed and killed daily. What was their future?

So should she and her husband emigrate as well? Within less than two years, the last of their five children would leave; why not go with them? What was holding them to this land? If the Israelis really wanted them to leave, why not accommodate them?

Then Nawal thought about the women all around her who were in despair – Muslims and Christians, it didn't matter. The depression permeated their lives as they shopped for fresh produce at the market, as they hung the laundry on their balconies, and, for the Christians, as they worshipped together at the local Greek Orthodox church. Nawal understood that deep depression, for she had lived with it herself for years – at times it was so deep she'd seriously contemplated suicide. That is, until 1982 and that marvellous evening when students from Bethlehem Bible College, with one of the teachers, had visited her home. Nawal and her husband had listened to the testimonies about how Jesus lived in their lives. She had laughed at the young people and kidded them for their naive enthusiasm, saying, 'I do not believe anything you say.' When they asked why, she explained,

'I have been sick with back problems for twelve years. I cannot sleep because of the pain. Doctors have told me I will be in a wheelchair for the rest of my life. I give up and I don't want to live.'

The students and teacher asked if they could pray for her. They prayed, and nothing happened. However, the next morning, after twelve hours of wonderful sleep, she had risen without pain. She had called the Bible College to report, 'The Lord healed me!'

That experience had changed everything. Her faith ceased being simply a cultural expression, something that the Qumsieh family had always practised. Now when she attended the liturgy, the words were alive. They were celebrating the risen Lord who was residing in her heart and in the hearts of her husband and children. It was Jesus who had healed her body and her depression – something neither doctor nor medicine could do. When she opened the Bible, she realised that its words drilled deep into her soul. She hungered to understand it, to live it out. With permission from her husband, she had enrolled at Bethlehem Bible College. She'd studied voraciously, earned As in every single course and graduated at the top of her class.

Nawal thought again about the conversation that evening at the dinner table. Soon her nest would be empty. What would she do then? Should she follow her children to freedom in the West?

She thought again of her neighbours, both Muslim and Christian. She understood their anxiety and hopelessness. They felt utterly alone, unable to bare their hearts to anyone. What if someone were to give them an opportunity to speak? Many husbands would never permit their wives to open up, but what about those who did? For even a few, maybe she could make a difference.

Instantly her thoughts became a prayer: 'O Lord, is there any hope for the people here?' She thought of the missions in the Bethlehem area. Many were leaving because of the intifada. Would they ever return? 'Lord, if there is any hope for these women who are my neighbours, I want to be part of that. I want them to experience You the way I have.'

At that moment she knew she would not be leaving the West Bank with her children. The Lord had work for her to do.

Jerusalem, 1988

The intifada was in full swing as I arrived to speak at a Christian medical conference. Bishara picked me up during a break in the programme and drove me up the Mount of Olives to Al-Maqassed Hospital. I had requested earlier that the delegates, consisting of many doctors, be allowed to visit this hospital, but the Ministry of Tourism, which had helped organise the conference, had denied every request. So I decided some of us would simply go on our own, without permission. As we wound our way up the hill, I couldn't help but recall some of my early trips to Israel when I'd stayed as a guest at a home near here that had a spectacular view of Jerusalem. The woman was a devoted Christian who had bought the home so she could have a front-row view of the return of Christ. She'd passed away several years ago – without witnessing the end of the age.

The hospital we were visiting was a private institution run by Muslims, though Bishara explained that it was open to Muslims and Christians. Many of the thousands of kids injured in the intifada were brought here. Every room was filled, and there were some patients lying on trolleys in the halls. Nearly every bed had family members around it. On several occasions I saw mothers crying over their children.

News accounts often reported that the soldiers used only rubber bullets, and they were supposed to aim below the knee. However, many of the injuries were horrifying. I stood by one bed where a boy paralysed from a bullet that had lodged in his neck was lying. His mother spoke Arabic, and Bishara translated.

'They cannot remove the bullet,' she said quietly. 'The doctors say he will never walk again.'

'How old is he?' I asked.

'Eleven years old,' she said, starting to weep.

I couldn't help but think, *Where is God in this?* The woman wore a traditional scarf that indicated she was Muslim. I wanted to respect her faith, but my heart went out to her. 'May I pray for the boy?' I asked. She nodded her head. I laid my hand on the boy's shoulder and asked Jesus, whom Muslims recognise as the Healer, to heal this boy of his injuries and his family of their emotional pain.

In another room I found an older woman, wearing a simple cross necklace, sitting with a teenage boy, whose leg was in a heavy cast and raised in traction. She spoke English, so I said to her: 'I see you are wearing a cross. Are you a Christian?'

'Yes,' she answered. 'Catholic.'

'And this is your son?'

'My grandson.'

'May I ask what happened?'

'He has two bullets in his leg. One shattered his hip. The doctors do not think he will ever walk again.'

'I'm so sorry . . .'

'I told him not to go. His parents told him not to go. But there is so much pressure. The boys feel they must go and prove they are good Palestinians. He is lucky he wasn't killed.'

'Where do you live?' I asked.

'In East Jerusalem.'

'Are you able to keep your faith in God in the midst of these hard times?'

The woman looked into my eyes, perhaps wondering how honest she could be with this stranger. 'Christianity is a daily commitment,' she answered with a steady voice. 'But it is a daily struggle to forgive my enemies. How can I forgive those who want to kill me and my brothers and sisters and who would deny me my homeland? But I *must* forgive. Every time I pray the Our Father, I struggle with the words "Forgive our trespasses as we forgive those who trespass against us." I want to say, "God, I forgive my enemies." I picture them; I see what they are doing every day. I see the dead bodies, the suffering, the blood. I try to forgive, but I cannot. So I pray, "God, You must help me forgive, because I cannot!" '

I was deeply moved by this woman's honesty. As Bishara and I walked to his car, I said to him, 'I think God is more impressed with that woman's prayers than He is with all the silly, foolish ones that attempt to clean the slate with one easy swipe: "God bless all our family and friends. Amen." That woman is struggling with issues the magnitude of which most of us in the West have never imagined.'

Bishara agreed: 'She's serious about forgiveness. I understand her struggle. I've gone through it and continue to do so.'

My friend had told me about his prayer years ago, that God would remove his hatred for Jews. He insisted that God had answered that prayer; he felt no personal animosity towards Jews. But the conflict between Palestinians and Israel was causing him serious problems. At the beginning of the year, Bethlehem Bible College was ordered to close – Israel had shut down most of the educational institutions in the West Bank and Gaza, deciding that they were a major source of the rebellion. However, with the schools closed, the boys had nothing to do but throw more stones.

Before the intifada had erupted, I had arranged for the Bethlehem Bible College choir to sing at the conference where I was speaking. 'I'm sorry the choir can't sing for us,' I said, as we arrived back at the hotel.

'Don't give up yet!' Bishara said with a grin. 'I have contacted all of the students in the choir. We are going to try to sneak them into the hotel tomorrow!'

'How long will the school be closed?' I asked before getting out of the car.

'The news is not good,' he admitted. 'As long as the intifada continues, I don't think we will be allowed to reopen. We've tried holding classes in homes, but that's not working very well. I've cancelled graduation ceremonies for this year because the students can't finish their courses. Honestly, if this lasts too long, I don't know if the college can even survive.'

'You must not give up!' I said to my friend. 'I will help you. Open Doors will help you. Your mission is too important. You are training the future church leaders, and I refuse to believe that it is God's will for that effort to fail.'

'Then we must keep praying,' he said with resignation.

'That is why we must keep Bethlehem Bible College going! Students need to learn the Scriptures and how to apply them. This will show Christians and the entire Palestinian community that there is another way. A better way!'

The next night, we were amazed when Bishara showed up with the choir from Bethlehem Bible College, as well as souvenirs of olive wood for sale. Hotel management was upset because Bethlehem Bible College's souvenirs were half the cost of the same items in the hotel gift shop. The young people presented a moving programme of music and testimony.

There was another highlight to the evening. Sharaf, the Hope School student I had supported for several years, showed up to see me. During our conversation, talk naturally drifted to the intifada. I told him about the boys I had seen at the hospital. Suddenly he told me, 'Brother Andrew, I have never thrown stones at Israeli soldiers while at Hope School.'

'And you know why?' I responded. 'Because someone prayed for you!'

What was the right Christian response to the conflict? What I saw in Sharaf was a little solution. He wasn't a Christian, but he had learned of God's ways in the Bible while in Hope School. We needed thousands and thousands of little solutions. Rather than curse the darkness in the land, we needed to light many more candles.

Gaza, 1988

Hanna Massad seemed too young to be pastor of the Gaza Baptist Church. In fact he was the first indigenous pastor of the congregation that Southern Baptist missionaries had founded, along with a hospital, in 1954. Until now most of the pastors had been from Egypt or Lebanon. Hanna was learning on the job, attending Bethlehem Bible College during the week, then dashing down to Gaza to preach the Sunday services.

While the intifada was raging, Gaza wasn't exactly the safest place to go. Still, I felt a desire to visit this congregation, the only evangelical church on the crowded strip. I wanted to support Hanna and stand with the congregation that bravely gathered in the centre of Gaza City.

For years the church had met in St Philip's Church in the grounds of the Christian hospital, the control of which the Baptists had transferred to the Anglican Church in 1982. Now they had moved into a new rented facility in downtown Gaza City. As Hanna welcomed me for the Sunday morning service, he explained, 'After the uprising started, there were ambulances coming all the time to the emergency room of the hospital. The noise disturbed the meetings, and we finally felt it was time to move.' The home where the church now met was owned by a lady I knew. 'She doesn't want to sell it, but we can use it for as long as we want. Someday, we will buy our own property.'

Hanna translated for me as I preached to a congregation of about seventy-five people. Afterwards, we talked more over a meal. Later that afternoon, he would drive back up to Bethlehem to resume his studies. 'I'm limited in what I can do right now,' he said. 'But there is a great deal of potential for this church. I want to start a children's ministry and minister to teens, and the women should be more active. Most important, I want to hold some evangelistic meetings.'

I affirmed his vision. 'In time, you will have a chance to do all of those things. But you aren't ready yet. Right now, you need to be trained.'

Hanna laughed. 'Right now, as soon as I learn something at school, I have an immediate opportunity to apply it here in Gaza!'

BRINGING THE TWO
SIDES TOGETHER

Bethlehem, 1988

Salim Munayer exuded energy even as he waited to talk with me after a meeting at Bethlehem Bible College. As the academic dean of the college, Salim managed the course programme and also taught several classes. Bishara relied heavily on him. I wondered what the secret of his enthusiasm was and thought that perhaps it came from his growing up in a mixed Arab-Jewish community where kids fought daily on the streets just for the right to play. I knew he was fluent in Hebrew, Arabic, and English. Though a Palestinian, he had helped to start two Messianic congregations, and he taught both Palestinian and Israeli university students. He had an amazing ability to move among Muslims and Jews as well as Christians.

As I turned to give him my full attention, Salim said, 'Brother Andrew, I would like to propose a project to Open Doors.' I followed him to his office in the administration building. As soon as we were seated, he plunged ahead: 'I want to share with you a dream. As you know, I have ministered among both Jewish and Palestinian believers. At Bethlehem Bible College I spend a lot of time explaining to Bishara and others what Israelis think. And when I teach in Jaffa, I spend a lot of time explaining to Jewish believers what Palestinians think. I've realised that rather than trying to explain one group to the other, it would be better if I could bring the two groups together.'

'You mean Christians from both sides?'

'Initially, yes. I think it's time that believers on both sides start talking to each other. You know, I have students asking me questions about what Jesus would do in the midst of this intifada. They want to know how they should act at checkpoints. Messianic Jews want to know if they should serve in the army. Palestinians want to know if they should do something about the settlement next door. Students at Bethlehem Bible College are saying that they know Jesus' teachings prohibit them from being involved in the violence, but if they are not involved in some manner, they feel they are betraying their people. They struggle with the Bible, which talks of their spiritual heritage coming from the Jewish people. Our Messiah was a Jew, but right now we are at war with the Jewish people. These are difficult emotional and theological issues.'

'Do you think there is an answer?'

'I believe that there must be a process of reconciliation of both sides.'

'I agree. But how does that happen?'

'It starts by building a relationship. Many of the people I work with have never spent time with a single person on the other side. I would like to try taking groups of people from both sides out into the desert for three days. I believe that when they are away from their normal surroundings, in a situation where they must work together, we can begin to break down the barriers and build a trust relationship.'

'Hasn't something like this been attempted before? What makes your project different?'

'In the past, there have been meetings between Israeli and Palestinian believers, but they centred on talking about political issues. These meetings turned out to be negative. There is a need to develop relationships before we try to talk about these issues. But in order to have relationships, we need to deal with our prejudices and the dehumanisation of each side. I believe that a desert setting is the best place to break down prejudices and build relationships so we can then deal with the issues.'

I reached over and grabbed Salim's arm. 'You are passionate. I like that! But really, do you think this will work?'

Salim handed me several papers, outlining a plan with first-year costs. As I glanced over it, he said, 'The reality of our situation is that Israelis and Palestinians are living as if in one house. As we live in such close quarters, intermingling is unavoidable and even necessary. There is no choice but to live side by side; therefore reconciliation and building relationships are essential.'

I looked up and, reflecting on his proposal, said, 'You intend to build a model among Christians from both sides?'

'Andrew, believers can play an important part in resolving this conflict, because as a result of our mutual faith in the Messiah, we are one body. We have been given the tools required for a transformation of hearts. We can answer hatred and bitterness with the message of forgiveness and love. Perhaps we can be examples and models, showing that it is possible to live side by side, free from the bondage of hatred.'

'I'm convinced that we must try,' I said. 'I will take this proposal back to my team and see what we can do.'

I took the proposal back to the Open Doors' leadership team, who agreed to take responsibility for a portion of Salim's budget. 'Let's see how it goes and maybe we can do more,' said Johan.

Salim called the project Musalaha, the Arabic word meaning 'forgiveness and reconciliation'. I realised this was just a small part of our worldwide work, but it had huge significance. This was a unique project conceived by the local Christian community that was attempting to deal with the root causes of the conflict in the Middle East. I was eager to see how it would work.

The Negev, spring 1992

Yitzhak couldn't help it.[1] He had been taught to hate Arabs. To him, the only good Arab was a dead Arab. And yet, here he was sitting on rugs inside a Bedouin tent with fellow Jews and Arabs, all because of his wife's gentle insistence that as a Messianic believer in Yeshua, he needed to meet believers from the other side.

'This is ridiculous!' he had exploded when she had

first proposed that they participate in this desert encounter. 'Arabs are not people you can trust.'

In another small group on the opposite side of the tent, Wa'el questioned why he needed to participate in this meeting with Messianic Jews. 'If they are believers in Christ,' the Palestinian convert from Islam had told his friend, Salim Munayer, 'then we don't need reconciliation. We are already reconciled.' But he knew that this theological truth didn't correlate with the realities of daily life on the West Bank. It bothered him that Jews, believers or otherwise, insisted on laying historic claim to the land where he lived, devouring the rights of Palestinians who had lived in this land for hundreds of years. He was also put off by the label of Messianic Judaism. 'They're Christian Jews, aren't they?' he'd insisted. 'Should we as Christian believers of Muslim background start a Messianic Muslim movement?' Still, he'd always insisted on being open-minded. He was willing to talk with Islamists who challenged his conversion to Christ as well as humanist Jews working for peace. So he'd finally accepted Salim's offer to meet and talk with these Messianic Jews.

The wary group of thirty participants – an equal number of Palestinians and Jews – sat in circles around common bowls of chicken and rice that was scooped out with pita bread. As it was Passover week, some of the Messianic believers were using unleavened matzo instead of pita. In one circle, Wa'el sat next to a Palestinian woman, who was watching Evan Thomas, co-pastor of a Messianic church in Netanya and a board member of Musalaha. The young woman stared at the matzo in Evan's hand and asked, 'Why are you still bound by the law?'

The question was asked with genuine concern, and Evan answered the same way, quietly stating, 'One way I have chosen to express my faith in Yeshua is by celebrating the Jewish feasts. The Passover celebration points to the final sacrifice of Yeshua, made once and for all for the world.'

The woman, who worshipped in an Orthodox church, seemed unconvinced. Wa'el, overhearing the exchange, wondered how such a wide gulf – of language, culture, and religious practice – could possibly be bridged in three days.

Early the next morning the group set off to explore the ancient Spice Route that ran from south Arabia to the Mediterranean shore. Each camel was loaded with more than one hundred pounds of food, water, and equipment and either a Palestinian or Israeli rider. A partner from the other side led the animal. Yitzhak took the first turn riding while his partner, Wa'el, walked. As the sun rose, the caravan headed south towards the Timna Valley, a three-day, three-night journey to the site of the copper mines of King Solomon.

Throughout the day, Wa'el and Yitzhak traded places several times. They didn't talk much, but they worked well together, especially coaxing their stubborn camel over a steep rocky slope to the first campsite. Exhausted from the day, everyone quickly fell asleep under the stars. They were awakened before sunrise by thunder and lightning that lit up the skies. Everyone was drenched in the ensuing rainstorm. Then the skies cleared and the heat returned as the group continued their journey, aware of another phenomenon – they all, along with the camels, shared the same smell.

That day Wa'el and Yitzhak, who found their defences coming down, began to talk. Yitzhak listened, rocking back and forth on the camel as Wa'el walked beside the animal and talked about his childhood, living in a West Bank refugee camp. When he was a boy, his home was severely damaged when the home next door was blown up as punishment for a family member's participation in an attack against Israeli settlers. 'We had nowhere to go,' Wa'el said. 'A neighbour family took us in until we could repair our home.

'Two years later my mother got very sick and though my brothers and sisters and I prayed for her recovery, she died. I was convinced that my mother was the best person on earth, so why didn't God save her? It was a very big disappointment for me.'

'You were a Muslim family?' Yitzhak asked.

'We were Muslims but not devout. When I was a teenager, my uncles started taking me to the mosque for prayers. But I didn't see why I should worship God since He did not give us any help with our problems. I started reading philosophy – Greek classics, Lenin, Marx. I spent long hours in discussions with Islamists. I could not join those who said there was no God. So I believed there is a God, but I was not sure that it was the God described in the Quran.'

Wa'el walked silently for a few minutes, until Yitzhak asked, 'So what turned you to Jesus?'

The young Palestinian man chuckled as he recalled, 'As a teenager I started reading the encyclopaedia. It gave me much factual information on many things, including Christianity. Then for almost two years, I received a Bible study by mail. Eventually I concluded that Jesus Christ is the way to God. That was like a light thrown by God into my heart. So I believed in Christ and I wanted to grow in Him and know more of Him.'

A stunning realisation came over Yitzhak as his new friend talked. He had more in common culturally and spiritually with this Palestinian than he did with many Jewish believers who had immigrated to Israel from places like America, Russia, and Europe. He was amazed at the parallels between his own testimony and Wa'el's. 'I was born in a traditional Jewish family,' he said. 'My parents moved here in 1948 from North Africa. By the time I had finished my three-year stint in the Israeli army, I considered myself an agnostic. Then I travelled throughout Europe for a few months. A friend gave me a Bible before I left, and I couldn't stop reading it. Shortly before I returned to Israel, I became a believer.'

'What did your family think about all this?' Wa'el asked, aware that, like Muslim families, Jewish families could be divided when one member professed faith in Jesus Christ.

'My mother became a believer. But my father was extremely against it in the beginning. By God's grace, he has become more open because he saw what happened to my mother and me, and he couldn't help admitting that it was good. He is not a believer yet, but he now accepts us and occasionally even comes to meetings.'

What Yitzhak couldn't tell Wa'el – it was much too soon in their relationship – was that on his return to his home in Tel Aviv, he'd become deeply involved in a Messianic congregation that celebrated their belief in Jesus as Messiah in the context of Judaism, the nation of Israel, and Zionism. Like his fellow believers, Yitzhak had totally ignored Arabs, until one year ago when he'd married another Messianic believer. She worked with Arabs in a hospital and shocked him by saying, 'I kind of like them!'

On their final evening together, Evan Thomas asked two men to build a stone table, which he then covered with a clean kaffiyeh.[2] As one of the founding board members of Musalaha, Thomas had shared Salim's vision for what was now happening in the desert. He and his wife, Maala, had immigrated to Israel from New Zealand in 1983. They teamed up with David and Lisa Loden to give leadership to a Messianic congregation, Beit Asaf, in Netanya. Thomas had first seen the possibilities for Musalaha during an evangelistic outreach in Haifa where a group of Messianic believers were joined by fifteen Palestinian Christians. Thomas smiled as he recalled that three-day event. There were eight Israelis who prayed to receive Jesus as their Messiah, and seven of them were led to the Lord by the Palestinian Christians. That had prompted him to visit Arab congregations in Galilee, and he found himself feeling empathy for those communities. It had been only logical for him to expand into an active ministry of reconciliation between the two groups.

All the participants were now gathered around the stone table on Bedouin mats as Evan placed matzo and wine on the table. 'This is the last night of Passover,' he said as the service began. Briefly he explained the origins of the sacrament of Communion within the tradition of the Passover meal.

Then he read slowly from Ephesians 2. Wa'el felt the words pounding with new impact into his mind: 'Therefore, remember that formerly you who are Gentiles by birth and called "uncircumcised" by those who call themselves "the circumcision" . . . remember that at that time you were separate from Christ, excluded from citizenship in Israel and foreigners to the covenants of the promise, without hope and without God in the world. But now in Christ Jesus you who once were far away have been brought near through the blood of Christ.'

Yitzhak too was impacted as Evan read the words of Paul: 'For he himself is our peace, who has made the two one and has destroyed the barrier, the dividing wall of hostility, by abolishing in his flesh the law with its commandments and regulations. His purpose was to create in himself one new man out of the two, thus making peace, and in this one body to reconcile both of them to God through the cross, by which he put to death their hostility.'

Listening to those words, Yitzhak had to admit before God that he did hate Arabs and that this countered what God had said. God had brought peace between Arab and Jew. And after listening to Wa'el's testimony, he had to recognise that God was working among Palestinians just as He was among Jewish people.

Evan Thomas raised up a large piece of matzo and broke it. 'This is the body of Christ, broken for you.' Then he lifted up the cup of wine. 'This is the blood of Christ that was shed for you. I would like each of you to come forward and take the elements, but do not partake. Rather, I am asking you to serve the elements to another brother or sister, whomever the Lord is prompting you to serve.'

For the next few minutes, there was a silence that was magnified by the arid landscape around them. There was no wind; no insect noises broke the silence; there was only the snort of a camel in the camp a few yards away. Evan began to doubt the wisdom of his instructions. Certainly, these people had never participated in the Lord's Table in this manner, but he couldn't think of a better way to break through the barriers and help them see that they were one in Christ.

Wa'el and Yitzhak stood at the same time, came forward to accept the elements, then faced one another. Many in the group had tears in their eyes as the two served communion to each other. The power of the picture trumped any need for words. All could see: Through Christ both Palestinian and Jew have access to the Father by one Spirit. Soon the rest followed their example, in the process catching the vision Evan and Salim had for Musalaha. An enormous gulf had been bridged; true reconciliation had begun.

If God could bring together one Jew and one Palestinian, why couldn't He do it with a million Jews and a million Palestinians?

WHAT WILL THIS
SUFFERING ACCOMPLISH?

West Bank and Gaza, December 1992

Two armed attacks had left six Israeli soldiers dead, and Sergeant-Major Nissim Toledano had been kidnapped. The Islamic fundamentalist group Hamas claimed responsibility for these events. They demanded that, in exchange for Toledano, Israel release from prison Sheikh Ahmad Yassin, the founder and spiritual leader of Hamas. Rather than capitulate to the ransom demand, Prime Minister Yitzhak Rabin ordered a massive search and rescue operation throughout Israel.

Three days later Toledano's body was discovered near the Jerusalem-Jericho highway.

Retribution was quickly planned. A list of names was drawn up. Soldiers were given their assignments. It would be a lightning-quick operation. 'This will cut off the head,' said one of the officers in charge, 'and put an end to Hamas.'

Abd al-Fattah al-Awaisi was relaxing in his living room, reviewing notes for his history lecture the next day at Hebron University, when soldiers burst through the front door. Two of them yanked the professor out of his seat while the others pointed their guns at his wife and children and ordered them to move to the back of the house. 'Prepare yourself. You will be next!' said one soldier in a menacing voice as al-Awaisi's wife raised her hands and backed away. A blindfold was roughly pulled over al-Awaisi's eyes, and a thin plastic wire was tightly wrapped around his wrists behind his back. Thirty seconds later, he was led out of the house.

The next morning, Sheikh Abdul Aziz Kajuk was in a small room awaiting treatment at Shefa Hospital when the soldiers came for him. He too was blindfolded, bound at the wrists, and led away.

At noon Taher Lulu, a paediatrician at Nasser Hospital in Gaza, was preparing his lunch when Israeli soldiers interrupted. He would not eat anything for the next two days.

Businessman Adly Rifaat Yaish received a phone call that afternoon. 'Would you please come down to the police station?' he was politely asked. 'We have a couple of questions. It will only take a few minutes.' Yaish thought that was strange. For a Palestinian, he was allowed unusual freedom to travel on business to Jerusalem and Jordan. He had never been detained or interrogated. He grabbed his coat, told his secretary he'd be gone for a few minutes, and drove to the station where he was immediately bound hand and foot with plastic wire, blindfolded, and shoved onto a bus.

Yaish felt another man seated next to him on the hard bench. 'What is going on?' he asked.

'Silence!' came a harsh order, accompanied by the blow of a stick across his back. 'There will be no talking in the bus.'

A few minutes later, Yaish heard the door of the bus shut and the diesel engine rev up. *Why?* he asked himself. *Where are they taking us? What have I done to deserve such treatment?*

No one spoke. No explanations were given. He was thankful he had grabbed his coat – it was the only thing protecting him from the draft blowing through the windows of the rickety bus.

Hours passed. There were no stops to go to the bathroom, no food or water. From the darkness, al-Awaisi judged that the sun had set. He tried to doze but, forced to keep his head lowered behind the seat in front of him and with his arms bound behind him, it was impossible to find a comfortable position. He was still feeling the effects from a night confined in a cold jail cell. His back muscles were cramped. He wondered how his weak health could hold up under such conditions.

Sometime in the middle of the night, there was a brief stop. Al-Awaisi heard voices outside. Then the door closed and the bus continued. The next morning, as he noticed daylight begin to appear from the bottom of his blindfold, al-Awaisi could feel the bus labouring up a steep hill. Obviously they were headed into mountains. Still, there was no explanation. He desperately needed to go to the bathroom, but there was no provision for any physical needs.

Finally – he wasn't sure if it was a few minutes or a few hours later – al-Awaisi felt a blast of cold air as the bus door opened. A soldier cut the cords around his ankles. 'Everyone stand!' came the order. 'Move, move!' The groans of the other men expressed al-Awaisi's discomfort, as cramped muscles rebelled. His wrists were swollen from the wire. He had trouble finding his balance as he stood and stumbled down the aisle. He nearly fell as he stepped off the bus.

The blindfold was yanked from al-Awaisi's eyes. A soldier grabbed his arms and sliced the cord around his wrists, in the process adding a fresh cut to his left arm. Then he was shoved towards a group of men huddled a few yards away from the bus.

It took a minute for his eyes to adjust to the light. It was a grey day, with clouds blanketing the surrounding mountains. Everywhere he looked, he saw jagged rocks and not a bit of vegetation. Another man bumped into him as he staggered from the shove of a soldier. He seemed unaware of al-Awaisi and rubbed his arms trying to restore circulation. He was keeping his hands low to cover the shame of a large wet spot – obviously he had been unable to hold his bladder any longer.

'Listen carefully!' a soldier yelled in fractured Arabic. 'You have been deported for a period of two years. Maybe one of your Arab neighbours will have you. Otherwise this is where you will stay.'

The soldier then stepped back onto the bus. Pebbles sprayed the men as the bus took off, rounded a bend, and disappeared.

'Where are we?' asked one of the men.

'I'm freezing!' said another deportee. 'I can't imagine a more miserable, desolate spot.'

'Two years,' muttered al-Awaisi. 'How will I survive here for two years?'

The Netherlands, December 1992

I was resting in the speaker's room of the International Exhibition Centre in Utrecht, Holland, taking a break from the exhilarating but exhausting challenge of speaking to seven thousand young people at the Missions '93 conference. An hour earlier I had completed a lecture about how, since the fall of the Iron Curtain, Islam had risen as the biggest challenge facing Christians and the Western world. 'What communism was to the twentieth century, Islam will be for the next one hundred years,' I'd told the college students who were evaluating their calls to the mission field.

I was about to review my notes for my next talk when the phone rang. 'Andrew, this is Len Rodgers.'

'Len, what a surprise!' Rodgers was an old friend from Lebanon who headed up a group called Venture Middle East. I wondered how he had tracked me down. 'Where are you calling from?'

'I'm in Beirut. Have you been following the news here?'

'About the deportees?'

'Yes. I'm going to go see them on New Year's Day.' That was two days away. 'I hear they are barely surviving in absolutely miserable conditions. Why don't you come with me and let's see what Christ can do for them?'

Via BBC news, I had learned a few facts of the story. A total of 415 Palestinians, many of them doctors, lawyers, university professors, businessmen, and other professionals, had been rounded up from West Bank and Gaza – snatched from their homes and workplaces, plus a few from prison – transported over the border into Lebanon, and deposited on the side of a mountain. The Israeli government declared that these men were the intellectual leaders of Hamas, the group that had claimed responsibility for killing the six Israeli soldiers. However, the world community had raised an outcry over the deportations, claiming they were a violation of the Geneva Convention. The United Nations had passed Resolution 799 condemning the action and demanding that the Palestinians be returned to their homes.

Without yet understanding why, I sensed that this was a trip I needed to take. 'I would love to go with you,' I told Len. 'But tomorrow evening, for New Year's Eve, I lead a concert of prayer for seven thousand young people. I will ask them to pray for these men. Then I'll get down to Lebanon within the week.'

As I hung up the phone, I tried to understand my compulsion to visit these particular men. In recent years I'd met leaders of Hezbollah, the radical Muslim group best known for its kidnapping of high-profile foreigners. While their actions were abhorrent, I came away impressed by their devotion to both their faith and their cause. They had a discipline I'd rarely found among Christians in the West. Even more surprising, these men were willing to enter into a dialogue. In fact Sheikh Fadlallah had invited me to discuss Christianity openly with him. I wondered if there might be a similar openness among the Hamas.

I had learned a little about Hamas through friends in Gaza in 1988. The group's founder, Sheikh Ahmad Yassin, was languishing in an Israeli prison, implicated in several violent acts against Israel, including the killing of two soldiers. During the 1970s, he had established a branch of the Society of Muslim Brothers (the first Islamic fundamentalist group, started in Egypt in the 1920s) in Gaza to call Palestinians back to core Islamic virtues. His method was to establish an Islamic centre from which various medical and social services were provided in Gaza City and throughout the strip. Thus he had built up a power base that eventually caused Israel to consider it a viable alternative to Yasser Arafat's Palestine Liberation Organisation (PLO). I'd even heard rumours that Israel had helped to fund the work in its early years, until they began to understand Yassin's radical political agenda.[1] In 1987 the group became known as the Islamic Resistance Movement (or Hamas, its Arabic acronym, which means 'enthusiasm' or 'courage'),[2] with an openly stated goal of confronting and destroying Israel.

A friend at Gaza Baptist Church explained the significance of this group: 'They have recruited thousands of young people through the university and mosques. They are attracted to a radical, passionate Islam, and attendance at prayers has dramatically increased. They've managed to impose reform of morals in much of Gaza, shutting down movie houses and places that sell alcohol. Then last March they mounted their first military operation. We're concerned, because they're totally committed to Islam, and they believe the uprising is an expression of their faith.'

I learned from my friend that Hamas had recently issued a charter. I obtained a copy and read it. It was a blatantly anti-Semitic document that declared as its objective 'to raise the banner of Allah over every inch of Palestine', rejected all peace conferences and other peaceful solutions, and declared that the solution to the Palestinian problem was 'jihad'.[3] At that time peace negotiations were occurring in Madrid, but Hamas was declaring that such talks were useless.

My friend at Gaza Baptist Church had reason to be concerned. There were hundreds of thousands of Muslims in the Gaza Strip, compared to perhaps two thousand Christians, with only a handful of them evangelicals. What could the Church do to counter such overwhelming odds if the Muslims were this organised and determined? I had met with a couple of the priests from traditional churches in Gaza, and they were so blatantly anti-Israel that I feared that they were not helping their flocks find a genuine Christian response.

Why should I, a Christian and a friend of Israel, even think about speaking with these Muslim fanatics? I got up and paced around the room. Something bothered me. Was it right, even legal, to expel these men from their homes? I could understand Israel's fear. By attacking Israel's military, Hamas was certainly a threat to the country's security, but these particular men had been accused of nothing; Israeli officials even admitted that the deportees had no complicity in the killings. They had committed no crime and faced no judge, yet they were dumped on the side of a rugged mountain in a foreign country that didn't want them, and they were left to struggle as best they could in miserable conditions. This wasn't right. This wasn't justice!

But perhaps more important, I sensed that by visiting these men, I could open a door on behalf of the Church in Gaza. There was no question that Hamas was already a significant influence. How should the Church respond? It could ignore these men, but fundamentalist Islam wasn't going away – it provided an attractive alternative to the PLO and a potential 'answer' to the Israeli presence. No, the Church needed to come forward and reveal an alternative to violence. The first step was to go to Hamas and allow them to see real Christianity. That, I believed, was what God was asking me to do.

The next night I led students from around Europe in an extended period of prayer. As midnight approached, I announced, 'Yesterday, I had a call from the Middle East. It was an urgent appeal to come and spend New Year's Day with 415 Palestinians who are shivering on the side of a mountain in Lebanon. I chose instead to be here with you and to ask you to pray for these men.'

An unusual silence descended over the auditorium. Several of the students had been waving various flags, their way of praying for various countries, and I noted some blue and white Israeli flags among them. 'Going to these men doesn't mean I agree with their politics. I do not. But they are people, and people should not be treated like this. So I am going to visit them and bring them the love of Jesus Christ.'

When the prayer time ended, several students came up to me with tears in their eyes and admitted, 'Brother Andrew, may God forgive me. I've never before prayed for an Arab or a Palestinian.'

There were also a few young people who were angry. 'Why do you love Palestinians?' they demanded. 'Don't you know that Israel belongs to the Jews?' I looked at one young woman, shouting at me as she waved an Israeli flag. Shaking my head, I asked her, 'How bad is it to pray for the Palestinians?' I don't think she heard me.

Marj al-Zohour, Lebanon, December 1992

Abd al-Fattah al-Awaisi felt hemmed in. He was having trouble breathing at the high altitude. When the clouds lifted briefly, he could see Mount Hermon to the east blanketed with snow. But most of the time the hills, where he and his fellow deportees had been left, were smothered by clouds, producing a bone-chilling mist. The men were agitated, eager to escape their wilderness prison, but where could they go? The Lebanese army blocked them from travelling north. Impassable mountains surrounded them to the east and west. About three miles to the south, the Israeli army patrolled the border.

The leaders, especially Dr Abdulaziz Rantisi, tried to bring order to the situation. Organised according to their hometowns, the men were divided into some forty tents. There were eleven doctors in the camp, and they were busy treating the men for lacerations on their wrists and ankles and counselling them on health procedures. The International Red Cross, who had erected the tents, provided the men with a minimal amount of food and water. Thus far no other relief agencies had entered the camp.

Four days after their arrival, al-Awaisi awoke with a jolt. He had risen earlier for prayers, then nodded off to sleep. 'Everyone out!' came the harsh shouts in Arabic. The men shuffled outside the tents to find members of the Lebanese army pointing machine guns at them. 'You will march!' came the order.

The men, prodded by the soldiers, trudged down a dirt road towards Israel. Al-Awaisi struggled to keep up. He gasped for breath; his chest ached. But as they approached the border, a surge of excitement filled him – they were going home! Tonight they would sleep in their own beds!

A rapid burst of machine-gun fire shattered those hopes. Bullets flew over their heads as the group dropped onto the soggy ground. The Lebanese soldiers backed away, while firing a few rounds back towards the Israeli army. The return fire tore up ground all around the terrified men. Deeper booms reverberated from tank cannons. Dirt from the explosions rained down on them.

Then it was quiet. The Lebanese soldiers had disappeared. With a strong voice, Dr Rantisi ordered the men to retreat back to their camp. As they trudged back, al-Awaisi saw one of the men holding his arm, apparently injured by a bullet or shrapnel. Another young man was bleeding from his jaw and chin. As he fell back into his tent, exhausted from the march, a terrible despair fell over al-Awaisi. He ached for his wife and eight children and wondered if he would ever see them again. And he wondered, *What is the point of this suffering? What will it accomplish?*

EIGHTEEN

EVERY TENT IS A MOSQUE

Lebanon, January 1993

Including passage through a couple of military checkpoints, it took about three hours to drive in the rain from the Beirut airport to the forlorn mountains of Marj al-Zohour in southernmost Lebanon. Early morning light struggled to break through the thick clouds as we passed through a village and stopped at a checkpoint blocking the road up to the camp. I was glad that the broadcasting organisation known as Evangelical Omroep (EO) had provided me with a camera and a cameraman, giving me a journalistic cover.

After checking our passports, a soldier carefully examined the contents of our car, looking for food and other supplies. 'What these books?' he asked in broken English.

'They are Bibles,' I said. I also showed him copies of my book *God's Smuggler,* in Arabic, and *The Hiding Place* by Corrie ten Boom.

The soldier spoke to his superior, and together they came back to the car. 'You cannot take all these books,' they said. They grabbed a stack, saying, 'Pick them up on your way back.'

How strange, I thought, that they confiscated only some of the books. Why not all? Why confiscate any books at all? I determined that I would not pick up the books on the way home – maybe these soldiers would read them.

We drove along four miles of switchbacks to the bleak camp, consisting mostly of army-green tents, which provided the only colour in the midst of jagged grey rocks. I got out and wrapped my muffler and overcoat tightly around me to repel the biting wind and chilling rain. There was little sign of activity – most of the men were huddled in their tents. A few empty water jugs littered the ground. Scraps of plastic swirled around the camp. Outside one of the tents, laundry was flapping from a makeshift clothesline.

In a moment two men in green raincoats met me. More boldly than I felt, I said, 'I am Brother Andrew, and I have come to visit you from Holland.'

The camp leader reached out his right hand to me while holding his coat shut with his left. 'You are welcome!' he said. 'I am Doctor Abdulaziz Rantisi.' From my reading I recognised the name. He was second in command of Hamas, behind the founder Sheikh Yassin. Rantisi was accompanied by the camp imam.[1] Together they offered to give me a tour.

We sloshed through a muddy path, with rainwater rushing in a stream along one side. It was bitter cold, and I wondered if it might even snow. At one point the imam stopped and pulled off each of his boots to pour out the water. My shoes were filling with water too, but I felt it would be futile to empty them.

How does one begin a conversation with cold, wet strangers who may also be terrorists? 'You know, in Holland, we do this on holiday,' I said. 'We collect wood and we live in tents and we walk in the rain. I suppose something in man wants to go back to a primitive lifestyle.'

Dr Rantisi glanced at me, perhaps wondering about my sanity, then chuckled. 'You actually do that by your own choice. But we are forced to, and this in winter.'

'I don't know how you can manage in these conditions,' I sighed. 'But if you have no humour, you cannot survive.'

The camp leader nodded his head and smiled, and I could tell that the ice was cracking. 'We are thankful that it is not snowing,' said the imam. 'We've been told that it can snow up to one-and-a-half metres deep. If that happens, it would be to the top of our tents.'

Outside one tent was a box of potatoes. 'This is what we have to eat!' Rantisi said, holding up a potato. 'This is all. And because it is wet, we cannot make a fire to cook the potatoes. We will not have anything to eat today.'

A boy stepped out of the tent, and I asked to speak with him for a moment. 'How old are you?' I asked through the imam who translated into Arabic for me.

'Sixteen years old,' he said.

I looked at him and thought of my sons at that age and wondered how they would have managed in these miserable conditions.

'Do you know why you are here?'

He shook his head to say no and looked as though he might break into tears.

As we continued on our tour, I asked the imam, 'Do you have your prayers every day, five times a day?'

'Yes, of course,' he answered.

'So, where do you pray? I do not see a mosque.'

The imam stroked his scraggly beard for a moment, then answered, 'Every tent is a mosque.'

The answer shook me. It suddenly dawned on me that Islam didn't rely on a building. For many Christians, the Church couldn't function without a building. What difference would it make in our world if we believed every home was a church?

Of Dr Rantisi, I asked, 'Are you a member of Hamas?'

'No. I was a member of Hamas. I'm not a member now.'

I was surprised by the answer and not quite sure what to make of it. Perhaps they didn't trust me yet. Or maybe they were playing a game of semantics. As we slipped under the awning of a tent to escape the rain, I noted, 'I am reading in newspaper articles that you are happy to be here because it gives you a chance to take over from the PLO.'

Dr Rantisi was confused and spoke to the imam, who translated my words. The two talked for a moment, then the imam translated Rantisi's answer: 'We are not seeking to take the position of the PLO. The PLO represents the Palestinians, and we are part of the Palestinian people. We are a group of intellectuals, a group of physicians, lawyers, businessmen, professors. We and the PLO are brothers – same as blood.'

'Before leaving for Lebanon, I talked with a PLO representative in The Hague. He told me the PLO are fasting two days a week for you.'

'Mondays and Thursdays!' the imam said with a laugh. I looked at him with surprise. 'That is our tradition when it is outside of Ramadan – we fast on Mondays and Thursdays. We want to be very close to our Lord and your Lord and the Lord of heavens and earth, our creator. We feel here we are close to Him.'

'This is a thousand metres closer to heaven,' I said, 'but it's not a very pleasant climate.' They laughed, and I sensed that I was connecting with these men. At least someone was here to share briefly in their misery. 'I am here as a Christian to represent Jesus Christ and to express sympathy to all of you because we think it's terrible what's happened.'

Rantisi answered me directly in English: 'Thank you very much. The Christians are the closest people in the world to Muslims because God is our Lord and their Lord. By being so, we are really brothers.'

'I have a very important question for both of you. After this is all over, do you think you could possibly forgive Israel for what they have done?'

Rantisi and the imam talked, and the imam then gave their answer. 'Actually, we as Muslims would like always to forgive. We can punish whoever punishes us. But Quran says if you forgive, this is best for you and for others.'

'I hope you can,' I said. 'We all need forgiveness.'

'If the Israeli government takes us back tomorrow, we will forgive.'

I didn't expect Israel to back down, and I wondered how these men would respond the longer they lived in such conditions.

We moved back out into the rain, which was falling even harder than when I had arrived. Our next stop was a tent with the word 'clinic' clearly written in English on the flap. No one was inside. On a bench lay four boxes of medicines and supplies. Another box was on the damp ground and lying next to it was a single wooden crutch. It didn't look like much for a camp of four-hundred-plus men. Meanwhile one of the men who had joined our little group to listen in on the conversation ran to find the doctor in charge. I suggested that we wait inside the tent: 'Otherwise we will drown.'

A moment later I was introduced to Dr Mahmoud Zahar. He was a short man, with a neatly trimmed black beard and dark, piercing eyes. The rain was causing a racket as it pounded on the tent, and I practically had to shout to be heard. 'Are there a lot of sick people here?' I asked.

In clear English, Dr Zahar provided a clinical assessment of the situation. 'We have chest infections from the cold and damp. Many of the men have dysentery and diarrhoea, because the water is bad. There are ten men in the camp who have diabetes, and all we have to eat are potatoes – that is not a good diet for people with diabetes. In this clinic, as you can see, we have no heat, no light. We've done a number of small operations with local anaesthetic.'

'I must say, these are miserable conditions. I wish I could have brought more, but I have here some pills to purify your water.'

I handed the doctor the plastic shopping bag. He was grateful: 'By being here you are speaking to the conscience of the world.'

'That is why I am here.'

'You are understanding our situation. You can't imagine how long we are going to stay here. I am speaking to the world. What is our fault? What is our fault? We are innocent!'

'Are you a member of Hamas?' I asked.

'No! We are members of associations. We are doctors and lawyers and professors – professional people. What is our fault? If they have accusations, take us to court!'

I was surprised by the intensity of this man. As he spoke, he pointed at me, emphasising, 'What is our fault?'

I responded by asking him, 'What gives you the strength to carry on?'

'It is our religion!' he answered, and that spun him into another speech. 'It is not forbidden for a Christian to be a true Christian. It is not forbidden for a Jew to be a true Jew. Also it is not forbidden for a Muslim to be a true Muslim. We are for peace. Our solution is peace. We are looking for a true peaceful method to achieve justice in our area.'

The methods of Hamas didn't seem very peaceful, but this wasn't the time for confrontation. I was here to meet these men, to observe, and to listen. 'My wish is shalom!' I said, intentionally using the Hebrew term.

'We are looking for peace! We believe Madrid peace-talking

will bring for us nothing. We are looking for a true peaceful method to achieve justice in our area.'

While we were talking, a man slipped into the tent and handed me a piece of paper, saying 'This is my wife's name and address. If you are in Israel, could you visit my family, please?' Over the next hour, others also gave me papers with names, addresses, and phone numbers of loved ones back home.

'I have brought you some books to read,' I announced in the now crowded tent. 'I know you men are intellectuals. And when it is raining, I'm sure you would like to have some good books.' I handed Rantisi and Zahar copies of *The Hiding Place* and quipped, 'This book will tell you how you can also become famous by saving the lives of Jews.' The two men looked surprised, but then they started to smile, then laugh.

'We want to organise a library,' said Rantisi. 'These books will be read.'

'Then I have some more. This is my book, called *God's Smuggler*. It is about my experiences in Russia and Eastern Europe. The Christians there had no Bibles, and so I made sure they got them. And I have brought some Bibles for you. This is the most important book I could give you. It will show you how to have real peace, peace in this world and peace in your hearts.'

I was starting to feel the cold and dampness in my chest and feared that, by the time I arrived back in Holland, I would be sick. As I said good-bye to the men, I knew they could not escape their awful conditions. No doubt, many of them would suffer from illness. I determined then that I had to help them in some way and that I would definitely return.

A gust of wind rustled the tent where Nabil slept fitfully. It took him a minute to orient himself and realise that what had awakened him were the groans of his younger brother, Ibrahim. 'Hey,' Nabil whispered. 'How are you doing?'

Hissing the words through his teeth, Ibrahim answered, 'The pain is unbearable tonight. The damp, the cold, the rocks . . .'

He didn't finish the thought, but Nabil understood. There wasn't much he could do for his brother except reach over and squeeze his arm to let him know someone cared. Ibrahim had been hit by six Israeli bullets during a protest at Rachel's Tomb and had spent several weeks in a Bethlehem hospital. Two bullets remained in his body, and he lived in constant pain. The doctors in camp could do nothing to help him.

Fully awake now, Nabil allowed his mind to drift to life before Marj al-Zohour. He had started to earn a decent income as a writer for a weekly Palestinian newspaper and a stringer for a couple of foreign magazines. His work helped ease the memory of dark times – the arrests, weeks in prison, often without any charges being filed. Nabil had dabbled in politics, even briefly participating in meetings of Hamas. He liked their emphasis on the return to Muslim fundamentals. Their agenda fit well with his aims of seeing Israel eliminated and all the land returned to the Palestinians. However, he wasn't by nature a fighter. He would do his part by writing articles about Palestinian suffering.

The soldiers had come one afternoon while he was away on a writing assignment. Ibrahim was arrested and a message left with his mother and sister – Nabil was to report to military headquarters in Bethlehem no later than six o'clock that evening. In hysterics, his sister, Hanan, told him, 'If you aren't there, they will demolish our house.'

Nabil knew the soldiers would follow through on their threat if he didn't show up on time. 'Quick, give me some food!' As Hanan hurried into the kitchen, Nabil went to his room and grabbed a warm shirt. Then he hugged his mother and sister. 'You must be strong, both of you,' he said, staring into their eyes. 'Ibrahim and I will be home soon.'

Of course, they hadn't come home, and there was no way to communicate with their mother and sister. That was why Nabil had given a note to the Dutchman who had visited camp a few days before, though Nabil seriously doubted anything would come of that. He worried about his family. His mother struggled with progressively worsening arthritis. Hanan, who was to be married soon, bore most of the burden for their home. How would his mother survive with no income and without his sister to help around the house?

A deep despair enveloped Nabil. He longed to cry out to Allah but wondered if God would listen to his prayers. Sometimes he wondered why he recited the ritual prayers five times each day. He wanted to scream: *Does anyone care?* Israel despised Palestinians. Arab nations did nothing to help. And the world ignored their plight.

For the first time Nabil felt life was utterly hopeless. No one would come to his rescue, because no one cared about Palestinians.

The Netherlands, January 1993

By the time I returned to Holland, my head was clogged, my chest felt heavy, and I was coughing. Still, I felt compelled to accept several interviews about what I had discovered at Marj al-Zohour.

Immediately before my first television appearance, the Israeli ambassador to Holland was interviewed about the deportees. The newscast had just reported that Israel had admitted that eleven of the men were deported by mistake, including the teenage boy I had met on my brief tour. The eleven would be allowed to return but not the others. I listened intently as the ambassador said, 'These are not innocent refugees. They are hardened criminals.'

Naturally, the interviewer asked why, if these were hardened criminals, they weren't arrested and brought to trial. The ambassador stuttered, then said, 'These people who are on the hills in Lebanon now are not people with blood on their hands, otherwise we would not have deported them.' So they were hardened criminals (though most of them had never been in prison), but they had no responsibility for the murders that had precipitated this action? So why did they deport them? The ambassador's reply: 'There have been six murders by Hamas until the banishment of this group. There has not been one since.'

On a Christian television show, I was asked, 'What did you learn from this trip?'

'This was the most bizarre trip I've ever made,' I answered, trying to avoid coughing. 'I visited a piece of land deserted by God and Allah. We live here comfortably in our own homes and countries. The 415 Palestinians live in tents in no-man's-land. It is absurd that people have to live in such misery, in the rain, cold, and terrible living conditions.'

'So why did you go?'

'The love of God for them motivated me to go. I wanted to be there. I wanted to see the need. And I wanted to find out what we can do. Maybe they just need a shoulder to cry on. If they never meet a messenger of Jesus, they will never get to know the love of Christ and experience real forgiveness. Also, to love Jesus they should be able to love me first. That's why we have to go and visit them, to build bridges between people and God.'

'But you were only there for a few hours. You could come home; they couldn't. Could you really do any good?'

'You are right. I was able to leave the misery of that camp. But at least they have the Bible now. Arabic Bibles, Gospels, and some of my books in Arabic. They had nothing to read before because it was not allowed. Now they can read the Bible.'

'But they are Muslims.'

'When you offer a Bible to a Muslim, he will never refuse it. But the secret is that we have to go to them. This is an opportunity to share the gospel.'

Several people were surprised that I would even consider reaching out to Muslims. They wondered if a Muslim, especially a fundamentalist like a member of Hamas, would listen to Christians. And what about Israel – these people I had visited were avowed enemies of Israel. Shouldn't I stay away from them?

When Len Rodgers and I compared notes over the phone about our respective visits to Marj al-Zohour, Len told me about his reception there. As he entered the camp, one of the deportees said, 'We knew that Christ would come to us!' That was an amazing statement, and I reflected on what it meant. I knew that in their eschatology, Muslims believe that Christ will return to earth – that will be a sign of the ultimate victory of Islam. But I sensed that this was more personal. Maybe it was their way of recognising that we cared.

Regardless of how they interpreted our visits, our purpose was to introduce these men to the *living* Christ who dwells within us. Christ said to go and make disciples of *all* nations. Did that include Palestinians or not? Did that include Arabs and Muslims? How could we ignore more than a billion people whom God says He loves? It is true that many Muslims are antagonistic towards the gospel, but many more are not. These men in Lebanon – yes, Muslim fundamentalists – seemed to respect Len Rodgers and me. My friend George Otis once said, 'Islam will never respect a church that is in hiding.' I am a Christian, and with aggressive love I went in obedience to God and proclaimed Christ to these men.

But it wasn't enough for me to go to the camp. The interviewer was correct – I could visit and return to my comfortable home in Holland. But millions of people lived without hope in the Middle East. It didn't matter that a single person once in a while visited a very few of them. God needed a permanent presence in Israel, West Bank, Gaza – everywhere that the conflict between Israelis and Palestinians raged. Not a few foreigners, but a living, breathing, vital local church was required. Committed Christians living in the area could demonstrate to Muslims, to fundamentalists burning with hatred, that God's way of love is far more powerful than their hate. But were Christians living as neighbours to Hamas and other fundamentalist groups prepared for the task? That was what I had to find out.

What was the next step? On my desk was a pile of little pieces of paper, each bearing a name and address. These four hundred men marooned in southern Lebanon had wives and children – at least another three thousand people were affected by their deportation. Didn't they need the love of Jesus too? I might start by going to them. But not alone – I would take a local Palestinian Christian leader. And I knew just the person.

I picked up the phone and called my travel agent. 'I need to book a trip to Israel.'

THE FAMILIES OF HAMAS

Marj al-Zohour, March 1993

Abd al-Fattah al-Awaisi listened as light rain tapped on the tent where he and a dozen other men from Hebron lay, waiting for the call to prayer. Late the evening before, the group had crowded around a transistor radio powered by two weak batteries. As a historian, al-Awaisi missed the many newspapers, magazines, and journals he studied regularly at the university. He had to be satisfied with news from the BBC and a local Lebanese station.

The news was that Israel's highest court had ruled it would not reverse the government's deportation order. However, it also had established a process whereby individual deportees could appeal their case. *How will we do that?* al-Awaisi had wondered. *We aren't even in Israel. We have no access to lawyers who can help us, even if we could file an appeal.*

But that wasn't the only news. In a compromise with the United States, Israel said it would allow approximately one hundred men to return immediately and would shorten from two years to one the term of expulsion for the others. A US government spokesman had praised the decision and stated that no further action by the Security Council was necessary. Al-Awaisi and his friends had hoped that the United States would put pressure on Israel to abide by UN Resolution 799 that required *all* of them to be returned home. Now it appeared that the international community had lost interest in their plight. *Just six short weeks*, he thought. *How quickly the world forgets us and moves on to some other issue.*

At the first call to prayer, al-Awaisi stepped out of his bedroll, bundled himself into his coat, and wrapped a scarf around his neck, trying to fight off the cold mist. He grabbed his prayer rug, which was rolled up with the others in the corner of the tent, and headed to the open area where the camp gathered for prayer and updates from the camp leader, Dr Rantisi.

At the conclusion of prayers, with the men remaining on their knees, Dr Rantisi stood to address the men, now numbering slightly under four hundred after fourteen 'mistakes' were returned home by helicopter and five more had been evacuated for medical reasons. Briefly he reviewed the situation, concluding that Israel knew they were violating international law and yet still refused to let them all return to their homes.

Rantisi put the issue to a vote. 'Let he who rejects the American-Israeli deal raise his hand.' Every man raised his hand. The only sound was the motor drive of a photographer's camera, recording the moment for the international press. 'Let he who agrees to this deal now raise his hand.' No hands were raised. Rantisi concluded the meeting by shouting: 'God take revenge on those who suppressed us. God take our revenge on those who expelled us!'

Bethlehem, spring 1993

Bethlehem Bible College had leased buildings on Hebron Road from the Bible Lands Society of England and hoped to eventually buy the buildings. Having formerly housed the Helen Keller School for the Blind, they were ideal for the college. From now on

I planned to make this my base of operation every time I visited Israel and the West Bank.

In the kitchen adjoining the guest apartments, Bishara Awad, president of the college, and I drank coffee and discussed my mission. I had told him about my visit to Marj al-Zohour and showed him the stack of names and addresses. 'I want to visit as many of these people as possible,' I said.

'You realise that these are probably all Muslim families,' my friend said.

'That is true, but they are people who need encouragement. This is an opportunity to show them the love of Christ.'

Bishara smiled. 'Do you know what you will find in these homes?'

'Probably people who are angry, scared, worried about their future.'

'That's right. The men you met in southern Lebanon were probably the primary breadwinners for their families. When the man leaves, the income leaves with him.'

'So should I be bringing them money? I couldn't do much.'

'No, that would actually complicate your mission. You go and tell them what you saw on the mountains. Tell them how the men are doing and how they miss their wives and families.'

'Would it be all right to read the Bible or pray with them?'

'Yes, in most homes, that would be okay. But we must be sensitive.'

Bishara had sorted through the addresses I had collected. 'There are several near here,' Bishara said, thinking through what order we might visit the families. 'Let's begin at Dheihshe refugee camp.'

There are three refugee camps near Bethlehem Bible College. All were formed shortly after Israel was declared a nation and hundreds of thousands of Palestinians fled from the conflict between Arab and Israeli forces, settling just over the border in Lebanon or on land controlled by Jordan and Egypt. Many had settled in Bethlehem, which belonged to Jordan at that time. The Al-Azza camp was directly across the street from Bethlehem Bible College; Aida just a few blocks away. Dheihshe, however, was the biggest of the camps and just a five-minute drive up Hebron Road from the college.

Bishara parked at the entrance. There was a small notice there, recognising various groups that had contributed aid to the camp. Bethlehem Bible College was included on the list; obviously the college was involved in the community. We passed by a revolving gate that once served as the military checkpoint to prevent refugees from leaving. By 1993, however, the people were free to come and go within Bethlehem. But the contrast between this camp and the rest of the town was stark. Hundreds of cinder block apartments were crammed into an area half a kilometre square. Two or more families often lived in each tiny apartment. As we walked down a narrow street, I realised that if I stretched out my arms I could touch walls on both sides of the alley.

I quickly lost my bearings and was glad Bishara seemed to know how to navigate these narrow alleyways. 'Here we are!' he finally said and stopped to knock on the door of a first-floor apartment.

There was a long wait, though we could hear women's voices inside. Finally, we heard feet shuffling towards the door, which was opened a crack. A woman dressed in a plain brown caftan and a white scarf, a baby balanced on her hip, looked cautiously at us. Bishara, pointing to me, explained in Arabic: 'This is Brother Andrew. He has just come from Marj al-Zohour and was asked to visit you.'

The woman's face brightened and the door opened wide. 'Come in; come in!' Cautiously we entered the living room. 'Come, sit down. Please!' she said to me in halting English. Then she spoke in Arabic, leaning towards the kitchen, and several faces popped out to observe us. One of the women called to a boy. After receiving instructions, he dashed past us and out the front door.

The living room was small. A couple of weavings hung from the wall. An oscillating fan stood silent in a corner, waiting for warmer weather. An old television was in another corner, and on top was a family photo that included two young men now living in a tent in Lebanon. A worn-out couch, a few folding chairs, and a small coffee table completed the furnishings. Three women crowded at the entrance to the kitchen. Peering between them, a young girl caught my eye and smiled. There was a knock on the door, and several men entered, followed a moment later by another white-scarfed woman carrying a baby. From the kitchen, a teenage girl came to us with a tray holding my favourite coffee and a plate of biscuits.

As we sipped our coffee, the room filled and several men crowded through the front door or listened from the street. Bishara asked some questions, then explained to me that the old woman smiling at me was the mother of two men in the camp – Nabil and Ibrahim. I smiled back at the woman and noted that her hands were swollen, probably from hard work.

'Next to her is Nabil and Ibrahim's sister, Hanan,' Bishara said. 'They have two older sisters who are married – they are the ones with the babies.'

'And who are the others?' I asked, referring to the curious neighbours crammed into the apartment.

'Probably cousins, all part of the extended family. They are eager to hear what you have to say.'

'I visited the camp a few weeks ago,' I explained and pulled out a stack of pictures for them to look at. For the next few minutes, I described the conditions at Marj al-Zohour. A couple of babies cried, and the mothers tried to quiet them as they listened to the news. Bishara translated for me.

When I finished my brief report, I nodded to Bishara, who opened his Bible and said, 'I want to give you a word of encouragement from our Scriptures.' He opened to Matthew and began reading in Arabic: 'Blessed are the poor in spirit, for theirs is the kingdom of heaven.' He read through the Beatitudes slowly, without any commentary. The crowd listened intently to the pastoral words. Then he asked the family if they would allow me to pray to Isa – Jesus – for them. Most of the people in the room nodded their heads.

We all stood. Many held their hands at their waist, palms up. I prayed for all in the room, that God would meet their needs. I prayed for their loved ones at Marj al-Zohour, and I concluded with a prayer that all of them would experience peace from Isa, the Prince of Peace.

As we prepared to leave, someone noted my camera and suggested I take a group picture. 'I will take these pictures back to Marj al-Zohour, so your sons, your brothers, your uncles can see you.' Several of the men and boys wanted a separate picture with me. As I knelt on the floor in their midst, a young man grabbed my hand and put his other arm around my shoulder, saying with more than words how much he and his family appreciated our being with them.

We visited several other families in the Bethlehem area, then did the same in Hebron the next day. The response was always the same. Each home we visited welcomed us and within minutes was filled with family and neighbours eager to hear news of their loved one. Bishara usually closed the visit with a word from Scripture and then I prayed.

AFTER THE VISITS in Hebron, Salwa and Bishara served me dinner in their apartment at the college. Bishara was quiet, obviously thinking about something.

'What is on your mind?' I asked.

'This was my first significant opportunity to minister in the Muslim community,' he answered.

'But you have Muslim friends,' I said. 'I noticed that Bethlehem Bible College was publicly recognised at the entrance to the refugee camp. And I've met several Muslims at college events.'

'Of course, I have made many friends in the community. We want to be good neighbours. But to actually visit Muslims in their homes, to show them how sad we are that their loved ones are deported – for me, that is the first time I've had this kind of ministry.'

Bishara's thoughts also put me in a reflective mood. 'What struck me today is that the media perception of these people is very different from what we see in their homes. When I read about Hamas in the paper, it's as if they have only one agenda. You never think of them having families. They were all very hospitable. Every one of them gave us tea and coffee, fruits, pastries.' I paused to enjoy some bites of the roast beef Salwa had prepared. Then I added, 'My friend, you and I can't do this alone. Surely there are many other Christians who can visit the homes of Muslims and show them the love of Jesus.'

Bishara sat back and thought. Then he said, 'I doubt whether that kind of outreach is being done at all.'

'The students here at the Bible college – surely some of them could do this. That is partly why you are training them, so that the local Christian community can be a light in the darkness.'

My friend nodded. 'You are right. That is why we must train them, so that they can do what you and I did today.'

TWENTY

A MEAL WITH TERRORISTS

Marj al-Zohour, spring 1993

Al-Awaisi knew something was wrong when the sombre delegation entered the tent. Several of his tent mates slipped out as the visitors sat on the ground. 'We have some bad news,' said Dr Rantisi. 'We have just received a report from Hebron. Your wife and children have been deported.'

'The authorities said your wife didn't have proper papers,' explained another member of the delegation.

Feeling his chest constrict, his breathing short, al-Awaisi asked, 'My family, where did they take them?'

'To Jordan. A refugee camp. We don't know which one, but we'll try to find out.'

That night al-Awaisi felt a searing pain in his head. The tent seemed to spin above him. He tried to speak, to tell his tent mates that something was wrong, but he could force out only some slurred sounds. Nevertheless, someone realised that there was a problem.

A few minutes later, Mahmoud Zahar entered the tent. A lantern and two flashlights provided minimal light. He carefully examined al-Awaisi. 'You have suffered a stroke,' Dr Zahar finally concluded. 'You need to go to a hospital.'

Deep despair enveloped the university professor. Though his friends would try, he knew there would be no trip to the hospital. At that moment, he felt his life ebbing away, and he wasn't even sure he wanted to live anymore. First he'd been removed from his home and his profession. Now he'd lost his family and his health.

He wondered, *Is there any reason to hang on?* Instinctively he prayed: 'Allah, is there any hope?'

Marj al-Zohour, August 1993

I returned to the camp at Marj al-Zohour with a member of the Bible Society in Beirut. It was a clear, sunny day, and I was amazed at how the camp had changed since the time I saw it in the dead of winter. The camp was a beehive of activity. Men were washing their clothes in large plastic tubs and hanging them on lines strung between the tents. Others were tending to fires, cooking rice and meat for the main midday meal. Several tents also served as shops, and they were doing a brisk business. I noted that the cigarettes and film were cheaper than in Beirut.

Still, all the efforts of the men couldn't change the location, which remained desolate. The dry, golden-coloured rocks reflected the sun, causing me to squint. However, the mountain air was cool, and most of the men wore light jackets or sweaters. There was a hint of snow on Mount Hermon in the distance. The only sign of plant life in the camp was in one protected corner, a three-foot-square garden where someone had planted mint and spices. The precious plants were protected from the bright sun by a small burlap awning.

The population of the camp had dropped since my first visit. Under world pressure, the Israeli government had taken about one hundred men back. The rest, it was said, could come home after one year – a reduction of one year from the original deportation sentence. It was clear that in the eight months since they'd landed here, the men had figured out ways to create an economy, trading with nearby villages for food and other needs. These men had not given up on life; indeed they were proud, hardworking, determined to make the most of a bad situation.

While the deportees still couldn't leave, Lebanese soldiers at the checkpoint down the road allowed most visitors to enter the camp. This time there was no limit on the number of books I could take in. My friend from the Bible Society and I had plenty of Scriptures to hand out. However, it was my stack of pictures of families in West Bank and Gaza that drew a big crowd. I had written the names on the back of the photos, and I handed them to each man as he recognised his family. A young man, speaking excellent English, introduced himself as Nabil and gazed for a long time at the photographs taken in his apartment. Frequently a man would run to find a friend to tell him he had a photograph from home. Somehow these men had obtained a video camera, and I was given videotapes to deliver back to their families.

Before touring the camp, I talked with Dr Rantisi. His tent was about fifty yards outside of camp to allow him privacy as he met with leaders, mediated disputes, and planned for the day when they would all return home. I gave him a copy of a brand-new Arabic translation of the Bible.

'We have a nice library,' he told me. 'I will show you.'

As we walked back into camp, Rantisi explained that the men in the camp had made good use of their time. He pointed to a bold sign: Marj az-Zohour University. Opposite it was a large tent. 'That is our assembly hall and our mosque. And here is our library.'

I stepped through the flap and into a beautiful room lined with shelves on both sides. A small table was in the middle. The shelves were full of reference books of all kinds.

I was amazed. 'How did you obtain all of these books?' I asked the librarian from Hebron.

The man gave a big smile as he said, 'At first the people in Lebanon brought us food. Then we told them we needed books. So we traded for books!'

'It looks like a wide variety of books here. What subjects are you studying?'

'Many subjects – mathematics, languages. We have English, Spanish, German, Russian, Italian, Hebrew.'

'There are seventeen professors here,' Rantisi explained, 'and currently sixty-six official, registered students.'

'You give exams and grades?'

'Yes, the students write papers and take exams and the professors grade them. The results are sent to the university back home, and the students are then given credit towards their degree. There are many others studying but not for academic credit.'

'What is the most popular subject?' I asked.

A chill went down my spine as he answered: 'Sharia law.'

Sharia law is the Islamic legal system. I knew serious Muslims believed that there should be no separation of government and religion. Sharia law was intended to govern every aspect of daily life. And what was the end result of such a system? If I was to believe the Hamas Charter, then these men were plotting to drive Israel out of the land and establish a state governed by Islam. The implications were staggering. Did the world realise what was happening here? These men had taken a terrible situation and used it to strengthen their resolve. There was no question that rather than destroying Hamas, Israel had made them stronger. Perhaps these men were naive to think they could defeat Israel and its powerful military might, but they and their followers back home were certainly going to challenge those they considered occupiers. I was sure then that Israel had created a time bomb![1]

Then Dr Rantisi said he wanted me to meet one of the professors from Hebron who was confined to his tent by illness. I was introduced to Dr Abd al-Fattah al-Awaisi. He was lying on a cot – the only bed I'd observed in the camp – paralysed by a stroke four months earlier. He was wearing a black-and-white-checked kaffiyeh on his head and was covered with a light blanket. He stared at me through his glasses with intelligent eyes. He spoke fairly good English, so I knelt by his bed to talk.

'How are you feeling?' I asked.

'I'm doing a little better. For the first two months, I couldn't talk. I am still paralysed on my left side.'

'Would you like to tell me a little about yourself?'

He seemed to welcome the chance to talk. 'I was born in 1959. I got my PhD from Exeter University in Britain. I am an assistant professor at Hebron University. I am married and have eight children.'

'Were you taken from your home?'

'Yes, from my home on the fourteenth of December.'

'Did the authorities say anything to your wife and children about the situation?'

'When they came to arrest me for deportation, they told my wife, "Prepare yourself; you will be next." At the time I could not understand what they meant because I didn't know where they were taking me. But when I heard they deported my wife and eight children to Jordan on twenty-seven March, I remembered this word and I understood it very well.'

'Do you know why your family was sent to Jordan?'

'They haven't Israeli identity. They are called visitors, and so they haven't permission to stay in Hebron. So all of them are now living in Jordan, in circumstances . . .' Al-Awaisi's voice caught from emotion. It took him a moment to finish his thought: '. . . I could not imagine. My wife, she has a Jordanian passport. My children, they haven't Jordanian passports. They are holding Egyptian travel documents. So they are not allowed to live in Jordan. The Israelis did not allow them to stay, and the Jordanians do not allow them to stay. So we are waiting the help of Allah, to see what will happen next.'

'May I ask a very personal question? How are they being supported now?'

'Since they deported me, my wife has taken my salary from Hebron University. But since they deported her to Jordan, nothing comes to her. She told me so two days ago when I phoned her.'

I wondered where there was a phone in the camp, but I didn't take the time to ask. Obviously these men were very resourceful. 'Does she live with relatives or is she on her own?'

'She and the eight children are living with her brother, who is married with two wives and has several children. They all live in one small house in Al Wahdaat refugee camp, near Amman. My children have not been allowed to go to the schools.' As an educated man, he was obviously troubled by this fact.

'When you are allowed to go back, will your wife be able to return to Hebron?'

'No, they issued to her a paper, showing that the Israelis will not allow her to go back to Hebron.'

'So do you plan then to join her in Jordan?'

'I am not planning for anything. I am waiting. I have spent

more than two months as you are seeing me now. The doctors say I need to go to a hospital.'

'So that is something we can pray for, that you can get medical attention and that you will be reunited with your family.' I grabbed his hand. 'I cannot make promises in this crazy world. But I'll see what I can do. I'll try hard.'

I meant those words. Dr Al-Awaisi's condition was deplorable. In a normal prison, he would have received medical attention. But here, even with eleven doctors, there was little that could be done for him without access to a hospital, and since an airlift early in the deportation, none of the men had been allowed to go to a hospital.

As I stepped out of al-Awaisi's tent, my eyes blinked in the bright sun. Then I noticed the young librarian running towards me. He caught his breath and said, 'Do you want to have a meal with us?'

'Of course!' I answered. 'I'd love to have a meal with terrorists!'

The man laughed while my companion for the day from the Bible Society looked at me in shock. 'Andrew, you can't say that!'

'Sure you can,' I answered. 'If you smile!'

'Come with me!' said the young man, eager to show me traditional Palestinian hospitality. He led me to the 'Hebron tent'. There a feast was laid out on a blanket on the floor – lamb, chicken, rice, various 'salads', and stacks of pita bread. About a dozen men stood to greet me, and then we sat together on the tent floor. I was offered a loaf of flat bread and I tore off a piece and dipped it into a plate of hummus.

The food was delicious and I complimented them. They seemed very proud of their feast, and they joined me in tearing their bread and dipping it into the various dishes. The conversation was lively and varied. One young man told me he was working hard on his studies and planned to return to Jerusalem University, adding, 'Also I am searching for a wife.'

'You won't find one here!' I said as I swallowed a bite of *kibbeh*, the traditional Arab dish of meat, cracked wheat, nuts, and raisins.

'I don't know why they arrested me,' he said. 'Between my job and studies and caring for my ill mother, there wasn't time for any other activities. My mother was in intensive care when they took me away. I didn't know for many days whether my mother was dead or not. One person, he is working for BBC World Service, he made a telephone call to my family, and they said she is now well.'

Looking around the tent, I saw many books – these were studious men. When I observed the books, the librarian said, 'Every tent has books. Your books that you brought, especially the Bibles, they are always checked out from the library.'

As we finished the meal, I thanked them for inviting me. 'This was absolutely wonderful. When you go back home, I want to visit you and you will be *my* guests for a meal!'

That was the spark for an idea. These men had responded so warmly to my visits. Maybe I could do something for them. I had joked about eating a meal with terrorists. What they didn't realise is that without Christ in my life, I might have ended up as a terrorist myself. I couldn't help but recall my own life as a boy under German occupation. Like so many Palestinian boys, I had thrown stones at soldiers – the German soldiers in my town. What if the Germans hadn't been defeated in 1945? What if the occupation had lasted for decades? That wasn't the case in Holland, but Palestinians believe they have lived under occupation since 1967, and for some Muslim fundamentalists it was motivating them to take drastic actions.

We were all religious. These men were committed Muslims; I was a committed Christian. So what was the difference between us? Why were they committed to wiping out Israel, while I was committed to strengthening the Church in the land so that Israelis and Palestinians could find their true identity?

In a single word, the difference was Jesus.

Why not give them all a meal and tell them about the hope I have, the only hope for real peace in the Middle East?

O N 17 DECEMBER 1993, exactly one year to the day after 415 'leaders' of Hamas were deported, those who remained in the camp at Marj al-Zohour were returned to Israel. Some were immediately sent to prison. Others tried to pick up their lives, reconnecting with family, returning to their work. However, that was difficult because all of them were confined by city arrest – they were not permitted to travel outside their community.

Abd al-Fattah al-Awaisi was in a dilemma. If he returned to Hebron, his family would not be able to join him. They remained trapped in a Jordanian refugee camp. Unfortunately, no Middle East country seemed willing to take them. So he turned to friends he'd made in England during his years of study. He was transported to London where his family eventually joined him. I phoned him a couple of times. The reunion with his family seemed to revive him physically and with much needed medical attention, his condition improved. But he lamented that he and his family would never again see their home in Hebron.

HOW FAR DO I GO?

Hebron, February 1994

Early on the morning of 25 February 1994, a Brooklyn-born doctor walked resolutely to the Ibrahimi Mosque in Hebron. He lived in the nearby settlement of Kiriat Arba, having moved there in 1983 after graduating from medical school in New York. He had grown up in a strict Zionist family that mandated separation from all non-Jews. He prided himself in never having treated an Arab patient.

To Dr Baruch Goldstein, the mere existence of the Palestinians was a problem, for he ardently believed that all of the Holy Land belonged only to the Jews. By his logic, even if they were peaceful, all Palestinians must still be driven out of Israel and the disputed territories, and he was prepared to do his part in that cause. He had often visited this particular mosque, built over the cave where Abraham and his wife, Sarah, as well as the patriarchs Isaac and Jacob, were supposedly buried. Several times he and other settlers had verbal confrontations with the Palestinians there. On this day there would be more than shouting.

Because this was the month of Ramadan, the mosque

was full. The doctor entered the back of the mosque and moved forward quickly while the men were bowing together towards Mecca. He opened his coat, took out a grenade, pulled the pin, and tossed it among the worshippers. Then the machine gun emerged and he began shooting.

Amid the screams, smoke, and echoing sound of gunshots, it was hard to find the source of the attack. Precious moments were lost as men scrambled for exits or stumbled over bodies, while others tried to locate the assailant. Finally, through the smoke, they saw the murderer. A group of men charged him and pummelled him to death.

In the ensuing confusion, it was hard to know exactly what happened in the next few hours. Ambulances screamed through the city, trying to get the wounded to hospitals. Gunshots and explosions sounded around the town. At Al Ahli Hospital, there were gunshots as patients were unloaded and doctors tried to do triage. More Palestinians were wounded and killed at the door to the hospital.

The official report was that twenty-nine men died that morning, killed by Dr Baruch Goldstein, and at least another one hundred were wounded. The unofficial numbers were much higher when casualties outside the mosque were tallied.[1]

Hebron, March 1994

Hebron was sealed off. Still, we made the short drive south from Bethlehem. 'Are you sure you want to do this?' Bishara asked me again. 'The city is under twenty-four-hour curfew. Nobody is allowed to leave their homes.'

'I appreciate your concern.' I repeated the answer I'd given him earlier that morning. 'But I gave my word that I would be in Hebron on Wednesday at 11.00. They know I am coming. Even if nobody turns up, I've got to be there.'

Bishara shook his head, smiling slightly. He knew me well enough to know there was no dissuading me. About three miles from Hebron, he turned off the main road, drove about half a

Brother Andrew visited Lebanon an average of twice per year during the civil war which raged from 1975 to 1990. Above, he sits on Lucien's balcony in a chair damaged during a missile attack. Note also holes from shrapnel on wall behind him. Below, Andrew prays in a Baptist church, one of many destroyed in southern Lebanon (see Chapter 4).

Top left: Bishara Awad, president of Bethlehem Bible College, and one of the members of the Light Force in West Bank. *Bottom left:* the destruction, just one block away from the college, was caused during the invasion in April 2002. *Top right:* Gaza Baptist Church in downtown Gaza City. *Bottom right:* during a Sunday service in December 2002, Al (facing congregation) and Brother Andrew pray for Pastor Hanna and his wife Suhad.

Brother Andrew began his outreach to Hamas when 415 of their leaders were deported from Israel in December 1992. As a result of his first visit to their camp in southern Lebanon in January 1993, he visited many of their families back home in West Bank and Gaza. He returned to the camp in August 1993 (top left) and distributed photos of their families. *Bottom left:* the central meeting tent that served both as a mosque and a university. *Top right:* during his second visit, Andrew had a meal in the Hebron tent.

That was the spark for an idea to host a meal and present the gospel when the deportees were allowed to return home in December 1993. Brother Andrew hosted five meals for Hamas, one in Gaza City drawing about 400 men. After speaking to the group, he distributed Bibles and copies of the *Jesus* video (see Chapter 22). *Bottom right:* Brother Andrew presents a Bible to Sheikh Yassin, founder of Hamas. Yassin was assassinated in March 2004.

Brother Andrew first met Yasser Arafat in Tunis in the early '80s. *Above:* Arafat looks at materials printed by the Palestinian Bible Society. Andrew used his relationship with the PLO leader to help expedite approval of the Bible book shop in Gaza City.

Top right: Andrew poses with boys in Gaza City. *Bottom right:* Andrew prays for a young victim of the first intifada.

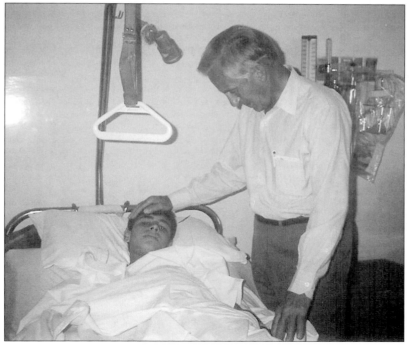

Musalaha is one of the ministries that has emerged from the Light Force in Israel, West Bank and Gaza. *Top:* A scene at one of the desert encounters that brings Arab and Palestinian Christians and Messianic Jews together for three days. *Below:* Salim Munayer leads a Bible Study for pastors from Messianic congregations and Palestinian churches in December 2003 (see Chapter 38).

mile, and then turned onto a narrow two-lane road. We'd driven about two more miles when we came to a huge pile of rocks and rubble, dumped in the middle of the road to prevent people like us from entering the city. Bishara parked and announced, 'From here, we walk.'

We climbed up the pile of rubble and saw an Israeli troop carrier parked about two hundred yards ahead. Obviously, this way was blocked. I was beginning to think that there was no way into town when I noticed a group of boys watching us. We scrambled back down the rock pile and asked the boys what they were doing there. They grinned and shrugged their shoulders.

Bishara was obviously worried. I tried to calm him. 'You should not go any farther. It's too dangerous for you. Me, if I'm caught, all they would probably do is deport me.'

I pulled out some shekels and showed them to the boys. Their eyes lit up. I pointed towards Hebron and said, 'I need to go into town, to a very important meeting. Can you help me?' Bishara translated.

One brave boy stepped forward, took my money, and motioned for me to follow. I grabbed my bag of Bibles and videos from the car and took off. Two more boys and Bishara tagged along behind me. 'You don't have to come,' I told my friend. 'I'll manage to find some way to get back.'

'If you go, I go too,' he answered as he hurried to catch up with me.

We scrambled through a rubble-strewn field towards a small group of houses, darted through that village and then along a footpath that led to the city. A few minutes later, we were in the outskirts of Hebron, but I was hopelessly lost. I had no idea how we would reach the meeting place. The boy knocked on a door. It opened a crack and a woman listened to the boy speak rapidly in Arabic. She closed the door and we waited as the boy stepped away. A minute later, the door opened and a man looked at Bishara and me and motioned for us to come in. When I looked back, the three boys were scampering away.

'What is the address where you need to go?' the man asked in clear English.

I handed him a paper. He looked at it, nodded his head, and said, 'Wait here a minute.' Then he went and made several phone calls. It was already 11.00, the time I'd promised to arrive. I had planned to buy food on the way, but there would be no stores open. I figured that just showing up was the best I could do. As we waited, the woman – I guessed, because of her age, she was the man's mother – served us coffee.

Five minutes later, our host told me, 'It is arranged. If you have finished your coffee, we will go.'

We stayed off the main streets, scurrying down alleyways and hiding in doorways as my new friend – I didn't even know his name – checked ahead to be sure the way was safe. Somewhere along the way, he knocked on a door and another man urged us to get into his car. Our impromptu taxi wound through more narrow back streets, avoiding main thoroughfares where tanks and armoured personnel carriers patrolled.

I thought about the man who was driving us. What would happen to him if he were caught? The answer chilled me. He could be shot on sight. And I would be arrested and deported. I hated to think about Bishara. The Bible College depended on his leadership. To fight the fear, I prayed another version of the smuggler's prayer I'd used so many times at checkpoints into Communist countries. 'Lord, You made the blind to see. Today please make the Israeli soldiers blind to this car. Protect these men who are risking their lives to get me to this meeting.'

A few minutes later, having driven down more narrow streets and even narrower alleyways, we reached a building that appeared to be a meeting hall. My driver jumped out and knocked. As soon as Bishara and I were out of the car, he drove away.

The door opened and there, grinning, was the camp imam I'd met at Marj al-Zohour. 'Quick, come in!' He welcomed me with a big hug. 'Honestly, we did not think you'd get here.'

As my eyes adjusted to the dark room, I'm sure my jaw dropped in astonishment. There were forty men waiting for me. I struggled to keep my emotions in check. These men had literally risked their lives to come and see me!

But the imam kept apologising for the conditions: 'These are very hard days. We have no freedom. No one can work. No one can buy food. We wanted to give you a nice present from Hebron.'

'I wanted to serve you a nice meal,' I said, matching his apology.

'But it was impossible to carry one in or to have one prepared here for us.'

I looked around the room for my friend, the librarian whose hospitality had prompted me to hold this meeting, but I didn't see him. I recognised one of the eleven doctors from Marj al-Zohour, who spoke up: 'Hebron is at the point of mass starvation. After the massacre at Ibrahimi Mosque, they shut down the city. For three weeks they have punished us. And we are the victims! Once a week, for two hours, we are allowed to go shopping. How can we survive?'

It was a typical Arab outburst. I understood the emotions, but I also noticed that the doctor who complained looked well fed, judging by the size of his belly. Still, these were trying days. Perhaps I couldn't provide a meal, but I could still feed these men. 'I am so sorry that we have to meet under these conditions,' I said to the men as the doctor translated into Arabic. 'While I have no physical food to give you, I have brought you gifts, which I hope you will consider spiritual food.' I brought out Bibles and copies of the *Jesus* film that had been dubbed in Arabic.

Holding up a Bible, I told the story of a Dutch boy who had noticed a Bible gathering dust day after day in the living room. Finally, he picked it up and took it to his mother and asked, 'Is this God's book?' The mother said it was. The boy said, 'Why don't we send it back to God because we don't use it!'

'I urge you, don't let the dust settle on these Bibles,' I said. Then I proceeded to tell the men about my spiritual journey. The heart of my message was the cross and how Jesus forgave my sins by dying for me.

As I started to relate how the cross applied to every life, a man, dressed in a white caftan, stood and, waving his arms, shouted to me in Arabic.

Now I've gone too far, I thought. I hesitated for a moment as the sheikh sat back down. The rest of the men watched me intently. *Well, I have their full attention. I might as well finish my message.* And so I talked about how much God loves the whole world, so much that He sent Jesus to die for each one of us.

After I was finished, the imam got up and said, 'I do have a gift for you!' Proudly he held up a pocket-sized Quran. It appeared worn, most likely the personal copy he carried around with him.

Then the doctor said, 'Andrew, don't let the dust settle on it! Use it!' Everyone laughed with me as I accepted the gift.

After visiting with the men, the imam made a phone call and arranged for a taxi, which would travel the back streets to pick us up and drop us off at the edge of town. As we waited, I asked the doctor, 'Why was the sheikh shouting at me when I spoke?'

'Oh, that's simple, Andrew,' he answered. 'You said that Jesus died on the cross but you did not speak about the resurrection.'

I was stunned. The sheikh was right. *Had I compromised the gospel?* Their only hope was in the unpolluted, radical presentation of Jesus – died and *risen* for our sins. I knew that Muslim doctrine believed that Jesus didn't die on the cross but was instead taken into heaven to return another day. Still, these men had risked their lives to hear me speak. *So why did I water down my message?* They knew I was a Christian, and just as they were uncompromising in their faith, they expected me to be uncompromising in mine.

I had been rightly rebuked by Hamas! I determined then that in future meetings, I would present the whole gospel.

A FEW DAYS LATER, a group of us headed down to Gaza for the next meal I was hosting for the men I'd met in southern Lebanon. Bishara had invited a young man named Labib Madanat, who had recently been named director of the Palestinian Bible Society. Labib had a most inviting personality that made me want to get to know him. Since we had more than an hour in the car, he started to tell me his story.

Mosul, northern Iraq, 1985

Labib Madanat sat on his bed late at night, reading his Bible. His three roommates were asleep. It had been a tough day emotionally. The Iran-Iraq War, which had raged for more than four years, had moved into a new phase, with major population centres being targeted on both sides. While Mosul University, 250 miles north of Baghdad, seemed outside the range of the fighting, everyone was on edge, worried about their families.

One of his roommates had just learned of the death of a cousin, who was in the Iraqi army. The evening prayers by the Muslims that night had been unusually intense.

Though born in Jerusalem, where his father had been pastor of East Jerusalem Alliance Church, Labib and his family had lived in Jordan since 1977. Labib was very comfortable around Muslims. All of his school friends were Muslim as were most of his fellow students at the university. Some were devout and many simply cultural Muslims. The five-times-daily calls to prayer from the nearby mosques were as normal to him as the chirping of birds at daybreak. The nearest evangelical church was so far away that he'd worshipped there only two or three times during his years at the university.

But Labib never hid his Christianity from his fellow students. He openly prayed, read his Bible and collection of Christian books, and talked freely about his faith. No one hated him for being a Christian. In fact it seemed he was respected. A member of President Saddam Hussein's Baath party had even approached him about becoming a member. 'I'm pleased that you would consider me,' Labib had answered. 'However, I must decline. I cannot serve two masters. My master is Jesus Christ.'

Labib felt at home among these people. He identified himself as an Arab and as a Christian, and wasn't bothered that most of his fellow Arabs were Muslim. But it was at times like this night, with so much pain and emotional suffering around him, that he yearned for his friends to know Jesus, the One who could give them genuine peace. He felt in his heart the love Christ had for these people. While he was studying irrigation and water management, he knew that whatever he did professionally, his real mission was to spread the love of Christ as far and wide as possible.

Jerusalem, 1992

Labib was running late. He was meeting a friend in the Old City, just on the other side of the Damascus Gate.

'May I see your identification?' An Israeli soldier barred his way, and Labib silently rebuked himself for not allowing time for this inevitable intrusion.

'Of course,' Labib answered, pulling out his Jordanian passport and Israeli visa.

'Stand against the wall,' the soldier ordered, indicating with a nod of his head that he should line up with several other Palestinians and wait. The message was clear – the soldiers were in control.

Or were they? Labib laughed silently at the situation. Sure he would be late for his meeting, but that didn't mean there wasn't a higher calling. 'May I say something to you?' he said in passable Hebrew to the soldier who was poring over several sets of papers. 'I am a Christian.'

Several of the other Palestinians, also being checked, looked at him in surprise, but Labib spoke loudly enough so that the soldier trying to ignore him couldn't help but hear the words. 'What I mean is that I am a believer in Jesus Christ, not just a Christian by religion only. Do you know about Jesus Christ? I will tell you about Him!' And so Labib began to tell the story of his Lord.

Suddenly the soldier snapped Labib's passport shut and turned to face the preacher. Labib stared into the man's eyes as he received his papers. 'I will pray for you,' he said with sincerity. 'I know you are away from home. I pray that when you are finished with your service that God will take you back safely to your family.'

'You may go!' the soldier spoke, turning to intercept another Palestinian headed through the gate.

Labib grinned as he passed through the gate and into the souk, the marketplace of the Arab quarter. *The soldiers think they're in control*, he thought. *But when I start preaching Christ, I am in control*. While most Palestinians dreaded these inevitable checkpoints that severely restricted their mobility, Labib had come to enjoy the encounters. And he knew the freedom he experienced at these moments was something worth sharing with fellow Palestinians.

Labib would soon be presenting that message to a far greater audience. He had returned to Israel looking for work in his field of expertise – irrigation. This was a land that could not survive without irrigation, and he figured that jobs would be plentiful. But every opportunity seemed to be blocked. Instead, after a few months as interim pastor at East Jerusalem Alliance Church, he had been approached about directing a new division of the Bible Society. Since 1967 the Bible Society of Israel had distributed books and Bibles throughout the entire region, but now people at the headquarters in England had decided to divide the work into two divisions – one for distribution in Israel proper, the other for distribution in West Bank and Gaza. Labib would be the first executive secretary of the Palestinian Bible Society.

Gaza, March 1994

Driving towards Gaza with Bishara and my new friend Labib, I was acutely aware that I was entering the cradle of Hamas. This was the last of five scheduled meetings in which I was returning the favour of that serendipitous meal in the tent at Marj al-Zohour. The first four, in Bethlehem, Nablus, Hebron, and Ramallah had averaged twenty to forty men in attendance. Since most of the deportees lived in Gaza, I anticipated perhaps fifty at this meeting.

These men had been home for about three months. Some, like the camp leader Abdulaziz Rantisi, were in jail. Others, like Mahmoud Zahar, had resumed their professions and leadership of the movement.

Dr Goldstein's attack in Hebron had produced a heightened tension in the West Bank. At the first four meetings, there was a resolve among these men that felt like a ticking bomb. I was curious to find if I'd sense a similar tension in Gaza. For one thing, the peace process was fiercely opposed by Hamas. Just one month after my second visit to Marj al-Zohour, Israel and the PLO had signed an agreement allowing for limited Palestinian self-rule in West Bank and Gaza. The Oslo Accords, named for the secret negotiations that had occurred in Oslo, Norway, were a breakthrough because Israel formally recognised that the PLO was representing the Palestinian people, and the PLO recognised the right of Israel to exist. Many questions remained to be resolved, but the agreement laid out several confidence-building steps by both sides that could lead to further negotiations.

However, Hamas wasn't buying into the process. They made clear that Yasser Arafat and the PLO didn't represent them and many other Palestinians. It wasn't so much that the Oslo Accords didn't answer the critical questions, such as statehood for Palestine; return of the refugees living in West Bank, Gaza, Jordan, and Lebanon; or the disposition of Jerusalem. The problem was much more fundamental. Hamas didn't believe that there should be *any* negotiations with Israel. They didn't believe that Israel should even exist.

There was another aspect of Hamas that few people seemed to understand. It was the sense of shame that had been inflicted on these men. Most of them were the primary breadwinners for their families, and they were unable to feed or protect their children. The deportations were an aching reminder that the Palestinians had no nation, no legal rights, and thus no future. Many held onto deeds for property that was now occupied by Israel. In vain they believed that someday they might be allowed to return to that land. Worse, the continual encroachment by Israeli settlements made them feel that the land they now occupied could be wrested away at any time. These were proud men who refused to accept such humiliation.

Further, these men felt isolated because the Arab world didn't rise up and defend them. Sure, those countries lent verbal support, but the work of securing their own state was theirs alone. The world's one superpower, the United States, firmly supported Israel. And they couldn't trust the United Nations, which issued resolution after resolution that Israel ignored. They were convinced that no one would help them, so they would have to act alone.

The problems were compounded by the intransigence of Israeli settlers. Already some were hailing Dr Goldstein as one of the great heroes of Israel. After my visit to Hebron, I had gone to Kiriat Arba, the Jewish settlement next to Hebron, and saw that Goldstein's grave site was becoming a shrine. Cabinets holding prayer books had been set up for spontaneous meetings. Several visitors were there, worshipping. One was an American settler, and he exploded in anger when I greeted him by saying, 'Shalom.'

'You have no right to say shalom to us!' he shouted.

While I clearly wasn't Jewish, I wondered at his anger. Perhaps he'd heard me talking in Dutch and thought I was German. 'Wait a minute,' I said. 'I mean no ill will towards you.'

The man stared at me with palpable hostility. With an icy scorn in his voice, he told me, 'We polish our guns every day. We are waiting for the Day of Purim when we will go out and kill *all* Arabs.'

I knew what he meant. The Day of Purim was celebrated each year, recalling the day recorded in the book of Esther when the Jews legally gained their revenge throughout the Persian Empire against those who had tried to destroy them. Some Jewish settlers were anticipating another Day of Purim when they would finally be rid of the Arabs and the land would be totally theirs.

I realised that many Jews didn't share this man's feelings. Still, I was shaken by the hatred I'd seen in the settlements. While I could never support Hamas, I could understand why they concluded they had no choice but to fight. But fight with what? They had no army, no heavy weapons to counter the firepower of Israel. So they might shoot a few soldiers – what would that accomplish? Their teenagers would throw a few rocks – which might be comical but for the tragedy of so many young lives being snuffed out and bodies permanently disabled. While I couldn't see any military resources, I felt certain Hamas would strike back. They were not compromisers. They were too certain about their faith and about their perceived right to the land.

So here I was going to speak to their leaders. What should I say? What could I offer them? I had no power to manufacture a peace deal or to give them a nation of their own. To these men, I represented the Church. Since they were completely open about who they were and their intentions, why shouldn't I be equally open about who I was as a Christian? I couldn't solve the conflict between them and Israel, but I could introduce them to the Prince of Peace.

Labib Madanat had been in Gaza only twice and both times it had made him homesick. His primary thought had always been to finish his business and escape as quickly as possible. As he waited for the soldier to process his papers at the Eretz checkpoint, he thought of his wife, Carolyn, who had lived in Gaza City with a Muslim family for a few months before they married. *I can't understand why she likes this place*, he thought. *I hate this place!*

Since assuming leadership of the Palestinian Bible Society ten months earlier, Labib had concentrated on two areas. First, he was trying to rebuild relationships with the historical churches in the area, including the Greek Orthodox and Catholic churches in Gaza. His second effort targeted hundreds of thousands of tourists who flocked to Israel. In an effort to improve cash flow for the society, he was selling Bibles with beautiful olive-wood covers, which pilgrims could take home as gifts and souvenirs.

Labib was making this visit to Gaza at the invitation of Bishara Awad, who was going to translate for Brother Andrew as he spoke to a group of Hamas leaders. Labib had come to Bethlehem Bible College to meet Andrew and hear him speak. He had read Andrew's first book as a boy and still remembered the impact it had on his life. In Arabic, the title wasn't *God's Smuggler* but an Arabic phrase that meant 'in spite of the impossible'. Well, this mission sure seemed impossible. And yet Labib was curious. Would members of Hamas really show up for this meeting? What would Andrew tell them? And how would these men respond?

In spite of his curiosity, as soon as the meeting was over, he would gladly escape this place and return to Jerusalem.

WHAT I SAW TODAY
ARE GOD SEEKERS

Gaza, March 1994

For our meeting, my contact had said that Hamas would rent a facility and order the meals and that I would pay the bill. Since the Israeli border guards wouldn't allow me to drive into Gaza, my friends and I carried the heavy suitcases, loaded with Bibles and *Jesus* videos, across the no-man's zone and hailed a taxi.

We were let off at the cultural centre in the heart of Gaza City. Dr Mahmoud Zahar met us and escorted us into the main auditorium, a large room bathed in sunlight from a skylight. I blinked for a moment, amazed at the sight. On row after row of folding chairs were seated Palestinians, some dressed in suits, many in the traditional Arab robes with white or white-and-red-checked kaffiyeh that were bound by black ropes (*iqals*). At the front of the room, next to the podium, was a table draped with a green cloth. Eight of us were seated there. As men continued to enter the room, I looked out over the audience and did a quick calculation. There were about four hundred men in attendance (and not a single woman). I had invited them as my guests, and I didn't have nearly enough money!

This was a joyful occasion. Four men who had learned to sing together at Marj al-Zohour performed for us – *an Arab form of barbershop quartet,* I thought. A man who had been released from prison just the day before was recognised with a rousing ovation. An imam asked us all to pray. He turned towards Mecca and began chanting from the Quran. He had a beautiful voice, and I was deeply moved as I held my hands open and prayed silently to my heavenly Father. I couldn't understand the imam's prayer, but I could sense the pain and anguish in his melodic words. Suddenly I realised that I didn't have to agree with Muslims to identify with their deep, heartfelt cries to God.

Something melted in me at that moment. I realised that I genuinely enjoyed being with these men. I had met them in their dire need and now I sat with them, a small Bible in my hand, ready to offer them hope. I wasn't there to fight Islam but I identified with them because they were suffering. Many of them had no job and couldn't provide for their families. They were angry, and I knew their anger was a prison as real as any physical prison in which they'd been locked. They needed to be set free. *Lord,* I prayed, *enable me to open the door so that these men may find real peace in You.* Calm enveloped me and I recognised that this meeting was a sacred moment.

There were several speeches, most of them concentrating on politics, before I was invited to speak. Mahmoud Zahar introduced me, saying, 'Our special guest, Andrew, came to visit us in Marj al-Zohour. He came to be with us and to feel with us in our trouble. He comforted us by his presence. Wherever the story of Marj al-Zohour is told, Brother Andrew will be in it. And now he and a team have come to visit us here in Gaza. He has invited us to come together and celebrate and have a meal together.' He turned to me and added, 'We appreciate your work to all peoples in distress – Christians and Muslims. We appreciate your visit and thank you.'

I stood up and for a moment was deeply moved by all of the men waiting to hear my words. The last time I was with them, I'd been sitting on a tent floor sharing a meal. Now I was feeding them and hoping to leave them with something of much greater worth than physical food.

'When I first got the call about you and the horrible situation at Marj al-Zohour, my desire was to come right away and be with you. But it was New Year's Eve and I was speaking to seven thousand young people, leading them in prayer. That night, I told them about you, and those seven thousand men and women prayed for you.' The audience interrupted with enthusiastic applause.

'I'm not here as a politician. Rather, I am here as one who seeks to understand what you are feeling.' I knew I could probably elicit a standing ovation by telling them that as a boy I had thrown stones at German soldiers, but I resisted the temptation. That wasn't my point. I wasn't looking for their approval. I felt it was more important that somehow these men understand that I identified with them, so that I could present the gospel. With this in mind, I began to tell them my own story.

'Many years ago, when I was only twenty years old, I lay in a hospital bed in Indonesia, where I'd been sent as a soldier to put down an uprising. A bullet had torn apart my ankle. I was alone, in pain, aching to go home to my family. I had no one to turn to, no one to fill the lonely days and even lonelier nights.' I knew these men had felt the same emotions. 'It was then that I began to read a little book my mother had given me when I left home.'

I held up a copy of the Bible and admitted that I had not wanted to receive that gift, and in fact I had buried it at the bottom of my trunk. 'But now, in the hospital with nothing else to do, I began to read, starting in Genesis with the story of creation. I read all of the stories and skipped over the laws and prophets. After a couple of weeks I started reading the Gospels and was struck by their deep significance. The person of Jesus was unlike any man who had ever lived. His story was so incredible that I wondered, "Could this really be true?" '

Muslims revere the man Jesus as one of the greatest of all prophets. I built on that respect as I told them that it wasn't just what Jesus taught that impressed me but also how He lived. I was astounded by how He handled controversy, how He answered critics, and how He endured suffering at the hands of unjust rulers. Then I told the men about how Jesus died on the cross. This time I also told them about the resurrection and the offer He made to come into my life, to forgive my sins, to change me into a new man. 'I finally cried out to God in this simple prayer: "Lord Jesus, if You will show me the way, I will follow You."

'I couldn't change my circumstances,' I told the men as I concluded my testimony. 'I still limped from my war wound, and I knew I might never walk normally again. I didn't know what my future held, but for the first time, I had peace. And I learned that anyone who comes to Jesus can have that peace. It's a peace that rises above the circumstances.

'I can't change the situation you face here in Gaza. I can't solve the problems you have with your enemies. But I can offer you the One who is called the Prince of Peace. You cannot have real peace without Jesus. And you cannot experience Him without forgiveness. He offers to forgive us of all our sins. But we cannot receive that forgiveness if we don't ask for it. The Bible calls this repentance and confession of sin. If you want it, then Jesus forgives. He forgave me and made me a new person. Now I'm not afraid to die because my sins are forgiven and I have everlasting life.'

The men listened to my words. Though I couldn't tell how my message affected them, I had at least earned a hearing. I had to trust God to use my words in whatever way He saw fit.

The programme wasn't over after I finished talking. Another leader, an imam I assumed, rose to speak. Bishara whispered the translation in my ear. This was an extended plea to me: 'What are some of our demands? First, we ask Brother Andrew to take to his people in Holland and the West the real picture of the suffering of Palestinians in Palestine – under Israel, who have taken our land and displaced hundreds of thousands and put tens of thousands in prison. They defiled our holy places, destroyed our homes, destroyed our trees.' Then he moved into a rebuttal to my message, saying that the Bible says the Jews 'killed the prophets without fair treatment. We believe they did try to crucify Jesus, but according to our belief God took him and a substitute was crucified. Please, take this story to your people.'

For several more minutes, the speaker told me that the men in this room were not terrorists, extremists, or fundamentalists. 'We are Muslims in general. We despise extremism and separation. We follow the Word of God.' He went on to quote from both the Quran and the Bible to explain how Christians had not followed the commands of Jesus to love their enemies, while the Muslims had protected Christian holy sites in Jerusalem, particularly the Church of the Holy Sepulchre. 'There are no real solutions until people come to God. All of humanity is suffering because they worship more than one god – work, money, materialism. That's why God sent prophets like Adam and Moses and Jesus. We Muslims stretch our hands to everyone who believes, to bring peace and happiness. Again, we welcome you and your team.'

Finally, it was time to eat. The meal, consisting of kebab, yogurt, pita bread, and sweets, was laid out in every room of the building and even in the corridors to accommodate everyone. On separate tables were our Bibles and videos. But I had a difficult time enjoying the party – I still had to pay the bill. For rental of the centre plus the meal, the total due came to $2,500. *Lord,* I quickly prayed, *Your reputation is at stake here. I committed to pay for the meal. Would You please provide me with what I need?*

I pulled Labib and Bishara aside and quietly asked them how much cash they had on hand. 'May I borrow it? I didn't expect so many people.' They were gracious, but it wasn't enough.

Then Bishara talked to my contact person and arranged to send him the rest of the money. I thanked my friend and promised to reimburse him those expenses as soon as I returned to Holland.

By the time that crisis was averted, the men were beginning to disperse. Right then, a film crew from ABC news dashed into the centre. 'I heard something big was going on here,' the reporter said, catching his breath. He looked at me, and I smiled but said nothing. 'Did I miss it? I heard there was a meeting of Hamas.'

'Yes, that is right. We're finished.'

'Well, can I interview you? We need something for the evening news.'

I laughed and shook my head. 'No, I have nothing to say to the press.'

Before we left, Mahmoud Zahar thanked me for coming and hosting the meeting. 'Andrew, I believe you know that I teach at the Islamic University. To my knowledge, we have never had any lectures about Christianity. While you were talking, I was thinking that it would be helpful for our students to know about real Christianity. Would you consider coming to the university and giving a lecture about the differences between Christianity and Islam?'

I was stunned by the invitation but felt inadequate. Such an opportunity needed to go to someone who spoke Arabic. I felt like Paul, the 'weakest vessel' for this assignment. 'Mahmoud, I am pleased that you would want me to speak to your students. Let me think about it. My concern is that I don't have the academic degrees. Perhaps I could arrange for someone to come who has stronger credentials than I do.'

M Y FRIENDS AND I were euphoric as we climbed aboard our van at the Eretz parking lot for the return trip to Bethlehem. None of us in our wildest faith had imagined that four hundred Hamas leaders would show up at this meeting. But now, as I sat down and loosened my tie, I was concerned about what would happen next. It was great to present the gospel to these men, but more was needed. Much more! It wasn't right to go in, have a great meeting, and then move on as though nothing had happened. We needed a follow-up plan of some kind.

'So what did you think of the meeting?' I asked my new friend Labib as we pulled away from the Eretz checkpoint.

'I think my God is too small,' he said. I turned to look at him and saw he had a big grin. 'Brother Andrew, I never thought that a Christian could speak to radical, fanatic fundamentalists. But even if someone did have that chance, it never occurred to me that they would actually want to sit and listen to the gospel. Today God showed me how big He is.'

As we talked, Labib told me about his years of study at university in Iraq. 'That experience was awakened today,' he said. 'I remembered how much I loved witnessing to Muslims. But for the most part, the Church hides here. It doesn't reach out to Muslims. Yet I believe they would listen if we could only find a way to reach out to them.'

'Well, let's think of a way,' I said, sensing this was a significant moment in my new friend's life. 'I had one meeting. That was the easy part. Now what do we do? There may be men there who want to know more. How will we get them that information? And there will be others who learn about the meeting and will want to hear the message too.'

'Local churches have generally avoided speaking to Muslims about Christ,' Labib said. 'Some Western mission agencies have come and tried to witness to Muslims, but many of their converts have been from the traditional churches. People think that Muslims aren't open to Christ, but frankly I think they are closer to Christ than secular Europeans or Americans. What I saw today are God seekers.'

'Exactly! Most Europeans are naturalistic. They are not generally God seekers. But if you're talking with one of these members of Hamas and it's time for prayer, he will not be available to you. He will pray. He's not there for you anymore. He's there for God. We rarely see that kind of devotion in Christianity. If we're in prayer and the telephone rings, we pick up the phone. Many of these men wouldn't. That's why it's easier to talk to them about Jesus. For Muslims, the time of prayer is a time of obedience to God. We don't want to change them from seeking God. We want to present them with the way of Christ – which is God seeking them!'

Labib's mind was obviously churning, and I was quiet so he could think. Finally, he said, 'Andrew, I would like to try to open a bookshop in Gaza.'

My heart leapt with excitement.

'I've limited my vision up to now,' he said, looking at me with great excitement. 'I've been thinking only about how to make the most of the Bible bookshop in Jerusalem. After all, that's where many of the Christians are. But the men I saw today need the Word of God too.'

'And we didn't have enough copies at our meeting,' I reminded him.

'If we'd had a shop in Gaza, I could have made sure they each received a copy of the Bible.'

I knew then that this was a momentous day because of what God had done, not only in the meeting but also in the heart of my friend. 'Labib, I will do whatever I can to help you fulfil this vision.'

We parked at Bethlehem Bible College, and Labib headed for his car, then stopped, turned to me, and put an exclamation mark on my day. 'I will always remember this day as the day I fell in love with Gaza!'

As POSITIVE AS my meetings in Hebron and Gaza were, I couldn't shake the nagging sense that the Hamas time-bomb was about to explode. After our meal in Gaza, Mahmoud told me calmly that the Goldstein massacre would be revenged five times. In the ensuing months, there were exactly five attacks. On 6 April, at the end of the Muslim forty-day period of mourning, I heard the news on the BBC. A twenty-five-year-old man had blown himself up with a car bomb, killing eight and wounding forty-four in Afula, a town just south of Nazareth. Hamas claimed responsibility, saying it was revenge for the massacre in the Ibrahimi Mosque.

One week later, a man detonated a bomb, killing himself and five others on a bus in the coastal town of Hadera. Again Hamas claimed responsibility. With horror I realised that the conflict had escalated to a new level with human beings willing to go into Israel and kill themselves, taking with them as many civilians as possible. For the first time I heard reporters use the term *suicide bomber*.[1]

The news made me ill. Surely, I thought, my words should have prevented these bombs. Did these men really listen? I felt like a failure.

I couldn't help but wonder what drove these men to take such desperate action. One explanation was the sophisticated perspective of shame and honour that permeated their culture. One Palestinian had explained it to me this way: 'We can live kneeling or die standing up.' Hamas had decided that they preferred literally dying as opposed to living in submission to a hated conqueror. I couldn't sympathise with them – I believed they were totally misguided – but I tried to understand that Hamas, from their perspective, was sending soldiers into battle. Every soldier realises he may not return home. The general tells him you don't have to come back; just go and kill as many of the enemy as possible. That was the logic of a suicide bomber. Added to that was the religious component, the belief that death in jihad sent the soldier immediately to paradise.

Could I have done anything to stop Hamas? I thought of Genesis 4, the story of the first terrorist attack in history when Cain murdered his brother, Abel. God spoke to Cain before he committed his criminal deed and tried to convince him to do what was right and to resist the sin crouching at his door. But Cain had ignored God and carried through with his revenge. I wondered: *Did God want to speak to Hamas? God had no one to send to Cain, so He went Himself. But how would He deliver such a message today? Probably through a willing messenger.*

For some reason God had sent me to speak to Hamas, to offer them a way to deal with the rage in their hearts, to show them God's answer through the person of His Son, but I couldn't force them to listen. If God couldn't turn Cain away from his murderous course, then I certainly had no power to change Hamas hearts.

At least I had gone to them, taking the way that was open to me. I had done what I could, but it wasn't enough.

TWENTY-THREE

IN A SMALL WAY WE'RE MAKING A DIFFERENCE

Jerusalem, autumn 1994

The hatred could return. Yitzhak realised that as he watched the news of the latest suicide bombing attack. 'It was easy when we were out in the desert with Musalaha. Nobody was watching us, and we could say we loved each other,' he spouted to his wife. 'But now we're back to reality.'

Gently his wife tried to remind him that only a minority of Arabs were terrorists. 'Remember, let the truth of Yeshua's word go deep into your heart.'

Yitzhak knew that he had been genuinely touched during the desert encounter two years earlier. But permanent change was harder when he was back home. With pain he recalled a recent incident when he was playing football with fellow Messianic Jewish believers at a field in Tel Aviv. On an adjoining field another game was taking place when several troublemakers showed up and started driving the players away. Yitzhak had stopped to watch and saw that the aggressors were kicking and beating the players and further realised that the thugs were Jewish and the players were Arab. The antagonists had shouted at the players that they were not allowed at the public park. Yitzhak knew that wasn't true, but he simply stood there and watched as the Arabs were driven away.

Ever since then, the incident had plagued his thoughts. How could he, who had been involved in Musalaha, who cared about the Arab and pursuing righteousness, who knew that these men had rights, simply stand by and do nothing? It didn't help that he belonged to a congregation that was very right-wing. Many of his fellow believers were far more interested in promoting Zionism than in reconciliation, and they didn't understand his involvement in Musalaha activities. They couldn't understand how a person could have faith in Yeshua and also love Arabs. He'd had several arguments and even lost some friends because of his stance. But the incident on the sports fields showed him that his transformation wasn't complete. It wasn't simply a matter of saying, 'Love your neighbour as yourself.' He really had to do it.

Then the terrorist attacks had increased, and the suicide bombings had started occurring regularly. He was horrified by the carnage and his natural reaction was to recoil from anything related to the Palestinians. As he watched the news reports, he felt his old hatred pushing its way into his heart, and he made no effort to extinguish it.

Then the phone rang. Yitzhak heard the familiar voice of Wa'el on the other end. 'I just saw the news and I wanted to know if you are okay.' Immediately Yitzhak felt ashamed for entertaining his old hatred.

After the call, Yitzhak admitted to his wife, 'Wa'el reminds me that we have to show the real gospel. We are saved by the blood of the new covenant, which means we are saved to be a light to the world. And you cannot be a light to the world if you stand for one people and you're not also standing for the other.'

A few weeks later, Yitzhak passed through the Bethlehem checkpoint to visit Wa'el's church. A room in that church was being renovated for use as a children's centre. Late that morning, as the two friends wielded their paintbrushes side by side, Wa'el expressed thanks for his help. 'I wasn't sure whether you would come, what with our differences and all.'

Yitzhak laughed. 'You think you and I have differences! You should hear the arguments we have about theology just in our church. We have a saying: If there are two Jewish believers, there are three churches!'

During lunch, Wa'el admitted he was thinking of leaving the country. 'This has been so hard. There is nothing here but frustration. I just want to leave because the situation here is too difficult. But . . . I don't know where I would go, where I would fit.'

For a moment, Yitzhak recalled with shame his past feelings that a good Arab was a dead Arab. He had often thought it would be best if the Palestinians just left, and many in his congregation openly espoused that view. But this was different. This wasn't a nameless Arab but a brother in Christ and a friend. 'I hope you don't leave,' he said.

Wa'el looked soberly at his friend, not knowing what to say.

'I know it's hard, but maybe in a small way we're making a difference. Maybe we can show those around us that there is a better way than fighting.'

'I don't see how.'

'I don't know if the answer is a Palestinian state or autonomy or just living together. I'm not in a position to solve the problem. I know I cannot save the whole world, but I can save the world for one person, the Arab in front of me – reconciling ourselves to one another, listening to each other's problems, understanding our fears of each other, our bitterness.'

An hour later, when Yitzhak had to return home, the two men, brothers in Christ, embraced. It would be a long time before the situation would allow them to meet again, but they were committed to staying in touch and praying for one another.

As Yitzhak returned to his home in Tel Aviv, he thought about the deep change God was making in his heart. He realised that as a Christian he was rising above the politics of the conflict to the perspective that everyone is created in God's image. Therefore, everyone deserves to learn about God's salvation. He wanted to spend his energy spreading that message to Jews, Arabs – it didn't matter who, he wanted *all* to hear.

WHAT KIND OF PEOPLE
DOES THE BOOK PRODUCE?

Bethlehem, spring 1996

There was a neighbour in the room next to mine at the guesthouse of Bethlehem Bible College. We met at breakfast in the small common kitchen/dining area opposite our rooms. He introduced himself as pastor of a church in Nazareth. 'I'm here to find some quiet and rest,' he said.

I looked into his face, and he looked exhausted. 'You've come to the right place. It's good to have a place to be quiet, to pray, and if you need, to talk with friends.'

He smiled a weary smile and said, 'I'm afraid I can't cope with the problems anymore.' I listened as he recited the list. I had heard most of them before in my conversations with pastors over the years. His congregation was dwindling as several families emigrated to the West. There was conflict between older leadership and younger members. A dispute was building in the city between Muslims and the Church of the Annunciation, according to tradition the location where the angel Gabriel visited Mary. The Muslims had a tent across the street and were planning to build a mosque. In addition, there was the ongoing stress of feeling like a second-class citizen in his own country – a common complaint I heard among Arabs who lived in Israel.

The pastor from Nazareth was doing much better the next day. He had been to visit a couple of friends, and in one of their homes he saw my book in Arabic: *A Time for Heroes*. 'I read the first chapter,' he said.

'The one on Job!'

'Yes. I can relate to Job, but I don't think my problems are as bad as his.'

'So what have you learned from our friend Job?'

'That God is with us in the midst of our trials. I needed to be reminded of that. Faith doesn't mean that God will eliminate my problems. Rather, I realise that God is with me and with my congregation in the midst of our problems.'

'And He is sufficient.'

'Job didn't have all of his questions answered, but he met God. He heard from God, and that was enough.'

At the core, this encounter was the emphasis of my work, to be with my brothers who suffer. I could still hear the words of the pastor in Poland in 1955 who had said, 'Your being here means more than ten of the best sermons.' Since I didn't consider myself a great preacher anyway, 'being there' would always be my primary ministry.

I N PART BECAUSE of encounters like this, Bethlehem Bible College had become my base of operation whenever I visited the area. The school had grown steadily since the days when it occupied one room in Beit Jala. The current facility, purchased from Bible Lands Society with help from Open Doors, was just a few blocks from Rachel's Tomb. The building had made a huge difference in the college's effectiveness. The student body now numbered forty and was growing, and there was a fully trained, academically qualified staff. Open Doors assisted in several ways, including funding one of the teaching positions. New programmes had developed. One of them trained Palestinian tour guides. Another was a medical outreach. Occasionally medical personnel would come from the West and three to four hundred patients could be served per day. Plans were being made to open a public library on the ground floor of the school's classroom building; it would be the only public library in Bethlehem.

I loved hanging around the students. It is a cliché to say that they were hardworking and full of youthful enthusiasm, but I felt their eagerness to learn and that gave me hope for the Church. If the Church among Palestinians in Israel, West Bank and Gaza was to be a bright light, it needed hundreds of dedicated leaders. Just what would they be doing? That was what I discussed with them when Bishara asked me to speak at the chapel service.

Since many of the students had enrolled after the exciting time in Gaza, when Bishara and I spoke with the leadership of Hamas, I began by telling that story. After that historic meeting, one of the Bethlehem Bible College professors had grabbed me and urged, 'Will you stay here and evangelise Arabs? All of them – Muslims, radicals, Hamas, PLO!' The enthusiasm was appreciated, but the implication of his statement disturbed me. 'Is it my calling to stay here and evangelise fundamentalists?' I said to my attentive audience, with Bishara interpreting. 'I don't think so. My call is to strengthen the local body of believers. That includes you – so that *you* can fulfil that critical calling.'

To illustrate, I told them of one of my five meetings with Ayatollah Fadlallah, the spiritual leader of Hezbollah in Lebanon. ' "Brother Andrew, you Christians have a problem," he told me. Well, I know Christians have many problems, but I was curious what this Muslim leader would tell me. "What do you think our problem is?" I asked. He answered: "You Christians are not following the life of Jesus Christ anymore." That was an interesting observation from a fundamentalist leader. It really hit me hard, so I asked him, "What do you think we should do about that?" He said, "You must go back to the Book."

'That's a terrific sermon, don't you think? Especially here at a Bible college! A couple of cups of coffee later, the ayatollah said, "Andrew, we Muslims have a problem." So I said, "What do you think your problem is?" He answered, "We Muslims are not following the life of the prophet Muhammad anymore." He was so sad and terribly sincere. I asked him, "Well, what do you think you should do about it?" His answer: "We must go back to the book." Of course, he meant *his* book, the Quran, not the Bible.

'The last time Fadlallah and I met, he told me that he wanted to open a dialogue between Muslim scholars and Christian scholars. I want to encourage such a dialogue. Let us witness to each other; we may be surprised. But I told him I wanted to narrow the discussion to a specific question: What kind of people does the book produce? I want to challenge you with that question this morning. What kind of people does the Quran produce? What kind of people does the Bible produce? You are students of the Bible. What difference is the Bible making in your lives? Are you walking the talk? In Jesus' final words to His disciples, He said, "You will *be* my witnesses." That includes not just what we say, but how we live and what we are.

'God has given you a job to do. It's a very challenging task. Look at all of the people around you in your community. Whether Muslims or Christians, all of them are people created in God's image. What kind of life are you showing them? Do you realise that you may be the only Jesus they will ever see? That is why your work here is so important.'

Holding up my Bible, I closed by saying, 'Allow this Book to mould you into the image of Jesus Christ.'

Bethlehem, autumn 1996

'Andrew, turn on the news,' said Bishara over the phone. 'There is an important development on the BBC.'

Immediately I went to the common room and turned on the television. There were scenes of angry Palestinians on the Temple Mount shouting at the cameras, obviously threatening violence. Then, before I understood what was happening, the news anchor moved on to another story.

Bishara showed up a few minutes later. He explained that the Israelis had dug many tunnels under the Dome of the Rock and Al-Aqsa Mosque. 'Naturally the Muslims are very sensitive about this. There was a near riot when the tunnels were discovered in 1982. Meanwhile, the Jews have quietly continued work. They claim they are not actually working beneath the Temple Mount, but I have it on good authority they've been looking for the Holy of Holies. Today they opened up one tunnel onto the Via Dolorosa,[1] which, as you know, is in the Muslim quarter.'

'So the Muslims are offended.'

'I'm concerned that there may be riots.'

The next day I had a meeting downtown in Bethlehem and walked back to the college when it was over. There was tension in the streets as I arrived at Jerusalem-Hebron Road. I saw many young men and boys walking or running past the college towards Rachel's Tomb. Most of them already had rocks in their hands. They were angry and didn't care who knew it.

My sensibilities told me I should quickly get into the college and take cover in Bishara's office or one of the basement rooms. But curiosity got the better of me and I continued with the boys towards Rachel's Tomb, which had been transformed into a military post by the Israeli Defence Force. Some of the boys pulled out slingshots to fling their stones at the well-protected soldiers. Others found empty lots and loaded up with more rocks.

The demonstration seemed so feeble. Boys threw rocks at the soldiers, who were wearing helmets and hiding behind large shields. There was deep-seated anger, but it didn't appear that the soldiers were in any life-threatening danger. Then I heard a thump, saw a whiff of smoke, and realised a canister had been thrown into our midst. Tear gas began pouring out. Several more tear gas bombs followed. One landed near my feet. I kicked it away and moved upwind so that the noxious fumes blew away from me. But the kids weren't thinking clearly about the danger. Many started coughing and retreating. I motioned to some of the kids, indicating they should move upwind from the smoke.

Then I was aware of another sound. A couple of boys screamed and clutched an arm or head. I figured, along with them, that I had better move away. The soldiers were firing rubber bullets, but there was steel inside that rubber, and those bullets could inflict a great deal of damage and pain.

Later that afternoon, after the crowd had dispersed, I cautiously walked back towards Rachel's Tomb, staying close to the buildings on the sidewalk so as not to attract attention. An eerie silence had descended on the town, as though the anger had simply moved indoors. There were hardly any cars on the road. I stopped at the spot where I'd observed the conflict. In the street, leaning against the curb, was one of the tear gas canisters. It was cool to the touch, so I picked it up. I sniffed it and jerked my head back. For a moment, tears rushed to my eyes. Holding it at arm's length, I read a series of numbers, followed by the words: 'For outdoor use only. Made in the USA. Do not fire directly at persons as serious injury or death may result.'

Scattered on the street were black rubber bullets, inch-long solid cylinders that were flat on each end. I picked up a couple for 'souvenirs' and walked back to the college.

Bishara was waiting for me. 'So you see what our friends from America have given to us,' he said with a wry smile. 'I've been on the roof when they fired tear gas into the playground of the school down below us and the wind was blowing in from the west. I couldn't stay on the roof – the fumes were so strong. And those "rubber bullets". They can break your ribs. Several kids no doubt wound up in the hospital today. And when one hits a young child in the head, it can kill him.'

'They sound so humane. Rubber bullets.'

'What you saw today is typical. These demonstrations start with boys throwing rocks and end with tear gas and rubber bullets and often one or two kids dead. Unfortunately, these demonstrations are happening all over the West Bank and Gaza.' He shook his head. 'I'm very concerned.'

I asked Bishara what this protest hoped to accomplish. I couldn't see the connection between the demonstration I'd witnessed and the news from Jerusalem.

'The occupation is the main cause of violence,' he explained. 'The tunnel under the Dome of the Rock was simply the latest excuse. People wish to be free, and this is the only way they know how to express it.'

When the unrest subsided a few days later, ninety-one Palestinians were dead (and no Israelis). It was frustrating, because these kids were throwing away their lives, and for what purpose? Was it because they really had no hope? This was so utterly futile. I thought again of the strategic placement of Bethlehem Bible College. Here we were, a light proclaiming the Prince of Peace as the crowd passed by. But these kids were too angry to stop and inquire about Jesus Christ. Tragically ninety-one would die without learning of Him.

Beit Sahour, 1996

Nawal Qumsieh was ready and eager to go into ministry. But where? And how? At a seminar in Bethlehem, Nawal responded to the challenge. 'If anyone wants to dedicate his life to ministry for Jesus,' the guest speaker intoned, 'now is the time to come forward!' The man stepped back from the podium and bowed his head in prayer. Nawal slipped out of her seat and hurried to the front of the room. Out of some fifty in attendance, she was the only one to answer the call.

The speaker opened his eyes and looked around the room, then down at Nawal. He shook his head and said quietly so only Nawal could hear, 'Go back to your seat, please. Women cannot help in this society. We need men.'

Again the speaker challenged the audience. 'We need men to stand up for Christ in this culture. Will you come forward? Will you be part of the solution?'

Fighting back tears, Nawal walked slowly back to her seat. She felt like she'd been hit in her heart by a rubber bullet. Not one man took her place in the front. Now weeping, she prayed, 'Lord, who will minister to my people?'

And within her heart, she immediately sensed the answer: 'I am calling *you* to be in ministry.'

HAMAS WOULD LIKE
A CEASE-FIRE

Gaza, 1996

While walking through no-man's-land – a half-mile of cement-paved corridor at Eretz checkpoint between Israel proper and the now Palestinian-controlled region – I thought of my discussion a day earlier with Labib. The director of the Palestinian Bible Society had eagerly told me of his expanding vision as we ate lunch.

'As I've thought about what we want to do in Gaza, I realised that there are other places where we also could use a Bible bookshop: Nablus, Beir Zeit University, Bethlehem – that could be a wonderful place for outreach with all of the tourists visiting!'

I loved Labib's enthusiasm and vision.

Then he told me about the property he had found in Gaza that would serve as a perfect location for the bookshop. 'But I'm having problems,' he said. 'There is so much bureaucracy in the Palestinian Authority. I'm simply not making progress as far as getting permission to open a shop.'

'Perhaps I can help you,' I said.

Labib laughed and said, 'How? Can you cut through the red tape?'

201

'No. But I do know someone who I think can.'

'Who?'

'Yasser Arafat.'

Labib paused for a moment, then smiled as he said, 'You're right. His approval would help a lot.'

'Why don't you give me a copy of your beautiful children's Bible in Arabic. I'll give it to Mr Arafat for his daughter's first birthday.'

Just this morning, Labib had handed me a letter for the Palestinian president, plus a letter of endorsement from the Orthodox patriarch in Jerusalem. I felt inside my coat pocket to make sure the letters were safe.

I T WAS SURPRISINGLY easy for me to arrange an appointment with Arafat, newly named president of the Palestinian Authority. After making the appropriate phone calls, I lay down on my bed at Marna House, where most international visitors stayed in Gaza, and reflected on how my first meeting in the mid-1980s had been arranged.

It had started with a phone call from a Baptist pastor from the United States who was living in The Hague. 'Brother Andrew, would you join me in visiting a very sick man?' He explained that this man was a former headmaster of a Christian school in Nazareth, but he was too sick to travel home to Galilee now. He had asked for prayer before he died.

Of course, I went with the pastor and we visited the old man, who was living in a large, nicely furnished home. We read to him from the Bible and prayed for him. After about an hour, we left his room, and a man in his mid-forties was waiting for us. 'I'm Mr Khoury,' he said, extending his hand. 'Thank you for taking the time to visit my father. It means a great deal. Please, may I offer you some coffee?'

As we sat sipping Arabic coffee that I rarely enjoyed in Holland, I observed the very nice surroundings and asked, in my blunt manner, 'Who are you?'

Mr Khoury answered, 'I am Chairman Arafat's right-hand man. I represent the PLO in Europe.'

Always looking for an open door, I blurted out, 'Can you get me in touch with Arafat?'

'All it takes is one phone call.'

He made the phone call, and a few days later I was on a plane to Tunis, where Arafat and the PLO were in exile after being driven out of Lebanon. I brought Arafat, who was labelled 'the Teflon Guerrilla'[1] by one reporter, a Bible and a copy of *God's Smuggler* and told him about my work. I had wondered at the time what significance there was in that meeting.

This time I would be going to him with an agenda – a very important request. 'Lord, go before me,' I prayed aloud, my voice reverberating in the stone-walled room. 'Give me favour in his sight.'

Arafat's office and those of many leaders of the Palestinian Authority were in a row of buildings bordering the beach of the Mediterranean Sea. The complex looked surprisingly plain for a man who was leader of three million people, who might soon, if the Oslo Accords played out as promised, be a head of state. The taxi dropped me off, and I walked a block past the checkpoint to the main office. During the day, Arafat's waiting room was typically packed wall to wall with news people, foreign figures and businessmen looking for investment opportunities. But this evening, only the president and one of his advisors, Nabil abu Rudeineh, were working late.

'I've come to see my friend Abu Amar!' I said, announcing my arrival as I entered the building.

Almost immediately an office door opened and I heard Arafat's voice. 'Brother Andrew!' He emerged, wearing his familiar kaffiyeh, carefully folded over his right shoulder in the shape of the land of Palestine. Grabbing my shoulders, he kissed me on both cheeks and said, 'Come in; come in!'

The famous man with the persistent three-day growth of beard was surprisingly short, only 5' 4" tall, and his appearance did not bespeak his powerful presence in Middle Eastern affairs. But behind his unassuming appearance was a charismatic personality. In his office I asked, 'Do I call you Mr President now?'

'No, no!' he laughed. 'To you I am always Abu Amar.'[2]

'I hear you are also a proud father of a baby girl. I have brought you a gift – a children's Bible in Arabic that you can read to her when she sits on your lap.'

Arafat received the book and looked at it reverently. 'This is a beautiful book. Thank you very much.'

'I also have a request for my friend.' I pulled the letters from my jacket pocket. 'In this envelope is a letter from Labib Madanat, who directs the Palestinian Bible Society. It is part of the United Bible Societies that produced this beautiful book. This particular volume was printed in Beirut.'

The president started carefully thumbing through the pages, looking at the artwork. Several minutes of silence passed as Arafat seemed mesmerised by the book. Finally, he said, 'We need more quality books like this.'

'That's why I am here,' I said, seizing my opportunity. 'The Bible Society would like to open a bookshop here in Gaza. Labib Madanat has found some empty office space that would work well, across the street from Al Ahli Hospital. We would like to get your permission.'

'Of course, of course,' Arafat said, looking up at me. 'You have permission!'

He read the letter, then grabbed his pen and wrote a note to Nabil abu Rudeineh: 'Please proceed with the registration of the Bible Society and the license of the bookshop in Gaza according to Palestinian law.'

Abu Rudeineh looked at the instructions, then said, 'Mr Andrew, I will make a copy of this for you to take back to Mr Madanat.'

ON SUNDAY MORNING I walked over to the Gaza Baptist Church, just a few blocks from Marna House. The church was located across the street from the Palestinian Parliament building, where the Legislative Council met. East of the Parliament, across the street, was a long park. When I'd first arrived here after the 1967 war, a huge statue of the Unknown Soldier had dominated the area. But it had been torn down by Israelis, leaving an empty pedestal. After the signing of the Oslo Accords, the Palestinian Authority had erected a new statue, one far smaller than its predecessor, and it looked out of place on the large pedestal. Already a bullet hole marred its left shoulder. I was sure this was symbolic, but of what I didn't know.

I walked across the street to the Baptist church that met in two rented villas behind a cement wall, which was covered with graffiti. Jaber, one of the leaders at the church, greeted me at the entrance. His wife was setting up refreshments in the social hall next to the small sanctuary. Two toddlers ran freely among the rows of folding chairs put out for the service. An old lady with gnarled hands practised on a piano that badly needed tuning.

By the time the service started, a few minutes past 11.00, only twelve adults were scattered among the folding chairs. We sang the hymn 'All Hail the Power of Jesus' Name', but despite the pianist's enthusiastic pounding out of the chords, there was little conviction in the congregation's singing. A few years earlier I had preached in this same church with seventy-five or eighty people filling the room. But each year as I returned, the number had dwindled. Despair hung over the room, as though the members were attending a death-watch and it was only a matter of time before the demise of a beloved family member.

I knew this must not happen. This little body, the only evangelical church in Gaza, must not die! I preached with passion to this small flock. Afterwards, as I drank a bottled soda, I talked with Jaber and two other long-term members of the congregation – Isam, a businessman, and Dr Attala, a respected physician. Attala recalled his early experience in the church. 'I moved here from Egypt in 1976 and worked at the Baptist hospital.' He was referring to Al Ahli Hospital, which since 1982 had been run by the Anglican Church. 'I was baptised in the chapel of the hospital in 1979 and have been part of Gaza Baptist Church ever since.'

I couldn't help but notice the sorrow in his voice. 'Gentlemen, you must not give up!' I said, wondering how convincing I sounded. 'God has a very important work for this church.'

The three men looked at me, saying without words that they wanted to believe me. Then one of them spoke haltingly, 'Brother Andrew, we've been thinking that we need to hold an evangelistic crusade. If we organise it, would you come and preach?'

On one level, this request made sense. The Baptists were known for their evangelistic meetings, and what better way to grow the flock than to bring in a host of new converts? However, this church wasn't ready. 'Gentlemen, I understand your request, and I would love to come and preach here in Gaza. But you aren't ready. What would you do with those who respond to the message? They will need counselling, teaching, Bibles, books. Until you have a plan for follow-up, you aren't ready for a campaign.'

'I've heard the Bible Society wants to open a shop in Gaza,' said Isam.

'That's exactly what I mean – we need resources,' I said. 'We need a place for men and women to go and be taught the Bible. Otherwise, as John Wesley said, it's like giving birth to a baby and leaving it in the Sahara Desert without food or water or nourishment.'

'When will the bookshop open?' Jaber asked.

'I don't know. We're working on it. Please pray.'

The men were discouraged, and I knew I couldn't leave them that way. 'There is great darkness here in Gaza, is there not?' My friends nodded. 'What conquers darkness? Light! And that light is in everyone in whom Christ dwells. This church is a light, perhaps not a very strong light, but it has not gone out. It must not go out! You must pray, and I will pray, that God will strengthen this little congregation so that it becomes a bright light shining in the darkness. This church is the hope for Gaza. I will pray and ask others to pray that this church will be revived and grow.'

Isam smiled and thanked me for those words. 'Andrew, every time you visit, we are encouraged.'

'That is why I come. And, the Lord willing, I will come back every year and do whatever I can to help you and this church grow.'

'And one day, we will be ready to hold a campaign,' said Isam.

Southern California, 1996

Hanna Massad stared at the open Bible in front of him on the table of the Fuller Theological Seminary library. Scattered around him were commentaries and other library books – most dealing with various perspectives on eschatology. When he'd started studying theology as a curious teenager recently baptised in the Baptist church, he'd been introduced to the doctrine of dispensationalism, which distinguished between God's plan for Israel versus His plan for the Church. The thinking spelled out God's intentions, according to Scripture, for various periods in history. According to that prophetic view, the birth of Israel in 1948 signalled the beginning of the end of the age that would culminate in the rapture and the return of Christ.

Now as a student in seminary, working on his PhD dissertation, Hanna struggled with that doctrine. He was surprised to learn in his early classes at Fuller that there were other perspectives about the Holy Land and God's plan for the Jews and the Church. He had lived away from home for several years now. His father, who had initially resisted his attempts to study in the United States, had passed away. His mother and two sisters were both in poor health. He missed his home and his family and the congregation he had pastored for four years. He wondered about God's plan for his family and that church.

He wondered too if it mattered to God that he was a Palestinian. Before beginning his doctoral studies, Hanna had reviewed the history of the conflict between Israel and the Palestinians. At the start of the twentieth century, the majority of the people living in the Holy Land were Palestinians, and all of them spoke Arabic. In 1917 Great Britain declared its desire to see the formation in Palestine of a national homeland for the Jewish people.[3] However, this famous Balfour Declaration, as it was called, also stated that this new nation would not 'prejudice the civil and religious rights of existing non-Jewish communities in Palestine'. He wondered, then, at the fairness of the United Nations in 1947, giving 52 per cent of the land to Israel and allowing only 48 per cent of the land for the far greater population of Arabs living in the area.

The refugee problem also troubled him. Of the seven hundred thousand Arabs who fled or were driven out of Palestine, at least fifty thousand were Christians. His parents were among those who had suffered. He wondered why the Church around the world didn't seem to care about them. Many Christians seemed far more eager to rejoice in the birth of Israel than to understand the suffering of their fellow believers. As one Arab pastor had said, 'It is hard to be told that for the return of my Lord Jesus to take place, I must first be expelled from my ancestral home.'[4] Hanna understood why so many Palestinians had responded violently. But as a Christian, that bothered him too. He knew that violence was not the answer.

What did all this mean for him as a Christian and as a Palestinian? How should he relate to the Jewish people? The Scriptures spoke about Jews and Gentiles being united into one body, but in actuality the two sides were not yet reconciled. Forgiveness was needed on both sides. Many of the Christians he'd met in the States didn't see the two sides of this coin. They blindly supported everything the state of Israel did, whether good or bad, right or wrong. He understood that many reacted this way as a response to the horror of the Holocaust – he still cringed at the pictures he'd seen and stories he'd heard. But should justice for one people come at the expense of another? Why did so few evangelical Christians seem to know or care about their brothers and sisters on the Palestinian side?

That personal struggle had caused him to choose as the topic of his PhD dissertation the theological foundation for reconciliation between Palestinian Christians and Messianic Jews. So many had attempted to find a political solution in the region. Perhaps, he concluded, it was time for the Church to demonstrate a different way.

Gaza, 1996

Sunday evening, after spending much of the day with my friends at Gaza Baptist Church, I took a taxi from my hotel. The driver stopped on a narrow dirt road across from a mosque and spoke to a boy who guarded a gate. I paid the driver and got out and walked through the gate.

Ever since my talks to Hamas in 1994, I had stayed in touch

with Mahmoud Zahar, trying to visit with him every time I was in Gaza. We had met at his medical clinic in one of the poorest sections of town and at the university where he lectured. My desire was to understand this man, what motivated him, and how he thought. I also wanted him to know a Christian man who was as committed to Jesus Christ as he was to Muhammad and Islam. Two days earlier, when I'd called, he had surprised me by inviting me to his home for dinner.

Mahmoud's home was very simple, with little furniture and almost no ornamentation. We sat in two red overstuffed chairs. The walls were plain white, but there were a couple of holes – they looked like bullet holes but I didn't ask. I could hear voices talking softly in the kitchen behind a curtain. But when Mahmoud invited me to the dining table, it was only the two of us. I assumed that his wife or a daughter fixed the meal, but I did not meet them.

I didn't know much about Mahmoud's background, because he didn't spend much time talking about himself. I'd learned that he was born in 1943 and earned his medical degree in Egypt, specialising in diseases of the thyroid. Inevitably we began our talks with the current political situation. Mahmoud's intensity showed in the way he leaned towards me to make sure I understood his points. He was articulate, and I could understand why CNN and other news services often came to him for interviews. 'We are fighting against occupiers,' he said. 'We are fighting against armies, against people who are oppressing civilians. But it's very important to see the strength of the Palestinian side. All Palestinians, Muslim or Christian, are one unit facing the Israelis.'

'But now you are autonomous,' I protested. 'Under Oslo, the Palestinian Authority is in charge. You make it sound like you are still fighting. Aren't the two sides moving towards peace?'

'We refuse to participate in the peace conference. We refuse to be part of PA [Palestinian Authority] because they are not representing the majority. PA indicated that Israel is owner of the land, and we are a national minority, which is not the case. *We* are the owner of the land. We are part of the pan-Arabic state historically, geographically. We refuse to accept Israel as a state. We are accepting of Jews as citizens, having full rights, full duties as Muslim, as Christian, as any citizen. But as a Zionist fabricated nation – it is not acceptable.'

'So what is the role of Hamas in this battle, where you also have the PLO and the radical Islamic Jihad? How do the people know where to turn?'

'Officially we are one, a respectable one. But nobody can decide without the acceptance of Hamas, because on the popular level, if Hamas calls for demonstration, there will be demonstration. If Hamas calls for cease-fire, there will be cease-fire. If Hamas calls for escalation of resistance, there will be escalation of resistance. The power of Hamas is from the power of popular support.'

Mahmoud chose his words carefully when speaking about the PLO, but I could tell his true feelings about the group. The fact was that Hamas and Arafat were enemies. When the heat of suicide bombing attacks became too much, the Israeli government put pressure on Arafat, who then arrested members of Hamas. Four times Mahmoud was incarcerated in a Palestinian prison because, he said, 'I treated people who were shot by Israelis.' Prison was a brutal experience. He told me how they had shaved off his beard and all his hair, a shameful insult, and beat him. He rolled up his shirtsleeve to show me where his arm was broken in two places. I was surprised that he wasn't bitter about the experience.

He insisted that Hamas was not tainted by corruption like the Palestinian Authority, of which it was common knowledge that officials were more interested in personal payoffs than in serving the needs of the Palestinians. I challenged him: 'Mahmoud, do you really maintain there is no corruption in Hamas?'

'If we have corruption, it is one or two. But here [the PA] you can see this man [Arafat] is corrupted, deeply corrupted, and he is still in authority. We are not speaking about angels in Hamas. But we are speaking about system. Who is punishing the criminals, and who is helping the people? So here in the PA, they are corrupting people and none of them are in jail. If we had the power, we would never become corrupt because Allah forbids it. That's the difference between us and the secular system.'

After dinner we drank coffee in the living room. Mahmoud was thoughtful for a few moments as we relaxed. Then he stunned me by saying, 'Andrew, please, we Hamas would like to make a cease-fire with Israel. Could you mediate?'

I stammered for a moment before saying, 'Why do you think I have any influence?'

'You have contacts in the American State Department. You have met Henry Kissinger.' I nodded. 'Would you tell them of our offer?'

'Of course I will. But what do I tell them?'

'Tell them that we guarantee that no bomb will explode. No suicide bombing, no shooting, no sabotage for as long as we agree with Israel – two years, three years, five years. They can set the time. Nothing will happen during that period. We want a cease-fire.'

I was shaking as I left his home. It was one thing for me to be a representative of the gospel, but I felt helpless in the world of statecraft. However, I couldn't avoid this; I had to try and do something. I was confident that when Mahmoud guaranteed Hamas would not strike at Israel, he would deliver on that promise. It was true that I had met Henry Kissinger, the former US Secretary of State, on an airplane from Texas to Los Angeles. I had told him about my work, and he had given me his unlisted phone number, saying, 'Andrew, if ever you need me, give me a call.'

Well, this situation qualified. Dr Kissinger still maintained close connections within the State Department. It was time to give him a call and turn this offer over to the experts.

CALLED TO A HIGHER STATECRAFT

Harderwijk, Holland, 1996

The letter arrived via fax. It was from one of Kissinger's associates in New York City. 'I am sorry I was unable to reach you . . . but I got no answer on your phone and I am leaving . . .' wrote the associate. He was a well-known man whom I respected as a Christian trying to live his faith in the world of diplomacy.

At Mahmoud's request, I had called Henry Kissinger's office as soon as I'd returned home. The reply didn't take long: 'I spoke with people in our government about your discussions with Mahmood (sic) Zahar,' wrote the associate. 'It turns out that our government does not believe that Zahar has any need for intermediaries if he wishes to discuss his ideas with the Israelis. Moreover, our government is under a strict policy of not having contacts with Hamas itself. I am sorry I was unable to reach you directly with this information but wanted you to have it before I left on my trip.'

I leaned back in my office chair and reflected that I didn't seem to have much success in statecraft. In my spirit I knew that this was not my profession and that I was called to a higher statecraft. I was representing the King of Kings and Lord of Lords to people who, though they didn't realise it, desperately needed to know Him. And I was encouraging others to do that work, people in the Middle East who could be far more effective than I.

Gaza, December 1996

The irony was unmistakable. It had been exactly four years since 415 Palestinians had been deported to southern Lebanon. And now, as a result of my contact with these men, I would soon speak to an audience at Islamic University in Gaza (IUG), one of the most fundamentalist Muslim institutions in the world.

For more than a year, I tried to find someone with strong academic credentials who could give the lecture at Islamic University. I felt this was a significant opportunity, and I wanted the right person, someone sensitive to the circumstances, to do it, preferably in Arabic. I made several calls to friends, but for various reasons the answer was always, 'No, Andrew, I can't.'

Finally, when Mahmoud reminded me that the invitation remained open, I said, 'Okay, I will do it.'

'Good!' he said. 'We will look for a good opportunity.'

The occasion was the dedication of a new auditorium where I was invited to give the very first lecture. Mahmoud met me before the event and we talked for a few minutes. I gave him a copy of the letter I'd received from the representative at Kissinger Associates. 'I'm sorry,' I said. 'As you can see, they don't want to talk.'

Mahmoud emphatically disputed that: 'It's not true. The State Department talked with us in Amman during the time we were deported to Lebanon.' Still, Mahmoud didn't seem terribly surprised. Apparently he had expected this response but felt it was still worth the try.

'Why don't you contact Israel directly, as the letter suggests?' I asked.

Mahmoud shook his head. 'They will not talk with us. There is no channel available. That was why I thought you might be able to open a way for us.'

In most conflicts around the world, there is a back door for communication between the two sides. Even if officially the combatants aren't talking, it makes sense to provide some unofficial way to work towards peace. Apparently this wasn't the case here.

The experience convinced me that there was little I could do to help in the peace process, at least politically. My simple attempt was rebuffed, which affirmed that my call was not to work in the political realm but rather to bring Christ to individuals. That was exactly what I intended to do at IUG.

THE IUG CAMPUS sits next to a second university, Al-Azhar, where Islam is not so rigidly practised. In many ways these two university campuses looked like any of thousands around the world. Students crisscrossed between buildings, hurrying to class.

As Mahmoud escorted me to the auditorium, a trio of co-eds, by their dress obviously from Al-Azhar University, passed in front of us. Mahmoud observed, 'Andrew, do you see that? See what the non-strict observance of Islamic law leads to?' The irony is that these girls were far more modest in dress than you'd see on most Western campuses, but they didn't wear the traditional black *jilbab* (long coat) and *hijab* (head scarf) favoured by the fundamentalists.

The auditorium was a nice, modern facility, and it was about half full with a mix of faculty and students. All of the women, dressed in *jilbab* and *hijab*, sat together in one section. Representatives of Hamas sat in the front rows. After Mahmoud's introduction, I expressed my appreciation for this opportunity: 'I've been given the privilege of speaking to you. Maybe we can clear up a few misunderstandings that are between us. Maybe we can also acknowledge a common need we all have. And since most of you are Muslims by choice, I want you to understand that I am a Christian by choice.'

Using the *Injil*, I read from Matthew 25:34–36. This is a passage about judgment – the greatest fear of every Muslim. 'Then the King will say to those on his right, "Come, you who are blessed by my Father; take your inheritance, the kingdom prepared for you since the creation of the world. For I was hungry and you gave me something to eat, I was thirsty and you gave me something to drink, I was a stranger and you invited me in, I needed clothes and you clothed me, I was sick and you looked after me, I was in prison and you came to visit me." '

Looking up and pointing at my audience, I said, 'You Hamas

know that all these things I have done in your midst.' The men in the front row, including Mahmoud, nodded. 'I did these things in the name of Jesus.'

I went on to read from Matthew 26: 'Now it came to pass, when Jesus had finished all these sayings, that He said to His disciples, "You know that after two days is the Passover, and the Son of Man will be delivered up to be crucified." '[1] As I had at other meetings, I spoke about the crucifixion, how Jesus had died for my sins and their sins.

There was a commotion in the audience, and I saw several young men, apparently objecting to my remarks, get up and walk out. This wasn't going to be easy. Some friends had told me that we should not talk about the cross to Jews or Arabs because it is offensive. I had countered their arguments by saying, 'So we let them go to hell.' I was going to make sure this audience heard the gospel.

But during this lecture I also wanted to talk about the effect of the gospel. I read from the book of Acts about the paralysed man who had an encounter with Peter and John. 'The paralytic was looking for a handout,' I told my audience. 'But handouts never change society. However, Peter and John had spent three years with Jesus, and they knew what He would do in this situation. They looked at the man and said, "We don't have gold or silver, but what we do have, we give to you. In the name of Jesus Christ, rise up and walk." A miracle happened; the man jumped up and rejoined society.

'I read a story some time ago about a man who visited the Pope. He looked around and observed the splendour and wealth of the Vatican. The Pope noticed his amazement and said laughingly, 'We cannot say anymore that we have no silver and no gold.' And the man answered, 'Neither can you say, "Rise up and walk!" ' There was laughter from some in the audience, and I hoped it would break the tension.

'We face this problem that we hardly know what we believe anymore. That's why we need to come together for a dialogue. The whole world is in a crisis. If there is no way that God can change people, then there is no future for mankind. I plead for verbalisation of what we really believe, what we are convicted and convinced of. That's why I do not make any apologies for my faith in Jesus Christ and for the spreading of the Word of God in all the world.'

There was a shout from one of the students, and he and another student got up and charged out of the hall. There was a murmur among some of the university administration seated in front. A couple of them whispered, then one got up, walked to the doors, and locked them so no one else could enter or leave.

I took a deep breath and continued. 'Destiny has thrown us together. It is not by chance that I am here at this university, because the two main influences in the world today are, and will continue to be, Islam and Christianity.' I proceeded into the heart of my message, the contrast between real Christianity and real Islam. 'Real Christianity is following Jesus Christ. He says that if you really want to follow Him, then you must deny yourself. Real Christianity is utter selflessness. Jesus said take up your cross daily and follow Me.' I pointed to my audience and said, 'You Muslims will never understand the real meaning of the cross until we Christians take the words of Jesus seriously.'

After my lecture there followed a time for questions. The first question dealt with the conflict between Christians and Muslims in Bosnia, to which I said, 'It has nothing to do with Christianity. If you think that Serbia as the aggressor is Christian, then I would ask your forgiveness.' Another student wanted to know why Christians seemed to be Zionists. I tried to explain that not all Christians are Zionists. 'My point is that first and most important we are followers of Christ.'

Another asked me to address the Christian view of justice. I had to admit that there is hardly any justice in the world today. Further, Christians have never learned to speak with one voice against injustice. 'But then Islam is not united either,' I concluded. 'So let's acknowledge that and seek personal contacts so relationships can develop and grow. Real changes in the world never come from the top downwards. Real changes always grow from the grassroots upwards. That's why there is hope. If we let Him, God can change things through you and me.'

The university leadership was gracious about the lecture, but I knew they would not want to embarrass me even if they were displeased. Personally, I didn't feel good about the event. Some students had walked out, and I assumed others had wanted to do the same. I wondered what good, if any, this had done.

Gaza, 1997
Nearly a year later, during another trip to Gaza, Labib Madanat and I went to meet with Mahmoud Zahar at his clinic, just as the neighbourhood mosque was broadcasting the afternoon call to prayer. Inside the front door was a large waiting area, and the wooden benches were full of patients. Off to one side was an area strewn with prayer rugs. Mahmoud emerged from his examination room, drying his hands, which he'd just washed as part of the Islamic ritual ablutions. He nodded to me and headed to the designated prayer area with his staff. I sat and waited with those patients who weren't praying as Mahmoud and his team recited from the Quran, then bowed towards Mecca and prayed. *This is the strength of Hamas,* I thought as I observed the ritual. Mahmoud didn't apologise for making me or any of his patients wait. Perhaps that was one thing that drew me to him – he was consistent in his faith. *If only there were more Christians as faithful in the practice of their faith, then the world might take us more seriously.*

After the prayers, Mahmoud invited me into his tiny office and asked if I had time to go with him to meet with Sheikh Ahmad Yassin, the founder of Hamas. I immediately agreed. The sheikh had been released from prison just a few days earlier in a dramatic deal between Jordan and Israel, after Israeli agents bungled an attempt to assassinate Hamas leader Khalid Misha'al in Amman.

Mahmoud drove me to a simple house in Sabra, a very poor section of Gaza City. When Yassin returned to Gaza, his home became Hamas headquarters, and many visitors were crowded in the foyer awaiting an audience. Mahmoud escorted me past the courtiers to the receiving room, while explaining that Yassin was nearly blind and had trouble hearing but that his mind remained very clear. When Mahmoud introduced me, explaining how I had become his friend, Yassin nodded, then greeted me in a high-pitched, almost squeaky voice.

Yassin didn't look like the kind of powerful charismatic leader who could motivate thousands of followers. He sat in a wheelchair – at the age of fifteen he'd suffered an athletic accident that left him paralysed. Though it was a comfortably warm day, he wore a

217

heavy sweater, with a wool blanket over his legs. He had a full white beard about six inches long, and a white scarf covered his head. It was hard to imagine how this frail man had survived eight years in prison during which neither his wife nor any of his eleven children were allowed to visit him.

Labib and I presented the sheikh with copies of an Arabic Bible, a children's Bible and one of my books. I placed each book on his lap. He thanked me. An assistant then removed each book and put it on the low table in front of him. Immediately another assistant grabbed the books and removed them from the room. I thought that was strange. Never before had anyone seemed embarrassed to have copies of these books.

While we visited, Yassin signalled that he was hungry. His assistant fed him a banana, then held a cup to his lips so he could drink. Yassin spoke to me in nearly a whisper, saying that prison had made him a much stronger man. 'My goal is not power. My goal is the end of the occupation.' If there was any weakening of resolve among Hamas, it was clear that this man would restore the focus. Indeed, you could tell that the rank and file revered him.

One other thing struck me. Many of the callers in the next room waiting for their audience needed help – medical, financial, or food. Yassin would make sure those needs were met. This was the popular appeal of Hamas. Numerous charities were funded and staffed by the organisation, providing low-cost or free services for a population with an unemployment rate pushing 70 per cent. The PA was right to fear Hamas – they had earned the popular support.[2]

THE NEXT DAY I visited the campus of Islamic University, and a young man came up to me and smiled, saying in good English, 'I know you!'

I smiled back and said, 'I'm afraid I don't know you.'

'I was at the lecture in the auditorium last year.'

'Then why are you smiling? I didn't think you accepted what I said.'

'No, it was great!'

'Why do you say that?'

'Because you did not put us down. You left us in our dignity. That is why me and my friends admired you and what you said.'

Later, I talked with a woman who had sat among the female students. She said that they were extremely attentive. 'We have never had the opportunity to hear about Christianity before.'

So maybe my lecture had served some useful purpose after all. Perhaps a few students' skewed picture of Christianity had changed by my being there.

TWENTY-SEVEN

THE TEACHER'S BOOKSHOP

Gaza, March 1999
The party started on board the bus from Jerusalem. 'Get into the spirit of prayer for Gaza!' Labib cheerfully shouted as he boarded. Applause came from the various international visitors representing ministries like United Bible Societies and Open Doors that had helped pray, counsel, and fund this project.

It had been nearly five years since the vision for the bookshop in Gaza was born. Bureaucratic red tape had slowed the project even after Yasser Arafat granted his permission. As a brand-new government, the Palestinian Authority managed to create many hurdles over which Labib and his team had to jump. In addition, because Gaza was one of the most crowded pieces of land in the world, it was far more expensive than initially expected to purchase the property and open the shop.

While working to fulfil the dream for Gaza, Labib was also aggressively expanding the Bible Society work into communities such as Beir Zeit, the location of the most prestigious Palestinian university. The actual village, about half an hour's drive north of Jerusalem, was home to about fifteen hundred Christians. A local Catholic priest, Father Emil Salayta, was the primary force behind launching a Bible bookshop in the area. It had taken a year to establish, with doors opening in December 1995.

Labib had enthusiastically thanked me for the support of Open Doors in that project. He reported on the first month of ministry: 'We have distributed thousands of Bibles over the Christmas holidays. Let us pray that families will read it together and turn to the Rock.'

Father Emil planned to give a Bible to every family and a *Jesus* film to every Christian family in the region of Beir Zeit, Abud, Jifna, and Taybeh. Next, Labib was working to open a bookshop in Nablus.

We were given VIP treatment at the Eretz border crossing into Gaza. The Palestinian Authority felt it necessary to provide us with a police escort, and the flashing lights and armed guards at every intersection seemed to me like a wonderful marketing device to call attention to the grand opening. To accommodate more than 150 guests, the opening ceremonies were held at the Anglican chapel on the grounds of Al Ahli Hospital, across the street from the new bookshop.

It was a joyful celebration. After singing, Scripture reading, and prayers, the Rev. Miller Milloy, regional secretary for the United Bible Societies, and I addressed the gathering. I observed that the official name of the store was The Teacher's Bookshop. Why? 'Because Jesus' own disciples repeatedly called Him "Teacher", not because Jesus was the greatest prophet, nor because He wrote a book, but because He was the biggest message. He was the fulfilment of John the Baptist's message, "Behold the Lamb of God who takes away the sins of the world."'

Then the party moved across the street to the shop, and people wandered through the upstairs and the main floor and spilled out onto the sidewalk. 'From today on, anybody in Gaza can walk into this store and buy a Bible for himself!' Labib declared as he led a group of us on a tour. He explained that because of travel restrictions, many of the strip's million-plus residents were unable to cross into Israel and purchase a Bible. Over the years, Bible societies around the world had received letters from Gaza asking for copies of the Bible. Even during the last months of preparation, the bookshop manager reported that a number of passers-by had stepped into the building to ask for Bibles.

There were floor-to-ceiling shelves, filled with Arabic Bibles, children's picture Bibles, biblical encyclopaedias, commentaries and books on church history, lining the walls of the first floor. The second floor contained a children's book corner, facilities for computer access to the Internet, and tables and chairs for the studies Labib hoped would be held daily.

I noticed Doron Even-Ari, the first Messianic Jew to head the Bible Society of Israel, beaming proudly as he examined the facilities. He and Labib had become friends and were working closely together on several projects, including a soon-to-be-published colour brochure in Arabic and Hebrew that would present God's plan for peace in the Scriptures.

As a young man, Doron would never have imagined himself in this position. His parents had moved to Palestine from Germany in the 1930s and he grew up during the exciting years following Israel's birth. Trained by the Ministry of Defence, Doron had served his country for fifteen years in various parts of Africa, until 'God found me', as he liked to tell people who wanted to hear his story. At an outdoor stadium event in Pretoria, South Africa, 'God revealed Himself personally to me and introduced His Son Yeshua.'

I also noticed representatives of the liturgical churches – Greek Orthodox, Anglican, and Catholic – as well as elders from the Baptist church. Labib estimated there were two thousand Christians living among more than one million Muslims in Gaza. Labib wanted this to be a centre for them as well as for the community – a place where 'affordable copies of the Word of God are available for every person'. He envisioned this being the starting point for outreach into schools and universities. 'And I hope this will provide for better relations between Christians and Palestinian authorities. We want to bless them, and we want to strengthen the Church in Gaza.'

A representative of the Norwegian Bible Society, observing the festive atmosphere, commented, 'After this, we will no longer associate Gaza with just violence and problems. Now we will associate it with hope.'

The only group not visible at the party was the one that had unknowingly provided the impetus for the store. I mentioned to Labib that I didn't see any representatives from Hamas. 'Oh, I wouldn't expect any of them to come to the dedication,' Labib answered. 'But you wait. I expect some of them will visit quietly in the coming weeks.'

I prayed that indeed these men would be drawn to the store, and many others – students, government officials, military. They all needed the Good News from the Teacher.[1]

Gaza, 1999

Hanna Massad was glad to be back in Gaza after earning his PhD. And with a wife too! Hanna and Suhad had married just a few weeks earlier in Jordan. He beamed with pride as Suhad served coffee and pastries to their guests.

One of them, Abu Yahya, was manager of The Teacher's Bookshop, and he had recruited a young man, Kamal, who was learning the ropes of ministry under his direction. 'The shop has been open for six months,' Abu reported. 'What is amazing is how many students from the university are coming in. We have on average a dozen new visitors every day. We have discussion groups almost every day on the second floor. It's a chance for students to ask questions about Christianity and the Bible.'

'We're also showing the *Jesus* film,' said Kamal. 'And we plan soon to start teaching courses in English. Both are good evangelistic tools.'

Hanna reflected on how different the situation was from when he was pastor of the Gaza Baptist Church eight years earlier. This time he knew he wasn't going into the work alone. His wife was opening up opportunities for work with the women. And these two men needed someplace to send the converts who were already emerging from their bookshop ministry.

Abu's wife asked Hanna what his priorities were as he resumed his pastoral responsibilities. 'First, Suhad and I have already started visiting homes,' he said. 'We want to visit every family and individual represented in this church.'

'What about bringing in new families?' Abu asked.

'That's one reason I would like to work with you and

Kamal. I would like to plan some evangelistic events. Out of those events will come more disciples. I can't do something like that alone.'

'And we are far more effective working with a local church,' said Abu. 'Our philosophy is one of multiplication. We want to make disciples who in turn will make other disciples.'

'I have an idea,' Hanna said. 'While I was studying in the States, I learned about a speaker and writer, John Maxwell, who specialises in training leaders.' Hanna held up one of the books, *The 21 Irrefutable Laws of Leadership*. 'I think this might be helpful to leaders in the Palestinian Authority.'

'I'd like to know those laws of leadership myself,' said Abu.

That was the start of a cohesive team that met regularly to pray, study, and strategise. This little church was going to shine its light into the government, schools, and the culture. Hanna realised that this time the ministry didn't fall on his shoulders alone. God had provided him with a team. As a result, the impact of Gaza Baptist Church would be significant.

DID YOU TRY TO PRAY?

Beit Sahour, 1999

Nawal Qumsieh saw many needs in her neighbourhood, but she couldn't just announce a Bible study or prayer meeting and invite women into her home. There were limitations. If she was to teach a woman or do any counselling, she first had to get permission from the woman's husband. Muslim or Christian, it didn't matter – those were the rules in this culture.

For several years, she had visited homes, talked to husbands and wives together, presented the gospel, but no one had responded. It was well and good to be called to ministry, but if there was no fruit, what was the point? One day Nawal poured out her frustration to a pastor friend in Jerusalem.

'God has prepared you for ministry,' the pastor gently told her. 'And God is ready to move in hearts.'

'I believe that,' Nawal affirmed. 'But to whom should I minister? No one I've approached has responded.'

'You need to move out. God can't do anything until you move.'

'God knows I'm ready!' Nawal protested. 'I've tried moving out. That doesn't work. It's time for God to *show* me where to minister. I'm going to know He is leading me when someone *asks* me for help.' It was spoken with determination. Like Gideon, Nawal had set out a fleece.

A couple of days later she went to her hairdresser. Unlike most times, the man was quiet as he worked on her hair. She sensed a deep sadness in her friend, so she asked, 'What's wrong?'

'Don't worry,' he answered. In typical Arab fashion, a man wasn't going to open up to a woman who wasn't a member of his family.

She persisted anyway: 'I'd like to know. That is, if you know, if you can say.'

She waited as the man combed out her hair. Finally, he said, 'My wife has had many miscarriages.' He ran the comb through her hair a few more times, then stopped, saying, 'I've spent all of our money trying to find out why. We've tried many doctors, but none of them have helped.' Nawal didn't interrupt. She understood that an Arab man didn't feel complete until he and his wife had children. Finally, he said, 'My wife is pregnant. And she's bleeding. At any minute she might lose the baby.'

'How far along is she?' Nawal asked.

'She is due in ten weeks. Most of the miscarriages have been right about this time.'

'Have you tried . . .'

'We've tried all the doctors, all the medicines, everything! Nobody knows why. There's not any reason.' The man stepped back. His anger was palpable.

'Did you try to pray?' Nawal asked quietly.

'What?'

Nawal was shaking, her senses hyper-alert, her spirit in fervent prayer. 'Did you go to Jesus? Did you pray for your wife, or have someone pray for your wife? Did you try Jesus?'

The man stood frozen, but his anger subsided. 'No, I never heard about that. I've never thought about what Jesus can do.'

Nawal knew this man had been born in an Orthodox family but hadn't been to church in years. 'Why don't you try?' she said.

'I don't know how to do it.'

'Okay, ask somebody.'

The man paused, then said, 'Would you pray for my wife?'

She knew this was the moment she had waited for. 'Yes, but your wife has to agree with you for me to come and pray with her.'

The hairdresser silently finished his work. As Nawal paid him and headed out the door, she said, 'I'll be at home. If you need me, I will be ready.'

The man came to her home at 7.00 that evening, dashing up the stairs to her door in the pouring rain. 'Would you come now to pray for my wife?'

All she had to do was grab her raincoat, but she didn't move. 'Why now?' she asked. 'I'll come in the morning.'

The man was in a panic. 'She will lose the baby in the morning.'

Why shouldn't she go now? Nawal wondered. But she sensed that this was not yet the right moment. 'No, she can't. She will not lose that baby. She will keep the baby until morning, and I will come and pray for her.'

Nawal barely slept that night. *Why, Lord?* she wondered. *Why should I wait?* But there was a peace, a divine confidence that she was doing exactly as God wanted. So she prayed for the woman and her husband. 'Lord, please keep that baby until morning. And when I pray with this couple, may they feel Your presence.'

In the morning, after a very brief night of sleep, she prayed again: 'May I be led by Your Spirit.' Then she 'heard' her final instructions: 'Speak My Word, and I will do the rest.'

She arrived at the couple's home at 8.30 in the morning. Frantically the man opened the door. 'We went to the doctor, but he said there is nothing he can do. The hole is open and the baby will come any minute.'

Nawal walked past him to his wife, who was lying on a couch. She knelt down next to the woman and grabbed her hand. The wife opened her eyes, which were red from crying. 'I don't deserve the baby,' she whispered.

'Why do you say that?' Nawal asked.

'Because I'm a sinner, and God is punishing me.'

Sensing the husband hovering over her, Nawal stood and took out her Bible. 'I have good news for both of you!' She pulled up chairs for her and the husband next to the couch. Then she read passages of Scripture, showing them that, while all have sinned and fallen short of God's standard, God had placed all of their sins on His Son Jesus Christ. Then, with all three of them in tears, Nawal laid her hands over the woman's womb and prayed: 'I bind the spirit of miscarriage and the spirit of death over this womb. Lord, I release the spirit of life in this baby.'

Then it was time to pray for new life for this couple. With her guidance, they prayed and surrendered their lives to Jesus. An hour later, she hugged the woman and left.

The woman phoned that afternoon, in a panic. 'I'm bleeding badly!' she said.

'Don't be worried,' Nawal counselled. 'Together, let's keep saying that we trust the Word of God, that God gave you this baby, and that He will keep it for you. Satan can't take it from you.' Nawal read her some verses to concentrate on as her husband took her to the hospital.

Later that night, the woman called. 'The bleeding has stopped!' she practically yelled in excitement. 'The doctor examined me and said the hole has closed. He's amazed. He said it's a miracle.'

A very healthy boy was born ten weeks later. The couple named him Jacob and started telling everyone their story. Nawal started receiving calls: 'We heard what happened. Would you please come and pray for us?'

Harderwijk, 2000

In 2000 I turned seventy-two. Since 1955 I'd worked to strengthen the Church in difficult situations, first in the former Soviet Union and Eastern Europe, then in China, Cuba, Africa and many parts of the Islamic world. In 1993 Johan Companjen assumed the presidency of Open Doors. He was well suited for that role, and the ministry thrived and grew. I'd never dreamed of starting, much less running, a big organisation, and when I was freed of those daily responsibilities, I concentrated my efforts on a few key areas of the world, particularly the Middle East.

Now Al, a professional writer who served on the board of directors for our US base, sat with Johan in my office, asking me to talk about what I'd learned over forty-five years of service to the Church.

'Nothing was planned,' I said. 'I came across opportunities and I grabbed them. Or they grabbed me.' How else could I explain my work with Bishara Awad and Bethlehem Bible College or reaching out to Islamic fundamentalist groups? One doesn't set out to do such things. You respond in obedience as God opens doors.

What had I learned? Well, there were a few important lessons. I verbalised one of them: 'There are no terrorists – only people who need Jesus.'

Johan had heard me say things like this many times, but that was a shock to my American friend. 'I'm serious,' I said. 'If I see them as enemies, how can I reach them? I've often said, if you see a terrorist with a gun, get close to him, put your arm around him, and then he can't shoot you. As long as we see any person – Muslim, Communist, terrorist – as an enemy, then the love of God cannot flow through us to reach him. Each of us has a choice. I can go to terrorists and love them into the Kingdom. And the moment I love them, they are no longer my enemy. You don't hate a friend.'

Al asked, 'So who is the enemy?'

'The devil! Never people!'

As Al chewed on that radical and biblical idea, I gave him a second lesson: 'Whoever is reachable is winnable. I think that's what my work has demonstrated,' I explained. 'The Hamas are reachable. Anyone could have gone to see those men at Marj al-

Zohour. I did what Jesus did in His ministry – I met them at their point of need. When they're sick, I'm with them. When they're in the hospital, I'm with them. When they're in prison, I'm with them. How else can they know my Jesus? They can only meet Jesus if someone in whom He dwells goes to them.'

Obviously Al's head was spinning. He asked cautiously, 'What results can you show? Do you know how many Hamas have responded to the gospel?'

Al was only verbalising the questions most Christians wanted to ask. 'I think we're on the wrong track with all of our statistics. We are too results-oriented. I aim to be destiny-oriented. I was with a Christian peace team recently in Hebron, and they asked me, "How many fundamentalists have you led to Christ?" I told them, "I don't think there's anyone." They rejoiced, because one of their supporters from the States wanted to know how many Muslims they had led to Christ. Now they could write back and say even Brother Andrew couldn't do it. It's our job to go. We don't judge evangelism by results, certainly not friendship evangelism.'

Johan reminded Al about the unique call to Open Doors and me. 'We don't go into a country to evangelise. We go to strengthen what remains. Where there is a church, we stand with them. We let them know we care. We find out what they need – Bibles, materials, training. We equip them to be the church in that area. Hopefully the church becomes alive in their community, and *they* start evangelising.'

'But Andrew, it sounds like you *are* evangelising,' Al protested.

'No, I show them how!' I answered. 'These visits with Hezbollah and Hamas aren't stunts. I take local Christian leaders with me, because I want to demonstrate that they can do it. If I can do it, a million people can do it! As Johan says, Open Doors strengthens what is there so they can evangelise.

'The Palestinian Church is threatened with extinction. That's why I concentrate on the Palestinian Church. People wrongly interpret that to mean I have chosen for the Palestinian side. This is not the case. I have chosen for the body of Christ. That's why I work with Bishara and Bethlehem Bible College. Everyone knows he's a man of faith and integrity, and I support his vision to raise up and train leaders for the Palestinian Church, so it will not just survive but thrive. Take another example – Salim Munayer and Musalaha. That ministry of reconciliation wasn't my idea. It was born out of the local church to address the conflict between Palestinians and Jews. We support it because we agree this is the only solution, and we want it to have a chance to succeed.'

I realised I was preaching, but I wanted Al to understand the distinctiveness of this mission. 'Let me give you another example. Two of the Hamas deportees came to see me when I was staying at Bethlehem Bible College, but Bishara and I were away. While they waited, several students talked to them and gave them each a Bible. Bishara and I were thrilled when we learned that! Those students now realise that *they* can reach fundamentalists. This is the process of discipleship. Admittedly, it is a slow process. One becomes two, then four, then eight. It takes a while to make an impact. But it doesn't mean we shouldn't start with that one. I started with Bishara. Over twenty years, he has multiplied the number of disciples through Bethlehem Bible College, and I don't believe anyone from outside the culture could have done that.'

The three of us took a deep breath, and our discussion moved to the future of the Church in the region. 'We have to prepare the Church for hard times,' I said soberly.

Johan observed that times already were hard in the Holy Land.

I responded, 'Nobody seems to understand how tough it's going to become.' I hesitated for a moment, because I'm generally a positive person and I didn't like what I had to say, but my years in the region left me no other conclusion. 'Despite the pledges made at Oslo, there will not be peace. The Palestinians are terribly disappointed. I foresee an eruption of violence.'

Within a year, the volcano did erupt, and it was worse than most anyone could have imagined. For me, there was only one consolation. Now there were people in the Church, trained and ready, who would be lights in the darkness. People like Salim, Labib, Hanna, Nawal, and many others.

All of them would be deeply impacted by the conflict. Early in the new intifada, much of the conflict swirled around Bethlehem Bible College.

THE SECOND INTIFADA:
A RELIGIOUS UPRISING

September 2000

Hopes for a permanent peace were dashed in the summer of 2000. For two weeks President Clinton met with Palestinian President Yasser Arafat and Israeli Prime Minister Ehud Barak at Camp David to try to nail down an agreement, which would define his presidency. This was to be the culmination of the process started in Oslo in 1993. While there had been many setbacks during the intervening years, hopes were high that finally the two sides would settle their differences.

Unfortunately, that didn't happen. Millions of words have been spoken and written trying to understand what went wrong and assessing blame. There was tension in Israel, West Bank, and Gaza. Among Palestinians there was frustration not just with the peace process but also with corruption among the Palestinian Authority who showed little ability to govern the territories they controlled. There was an economic malaise that left more and more men unable to provide for their family. One-fifth of the Palestinian population was between the ages of fifteen and twenty-four, and a majority of them were undereducated (generally because of time lost when schools were closed during the first intifada) and unemployed. I had seen them lounging around the streets with nothing to do and had thought that they were the fuel for an uprising that needed only a spark to ignite.

That spark occurred on 28 September 2000, when Ariel Sharon visited the Temple Mount. With a big smile for the television cameras, he stated, 'I am a man of peace.' Most cameras didn't show the one thousand policemen and soldiers surrounding him. They didn't show the humiliation felt by Muslims at the presence of Jewish military on their holy ground. The next day after Friday prayers, young men began throwing rocks at the police. Seven Palestinians and one Israeli died that day. Thirteen more Palestinians died the next day. The protests spread like a dry brush fire. During the first two weeks, eighty-five Palestinians and seven Israelis were killed, and there was no letup in sight.[1]

For many, one picture defined the conflict. On 30 September Mohammed al-Dura, a twelve-year-old boy, was shot and killed during an exchange of gunfire between Israeli soldiers and Palestinian demonstrators in Gaza. Moments before his death, a photographer took a photo of the boy, a look of terror on his face as he crouched behind his father for protection. Palestinians were in shock, wondering how to protect their children. For some, the reaction was an intense desire for revenge that seemed insatiable. Many others felt that the rules had changed and nobody had told them. Always before, demonstrators had faced rubber bullets and tear gas; now the bullets were lethal.

This uprising quickly acquired a different character from the first intifada that began in December 1987 and raged on and off until the Oslo Accords were signed in 1993. The primary image of that uprising was of children throwing rocks against the military might of Israel. Much of the world sympathised with them. There were also various forms of non-violent protests. Death totals were far lower than during the second uprising.[2]

This time there were forty thousand armed security personnel operating under the Palestinian Authority within the territories, though their firepower was far less than that of the Israeli army. Plus the Islamic fundamentalist groups were playing a huge role; the suicide bomber quickly became a prominent image of the second uprising. It was harder for the world to sympathise with this rebellion when it saw horrific images of destruction by jihadi 'martyrs'.

For the Palestinian Christian community, this second intifada had serious religious overtones. Since the inciting incident had occurred on the third holiest Muslim site, the uprising became known as the Al-Aqsa Intifada, named after the mosque on the Temple Mount. Many Christians told us emphatically that they had no part in this violence. But Israel didn't differentiate between Christians and Muslims in their efforts to quell the uprising. Certainly believers understood and felt the anger and frustration of fellow Palestinians. They suffered from the same problems and humiliations as Muslims in West Bank and Gaza, and under these circumstances they stood with their fellow Palestinians. While they didn't want to be considered traitors, they also believed it was wrong to take up arms. They were angry at the militants for choosing violence, angry at the PA and Yasser Arafat for not doing a better job of running their government or negotiating the peace, and angry at Israel for exacerbating the conflict with the expansion of settlements and with constant restrictions placed on their movement.

Then it got more complicated. Palestinian militants started shooting from Beit Jala at the Jerusalem suburb of Gilo. It was mostly a symbolic gesture, for their guns did little damage. But Israel retaliated with massive firepower, shooting from their tanks and Apache helicopters. Hundreds of homes were destroyed. Christians set up roadblocks in Bethlehem and Beit Jala at night, trying to prevent militants from getting in position to shoot at Gilo, but without much success.[3] Fighting escalated as the Israeli army entered Bethlehem. One seven-storey building across the street from Bethlehem Bible College was commandeered. The college buildings lost most of their windows during the ensuing battle.

The reports were grim. I was on the phone to Bishara almost every week, encouraging him, praying with him. But it was several months before I could actually visit him. I thought constantly about my brothers and sisters in the midst of the conflict and prayed for them. I wondered if Christians should die fighting or live kneeling, and were those the only alternatives?

Bishara was a realist about the problems confronting the

Church, but his solutions were very different from those of most Palestinians. He had an alternative to violence. He was building up the Light Force.

THROWING THE
JESUS STONE

Bethlehem, June 2001

'Things have been quiet the last couple of weeks,' Bishara said as Al, making his first visit to the Holy Land, and I climbed to the roof of the main classroom building at Bethlehem Bible College. 'During Easter week, sixty-seven of our windows were shot out. Because of your help, we were able to get them all replaced.' He was referring to a special gift Open Doors made when we heard that Bethlehem Bible College had been caught in the middle of the shooting between Palestinian militants and Israeli soldiers.

From the roof we had a 360-degree panoramic view of the area. Across the street, on an empty dirt lot strewn with several weeks of uncollected garbage, boys were playing a lively game of football. Bishara pointed across the Jerusalem-Hebron Road to a seven-storey building no more than one hundred yards away. It was only a shell – every window was gone. 'That was where the Israeli soldiers were shooting from – right over our heads.'

'Or at your heads,' I retorted as we turned and stared at the steel door that opened into the stairway we'd just climbed. Three bullet holes had penetrated the door, leaving sharp extrusions, like flower petals, on the other side. The actual bullets were buried in mattresses being stored on the top landing. We walked around to the other side of the roof, stepping over some pipes so we could see the solar panels that provided heat for the college. They were shattered, gazing uselessly up at the sun. Behind them were new water tanks – the old ones had been riddled with holes. 'Almost every home and business lost their water tanks,' Bishara explained. 'It seemed like the soldiers wanted to shoot the tanks for target practice.'

We understood the implications. Bethlehem shared water with the settlements in the area. In recent months, the flow of water had become more and more infrequent. Often the water service was shut off for one or two weeks. Storage tanks were filled every time the water did flow. We were conscious of how precious this water was when we stood under the trickle of the shower, determined not to waste a drop.

Bishara pointed across a small lot containing about fifty olive trees. An impressive building rose beyond it. 'That's the Intercontinental Hotel,' he explained. 'It was built for the celebrations surrounding the year 2000 and the new millennium. We expected thousands of tourists for Christmas. But then the intifada started. Since then, the only time it's been used is by Israeli soldiers.'

We walked back downstairs to Bishara's car, which was parked behind the college. On the way, we passed a huge mural depicting the announcement of the birth of Jesus to the shepherds. That glorious event occurred less than five miles away from this spot. Several bullets had gouged holes in the mural. One bullet had pierced the head of a lamb. Somehow, it seemed symbolic.

BISHARA DROVE OVER the cobblestone streets of Beit Jala to the easternmost edge of town, before the hillside drops into the valley. Perched on another hill about half a mile away was the community of Gilo – the flashpoint of the recent conflict. Palestinians claimed that Gilo was a Jewish settlement built on land owned by residents of Beit Jala. Israel claimed that it was part of Jerusalem, that they'd owned the land before 1948 and had only reclaimed it after the 1967 war.

Like an ugly gash below us, standing on cement pillars, a

four-lane highway connected tunnels on each side of the valley. 'That's the tunnel road,' Bishara explained. 'It's for Israelis only. They are able to drive from Gilo to Hebron by going underneath Beit Jala.' Al noticed that cement walls had been erected on the Beit Jala side of the road. 'So militias can't shoot at the cars,' Bishara explained.

We turned and stared at the homes riddled with bullet holes. Many of the walls were simply gone, allowing us to gaze into rooms where families had eaten, talked, studied, and relaxed. The homes were now uninhabitable. 'More than 450 homes have been destroyed,' Bishara said softly. He pointed to one where an entire floor was blown away. 'Four Christian families lived in that house. One of our students lived there.'

'Where are they now?' I asked, trying to imagine the horror of that night when their home vanished under a barrage of tank and machine-gun fire.

'They have family in the area, but the homes are very crowded. It's a tremendous burden on the families.'

'Can you explain why this happened?'

Bishara pointed above the house and said, 'The militants are not from Beit Jala. They come in – Hamas or Arafat's Tanzim militia – and fire automatic weapons towards Gilo.' He pointed to the apartment buildings across the valley, gleaming in the morning sun. 'Their guns can barely reach Gilo. But as soon as the militias shoot, Israeli tanks start rumbling across the valley, firing at the places where they think the militias are.'

'Of course they are gone by the time the Israelis shoot,' I reflected, 'and the people in these homes are caught in the middle.'

'Yes, they are caught in the middle. The Muslims think they can force the Christians who live here to be on their side. But the people living in these homes are angry at the Palestinian militias, and they are angry at the Israelis for the harsh retaliation.'

We drove several blocks and stopped by a boarded-up building with a sign indicating that this was a children's theatre. Nearby was another home, with the second floor open to the elements. 'This house was hit by a tank shell. The wall crumbled and killed an eighteen-year-old Muslim boy.' Bishara sighed, then said, 'These people have nothing to do with the conflict, and the Israelis know that.'

On another street, we stopped and looked at a blackened car incinerated by a tank shell. Across the street, Bishara recognised a couple who had returned during daylight hours to collect some of their belongings. They invited us in, apologising that they couldn't serve us coffee. The man did have a bag of fresh apricots. I accepted one and savoured the wonderful flavour. 'That's the best apricot I've ever tasted!'

The man beamed. 'They are the best in the Middle East!' he agreed.

Inside the living room, most of one wall was lined with sandbags. Even so, a great deal of plaster from the walls and ceiling lay in a pile on the floor.

'Israeli Prime Minister Sharon threatened to take out the first row of homes,' the man said as I looked over the room. 'If the militias still shoot, then he'd take out the second row of homes. And he would keep going until the town was destroyed.'

'You can't fight tanks,' I said.

'We don't want to fight!' the man said. 'We have no weapons.'

On the way back to the college, we passed by Hope School. We couldn't actually drive there – the road was blocked, and we had to park and climb over the rubble. 'Hope School is in Area C,' Bishara explained. 'Bethlehem, Beit Sahour and Beit Jala are Area A, which is run by Palestinian Authority. But Area C is under Israeli control.'

We stood on the top of the heap and gazed at the place where I'd first met Bishara. I remembered that they had some chickens to provide eggs for the children. 'They have six thousand chickens now,' he said. 'They sell most of the eggs to help support the school. Every day they load the eggs in a car and drive here, then carry them over this heap to another car so they can deliver them to the stores in Bethlehem.'

GRADUATION IN ANY culture is a time of celebration. However, this ceremony felt unique because of the context. The fifty-four students attending Bethlehem Bible College and the fourteen who were receiving diplomas had paid a high price to learn the Scriptures and prepare for ministry. How many young people in

Holland or America would endure checkpoint searches, gunfire that kept them awake at night, fear for their safety and the safety of their families and continue to study diligently in a noisy house crowded with several families because their homes had been destroyed?

These students had suffered much, and now parents and family members, dressed in their Sunday best, sat proudly on folding chairs in the largest meeting room of the college. Among the music that the college choir sang in Arabic with great enthusiasm was 'A Mighty Fortress Is Our God'. That hymn, one of our favourites, took on new meaning when we thought that these people truly needed protection and trusted God to be their fortress.

The commencement speaker was Father Peter Du Brul of Bethlehem University. 'What does a Bible college do?' he asked early in his speech. It was a great question. 'It does something very dangerous. More dangerous than a dynamite factory. More dangerous and more powerful than a nuclear reactor. It produces not bombs nor electric power but students and teachers of the Bible – the most dangerous of books and the most healing of books.'

Given the context, with suicide bombers having struck again just a few days before and seeing the devastation left by tanks and rockets, did we really believe that these students had something more powerful than bombs?

'To study the Bible is not just learning how to quote it but how to live it,' Father Du Brul continued. 'For students in Bethlehem to study and to live the Bible is more dangerous than in any other country in the world, because you are right up against and under the very people that most of the Bible is about. You are very much oppressed by a certain interpretation of the Bible that allegedly delegitimises your right to your land, your God-given identity, and your future.'

Father Du Brul was pulling no punches as he expressed the tension among people of the Book. Orthodox Jews, Messianic believers, Palestinian Christians – all looked at the Scriptures from a different life context. So how would these students respond? After years of hard study, were they prepared to make a difference in this divided land? Father Du Brul believed the answer was yes!

'The solutions to these issues are not found in books or memorised as answers to questions. The solutions are to be lived by persons who are willing to risk their lives and their reputations, to risk showing their own ignorance and inadequacy out of their faith in Jesus Christ. What a challenge to live the Bible, to teach it, to study it, from the very position of one who is largely excluded from the pages of the Old Testament! But remember, the "unchosen" were there, and they sometimes saved the "chosen" themselves.' Du Brul rattled off several New Testament examples of outsiders pointing to the truth: the magi, the good Samaritan, the Roman centurion on Golgotha, and Sergius Paulus, the Roman governor on Cyprus. 'They came not to displace the chosen but to join them.'

Just how would these graduates point the way? Du Brul used an image familiar to those watching television news around the world of Palestinian boys throwing stones at well-armed and protected soldiers. He drew from the message to the church at Pergamum in Revelation 2: ' "To him who overcomes . . . I will also give him a white stone with a new name written on it, known only to him who receives it." I think the Palestinian churches receive such a stone as this. And this is the stone they should throw. This is the stone that I hope the Bible College has taught you to throw well, not to kill Goliath or to stone the adulteress, but to heal them. Because the name written on the stone is Jesus' name. What more can Jesus give as a reward to any conqueror but Himself! That is your job, your vocation, your mission. As the very people who were "not chosen", planted right in the midst of the people that claim to be "chosen", your very existence witnesses to something else, to Someone else who has a far deeper, grander, stronger plan – the assembly into unity of all the nations.'

Al and I were deeply moved by the words, by the challenge to these people who felt excluded yet were called by God to be part of His Great Commission. They were to take the Good News to fellow Palestinians. They were to live the Good News among Christians and Muslims. They were to be light, showing the way of real peace in the midst of turmoil.

Father Du Brul's conclusion brought home the challenge these young people would face: 'Get ready for a harder life. You are not going to know an easier road than the one that Jesus walked. But you will know no greater joy than the joy of walking with Him. We are not sending you into discos or malls to blow yourself up in the name of justice or mercy or the name of Christ. We are sending you to heal and to be healed of your own wounds in the act of caring for others.'

STILL MEDITATING ON Father Du Brul's powerful words, we gathered in the dining room for cake and punch. In the course of meeting members of the college faculty, we talked with Samia, a part-time English teacher. 'My regular job is at Notre Dame in Jerusalem,' she said.

'And are you able to get to work each day?' Al asked.

'I'm not allowed past the checkpoint,' she answered. 'I haven't been able to get to work since last October.' In other words, she'd been out of regular work since the start of the second intifada.

'So that means you haven't been paid?'

She smiled sweetly at the naive American stating the obvious and answered, 'I can't get paid if I'm not allowed to go to work.'

Bishara joined us for a moment and mentioned that Samia had been injured two months earlier, during Holy Week, by shrapnel from a grenade. We asked Samia to tell us what happened.

Samia had finished teaching a class. It was late afternoon on the Tuesday before Easter. As she stepped outside, she instinctively listened for any sounds of gunfire or fighting. 'If I'd heard any shooting, I would have headed to the basement.' The street was quiet, with only a single boy on the sidewalk. As she headed for her car, which was parked on the Jerusalem-Hebron Road, she heard the distinctive whistle of a grenade, and an explosion knocked her to the ground.

It took a moment for her ears to clear after the initial blast before she realised she was screaming. But no one seemed to hear. The street was deserted. She looked at her legs and saw they were covered with blood. Unable to stand up, she crawled to her car, climbed into the driver's side, and drove herself towards downtown Bethlehem to the hospital, which was only a mile away. That night a doctor removed ten pieces of shrapnel from her legs.

'Two pieces of shrapnel are still in my foot,' Samia said. She slipped her left foot out of her sandal so we could see the ugly red scar on her big toe.

'Besides those injuries, how are you doing?' I asked.

'I still have nightmares,' she said, fighting back tears. 'The next day, while I was in the hospital, there was a terrible shelling of Beit Jala. They brought a boy into my room; he died from injuries.'

I asked about the boy she'd seen on the street just before the grenade blast. 'Someone told me that he had only six pieces of shrapnel. But his injuries were much more serious than mine.'

We were quiet for a moment, reflecting on the terror this gentle woman had endured. Then she said, 'Two days later I walked over to Rachel's Tomb, from where the soldiers had launched the grenade. I walked right up to them and showed them the wounds that they had inflicted. They just laughed at me and told me to go away.'

By the way she spoke, it was clear that the mocking laughter of the soldiers was more painful than the physical injuries she had endured.

IT IS NOT SUICIDE –
IT IS RELIGIOUS

Gaza, June 2001

Hanna Massad, pastor of Gaza Baptist Church, stepped out of a minivan taxi and warmly hugged Al and me as we entered the Palestinian-controlled area of Gaza. As usual, Hanna was dressed in a coat and tie, befitting his role as a leader in the Christian community. His big smile told us how encouraging our visit was.

Accompanying us were two academics, one from England, the other from the United States. We had a full schedule, so Hanna had hired the taxi for the day to take us to all of our appointments. Our first stop was at Islamic University in Gaza for a meeting with Mahmoud Zahar. It was important for my friends to hear what this leader of Hamas had to say, unfiltered by the media.

For the benefit of my guests, I asked Mahmoud about his faith and how it intersected with his politics. 'There is no place for a secular state headed by Muslims if it is not controlled by Islam,' he explained. 'The Islamists are not accepting the leadership of Arab countries now (for example, Saudi Arabia), because they are implementing a secular, nonreligious regime.'

Since the Taliban were then firmly in control of Afghanistan, I asked if that was the kind of system he advocated.

'They are not representing proper Islam. We believe in the human rights of the Muslim. For example, who said that it is forbidden for women to be educated? Islam encourages women and men in every respect, but there are a few restrictions. For example, a woman is unable to be the leader of the army. But we are not depriving women.

'Islam is my religion, but Islam here is cultural.' Then recognising his Christian audience, he added, 'We are very proud of the Christian roots here, because they are as national as any Palestinian is national. We are serving the same national cause. For this reason I can say that we are enjoying a popular support for this political attitude. For our participation in the intifada, we succeeded to send a very hot message for the Israeli people that your security is not available without withdrawal, not redeployment; without dismantling settlements, not just stopping expansion. I'm speaking about national goals. We are helping our children, Muslim and Christian, and we are helping even the Jews, because if they are going to continue their occupation, the Arab world will sooner or later unite against the Israelis. It will be!'

'You really believe that?' I interrupted. 'You hope it will?'

'No, it will be! It is written in the Quran that the people under our rule will come, and we are going to enter the mosque together. We believe that Israel as a state will be dismantled. Arabs will unite and establish a pan-Islamic state without any borders. We are not speaking about hopes. We are speaking about reality.'

'But then there will be no room for Jews or Christians.'

'Andrew, there will always be room for Christians like you!'

We all chuckled at that nice statement. But Al and I felt we needed to confront him on the horror of suicide bombings. Just a week before, an attack on a Tel Aviv disco had killed twenty-one teenagers, mostly girls. The horrific attack had caused outrage around the world. Taking his first hesitant step to question the internationally feared leader of Hamas, Al asked, 'Mahmoud, doesn't the Quran condemn suicide?'

'Yes, it is forbidden.'

'Then how can you condone the actions of the men who commit suicide . . .'

'It is not suicide,' he interrupted. 'It is religious.'

I challenged him: 'Now you make it worse. Now you have a

million – an endless supply – of "martyrs". And they are killing innocent women and children. How can you as a good Muslim condone that?'

'Are they innocent?' He aggressively leaned forward over his desk. 'Tell me, who in Israel have we killed who is innocent?'

'Those teenage girls in Tel Aviv. They weren't a threat to you.'

'Okay, I will speak very simply. Nobody in Israel can be described as a civilian. Nobody!' He noted our shocked expressions. My guests shifted uncomfortably in their seats. But Mahmoud bored in. 'Because every man or woman, at age of seventeen or eighteen, he will be in the army. It is obligatory. They are spending at least three years carrying guns and they are here, shooting our people in the occupied territory. And those who are not professional soldiers, after their service, they will be in reserves, up to the age of fifty-five. So give me one example in Israel of someone who is not military. They are all of them military!'

There was a perverted logic in his statement. Another Hamas leader, Mousa Abu Marzouk of Damascus, had said, 'There shouldn't be any distinction between an occupier in uniform or civilian dress. If a man dressed as a civilian carried a gun and took my house, my land, and my right, how can I say that he is a civilian and had nothing to do with it?'[1]

Now Mahmoud leaned back in his chair and softened his tone: 'Look, we are not admiring bloodshed. We are human beings who are suffering from seeing bloodshed. We are deeply suffering from frustration at not having any peaceful channel to achieve our goal. So we have no option. We have no alternative.'

I WAS SCHEDULED TO preach three times in less than twenty-four hours at the Gaza Baptist Church. The first meeting on Saturday night brought a full house, with even a few people standing at the back. Under the leadership of Pastor Hanna Massad, the church had grown significantly. 'I have not done it alone,' he said. He named several young leaders and emphasised, 'We are a ministry team. The Bible bookshop has had a strong evangelistic witness, and that has contributed to our growth.'

The results were impressive. There were two choirs, one for adults, another that included half a dozen children. The singing was enthusiastic, and Al and I were even able to join in when they sang 'Tell Me the Old, Old Story' and 'Oh, How I Love Jesus'. The pianist, who had suffered through the lean years, often turned to us and grinned as she pounded out the tunes. This sure was more fun and lively than when there were only a dozen attending services. Silently, I thanked God for reviving this congregation. *May this be part of Your Light Force in Gaza.*

At the Sunday morning service I felt led to preach on persecution. 'If there is no life in us, we will never be persecuted,' I said. To set up my message, I read from 2 Corinthians 3: '"You yourselves are our letter, written on our hearts, known and read by everybody. You show that you are a letter from Christ." We should all read the Bible. But we shouldn't expect non-Christians to read the Bible. We are the Bible non-Christians read. We are God's epistle, and everyone should read our lives.'

My primary text was 2 Corinthians 4:7–9: 'We have this treasure in jars of clay to show that this all-surpassing power is from God and not from us. We are hard pressed on every side, but not crushed; perplexed, but not in despair; persecuted, but not abandoned; struck down, but not destroyed.' Those were the verses highlighted on a blood-spattered page that I held up for the congregation to see. The words were in Russian, and the page was from the Bible of one of ten people killed in a church eight months earlier in Dushanbe, Tajikistan, by Muslim fundamentalists.

'There is a large suffering Church around the world,' I said. Over the years I had found that churches in difficult circumstances were encouraged to know that they were not the only ones struggling. 'A tree that has never been exposed to a storm is not strong.' As I spoke, we heard a roar outside the church building. Two F-16s were making a run over Gaza. 'We are persecuted but we do not lose heart. Your brothers throughout the world are suffering. But one part of the body takes care of the other.'

I reminded them of the story of Stephen in Acts and how his last words were of forgiveness. 'Forgiveness is the key that opens your enemy's heart. The Islamic world is looking at you to see how Christ is living in you. You may not win an argument, but will they see Jesus in you?'

During the social time after the service, a middle-aged man with a panicked look approached Al. With wide eyes and standing practically on Al's feet, he explained his desperate situation. 'Can you talk to the American embassy for me?'

'You are an American citizen?' Al asked.

'I have American passport. But not my wife and two children; they are not allowed to leave Gaza. How can I get them out?'

'I'm sure the embassy can help.'

'I'm not allowed to go there,' he said. 'They stop me at the border. I call and no one can help me. No one cares!'

We felt for this man who desperately wanted to escape Gaza with his family, but there was really nothing we could do to help him. I had heard similar heartrending stories. Once, when I had tried to intercede for twenty-seven Palestinians from Bethlehem with American passports at the American consulate in Jerusalem, I had been told by the consul, 'We treat Palestinians with American passports as we treat all Palestinians.' The implication was that there was no hope for these people. That was why so many left for good when they had the opportunity.

Before everyone left for home, Pastor Hanna called for our attention. Deeply moved, he invited the congregation to think about the church in Tajikistan that had lost ten members. 'I believe we should take up a collection for that church,' Hanna announced. 'Tonight we will have a special offering for our brothers and sisters.'

A T THE EVENING service, Pastor Hanna took that special offering. After I preached and we'd sung a hymn, Hanna, with a big grin on his face, called me to the front of the sanctuary and placed in my hand the proceeds of the offering. 'We want you to take this to our brothers and sisters who are suffering so much. It is $800. We want this to be a blessing to them.'

I was stunned. *This is too much!* I thought, knowing that many in the congregation were out of work – more than half of the residents of Gaza were unemployed, and the number was increasing rapidly. And yet these people had dug deep into their pockets and had lovingly given to another church they'd only heard about in a sermon. I was deeply moved and promised to deliver the gift.

ESCAPE FROM BETHLEHEM

Harderwijk, March 2002

The intifada intensified in early March 2002. Often I found myself glued to CNN or BBC news in my office, horrified by the sights from Israel and the West Bank. Every day there was another report of a suicide bombing attack or a Palestinian gunman shooting settlers, but the death toll among Palestinians was rising alarmingly – three times that of Israelis. There seemed to be no calm heads in the midst of the chaos.

North, in Beirut, Arab leaders met for a summit. Among the topics of discussion was a land for peace proposal from Crown Prince Abdullah of Saudi Arabia, promising Arab recognition of Israel if a Palestinian state was established. But several leaders didn't show. Yasser Arafat wasn't allowed to travel to the event, and Palestinians walked out of the meeting when Arafat was denied permission to address the leaders via a satellite link.

On 28 March a suicide bomber killed twenty-two during a Passover meal at a Netanya hotel. Ariel Sharon called up twenty thousand reservists. Tanks moved into Ramallah, surrounded Arafat's compound, and began bombarding. Soldiers stormed the Palestinian Authority offices and captured dozens of bureaucrats and security personnel. Arafat, proclaiming he would die rather than surrender, was trapped in a basement with his aides.

The suicide bombings continued – five in five days. The army was staging troops and equipment outside other West Bank cities, including Bethlehem and the adjoining towns of Beit Jala and Beit Sahour.

Bethlehem, March 2002

The rumbling of Apache helicopters, followed by loud explosions, jolted Bishara and Salwa out of their sleep. Bishara glanced at the clock. It was 1.00 am. He had just returned from a speaking tour of Singapore, and he was scheduled to leave on another trip soon. 'Please don't go!' his wife had urged him. The army had entered Bethlehem for several days while he was away, then retreated to the border of Jerusalem. The day before, two suicide bombers had struck in Haifa and Efrat. Everyone knew it was just a matter of time before Israel re-entered the town.

Bishara and Salwa tried to sleep, but it was impossible. They waited. They prayed. At 3.00 am a long line of tanks and armoured personnel carriers began rumbling down Jerusalem-Hebron Road. The whole building rattled and shook as each tank passed by. The vehicles were leaving the formation and making their presence felt on every street of the area. There was a sickening crunch as a tank squashed a car. In the distance, Bishara could hear big guns booming. All of the noise bounced off the surrounding walls and hills, magnifying the terror.

This invasion was more massive than any before. There was a sense of unbelief – how could this be happening in Bethlehem, the holy city for Christians all over the world? Just three years ago for the millennium celebration, it had received a beautiful face-lift. Now it was a war zone.

Bishara thought about his son, Sami, whose wife was expecting their first child – Bishara and Salwa's first grandchild. The baby was due any day. He could imagine the tanks rumbling past his son's apartment building. There was a possibility that the army might choose it as a good vantage point for their snipers, and then Sami and Rana would be trapped in their apartment. Bishara grabbed Salwa's hand, and she clutched his, no doubt thinking the same thoughts.

Prayer naturally poured out. 'Lord, please protect Sami and Rana and the child that she is carrying.' Then Bishara thought of the staff and students, scattered throughout the region, surely all experiencing the same sleepless fears and astonishment. Some of their homes would probably be searched. He started praying aloud for each of the faculty, staff, and students. Salwa's grip relaxed slightly as they poured out their hearts to the One who could calm their fears and bring resolution to the crisis.

One tank stopped directly in front of the college. Bishara froze, wondering whether or not he should get up and peer through a window. But if a soldier were looking his way, that could be dangerous. He could hear a loud squeal as the turret turned. It was probably aimed at the refugee camp across the street. He prayed for the residents there who were literally looking down the barrel of a gun.

Cloud cover delayed the arrival of daylight but not the arrival of F-16s, which buzzed low over the town. In the distance, from the vicinity of Manger Square, Bishara could hear an extended exchange of gunfire. During occasional lulls in the noise, he heard men shouting, children screaming, women yelling and crying in the neighbourhood. Bishara tried to switch on a light, but the power was out. When it was safe to venture outside, he would start up the generator. Not many in Bethlehem had generators, but Brother Andrew had insisted that it was needed to keep the ministry functioning and had made sure one was provided. Bishara tried the telephone – the line was dead. He was glad he had a mobile phone. He pulled out a portable radio and turned on the news.

Shortly after 7.00 the announcement was made that Bethlehem was a military zone. People were warned in the most severe terms to stay indoors. Anyone venturing out of his or her home would be shot. Soon afterward, the rain began. Even the sky was weeping, Bishara thought. His anger followed. Just what would be gained by such a show of force? How would depriving the people of food, electricity, water, and safe shelter prevent suicide attacks on Israel?

There was little to do during the day but listen to the continuous news reports. They said that the most intense fighting was in the narrow alleys around Manger Square. There were casualties, but no one knew how many. Bishara could hear the gunfire echoing through the stone streets no more than a mile away. A nun was reported shot as she tried to prevent soldiers from entering a convent to search for Palestinian resisters. A woman and her thirty-eight-year-old son were critically wounded and died waiting for an ambulance that never came.

Then the announcer reported that people had taken refuge in the Church of the Nativity, and several Palestinian gunmen had followed them inside to escape the Israeli sharpshooters. After several conflicting accounts, it was determined that more than two hundred men, women, children, and gunmen had taken sanctuary in the oldest church in Christendom. They were surrounded on all sides by tanks and soldiers ready to shoot anyone who moved outside the church's thick walls. That was the greatest shock of all. One of the most holy places for Christians was now under siege.

Bishara recalled how this church had been used as a sanctuary for those who felt their lives were in danger, most recently in 1967 during the Six Day War when Israel conquered Bethlehem. In the Bible, God provided 'cities of refuge'. In Numbers 35 it says that even a murderer could go to the city and be protected. Bishara felt the church was like a city of refuge, but unfortunately the presence of militia gunmen and their pursuit by Israeli soldiers endangered everyone.

Salwa took Bishara's hand and urged her husband to call their son. 'Please, find out how Rana is doing.'

It was evening, but Sami Awad couldn't relax. 'How often are the contractions coming?' he asked his wife while nervously pacing the cosy living room of their apartment.

'They are too far apart,' Rana answered. 'The doctor said this is false labour. Now, would you please sit down? You're making me nervous.'

Sami plopped down on the couch next to his wife, but he could hear the sound of tanks rolling just a couple of blocks away. In the distance there was an explosion, followed by the sound of machine-gun fire. His mind was racing. This was the most serious invasion he'd seen, and it didn't look like the Israeli army would be leaving soon. The main checkpoint along the Jerusalem-Hebron Road was closed. The entire area was under twenty-four-hour curfew. He figured that within twenty-four to forty-eight hours all other roads out of Bethlehem would be blocked. And his first child was due any moment.

Sami jumped to his feet and went to the bedroom. As he grabbed a suitcase, he yelled, 'We need to get out of here *now*! We're not going to risk being trapped in our apartment when you go into labour. Our child is going to be born in a hospital.'

Rana shifted her weight and struggled to her feet. 'We can't go to the hospital now. They'll send us home.'

'Call Alex and Brenda.' Alex was Sami's uncle, his father's brother. Alex and his wife lived just beyond the border of Bethlehem, in a suburb of Jerusalem. 'They said we could use the lower level of their apartment for as long as we need.'

After Rana talked with Brenda, she said, 'I'm calling your parents too.'

'Tell them to pray hard!' Sami said as he shut a suitcase.

A few minutes later, the car was packed. As an added measure of protection, Sami took blue electrician's tape and taped a large 'TV' on the hood. This way, if they ran into a patrol, they might be allowed to pass as members of the press. And it wasn't really a lie, for he had done some filming for documentaries with his organisation, the Holy Land Trust.

The streets were empty. Sami stayed off the main roads. There was a nervous moment as he crossed over the Jerusalem-Hebron Road and noticed a military jeep in the distance. Fortunately, it was driving away from them. Heading north into Beit Jala, he took the narrow side streets, his side-view mirrors nearly scraping the walls on some of the turns. Before reaching the top of the hill that marked the northern border of Beit Jala, Sami turned onto a rocky dirt road that wound through the valley between Gilo and Beit Jala. It was a dangerous place because of the frequent shooting between the two communities. Rana winced as the car rolled awkwardly over the numerous bumps, and Sami slowed down to a crawl as they started climbing another hill that would take them into Jerusalem.

It was an agonisingly slow trip, but the rugged terrain and his wife's discomfort made it impossible to go any faster. Sami thought about Mary and Joseph riding on a donkey, trying to hide the baby Jesus from the evil eyes of Herod's army. His Holy Land Trust sponsored a special children's programme in Bethlehem on the day designated by the Church to remember the Slaughter of the Innocents. Two thousand years ago, troops had entered Bethlehem from all corners to search for and kill the potential baby 'terrorist' who was someday going to lead a revolt against King Herod. Now Israeli army troops were entering from all corners into Bethlehem in order to root out terrorist cells.

As the narrow dirt road emptied into a back street of Jerusalem, he saw an army jeep and three soldiers motioning for him to stop. Sami wondered how Mary and Joseph would have handled this situation. No doubt they would have hidden the baby Jesus. But Sami wanted the soldiers to see his wife, nine months pregnant. Maybe they would have compassion.

'May I see your papers,' the soldier said as Sami rolled down his car window and handed the man his US passport.

Another soldier ordered him out of the car. 'Take your jacket off!' Sami slowly removed his coat jacket while two soldiers were pointing their rifles at him. 'Open your shirt!' Sami unbuttoned his shirt and lifted his undershirt so the soldier could see his skin and realise that he was no threat.

'I am an American citizen,' Sami said as he held up his arms, making sure not to make any sudden movements. 'My pregnant wife is ready to deliver our first child. I am taking her to the hospital.'

'Where is your wife's passport?' asked the first soldier as he waved Sami's passport at him.

'She doesn't have one yet.'

With a smirk, the soldier sarcastically said, 'Then you may pass, but she cannot.'

Sami stared at the guns pointed at him. There was no way to argue with them. He would simply have to find another way of escape.

As Rana prayed, Sami weighed his options. Obviously all the main streets would be blocked. There were other back roads, but there was a greater chance of being trapped farther away from their destination in Jerusalem. The most direct route was the tunnel road that passed under Beit Jala to Gilo. It was a challenge getting there, and he would likely be stopped, but he figured the worst that could happen was that the soldiers would make them turn back.

As he merged onto the busy road, he entered a long line of cars and trucks backed up at the checkpoint. The soldiers had ordered the occupants of one car out and were doing a thorough inspection. Impatient drivers were honking their horns. Obviously Israeli drivers didn't want to be personally inconvenienced by security procedures, and the soldiers were feeling the pressure. Finally, they cleared the car they were inspecting and sent it off. Eager to ease the traffic jam, they waved the next few cars through, including Sami's. They were now safely in Jerusalem!

The next morning, as Rana slept, Sami and his uncle watched via satellite an international news station. The previous night, while Sami and his wife were escaping, another pregnant Palestinian woman was forced to have her child in a car near a new army checkpoint established a short distance from Bethlehem Children's Hospital. The Israeli soldiers had refused her passage. The child had died. Sami and Alex wept.

I T TOOK SEVERAL days for me to reach Bishara by telephone. 'Absolute fear has taken over the city,' he told me. 'We are not allowed to leave our homes or even look out the windows.' Obviously the college was closed and they had no idea when it would reopen. Besides Bishara and Salwa, Doris, a volunteer from Germany, was the only other person in the compound, helping take care of the facilities.

As long as the siege continued at the Church of the Nativity, no one was moving within Bethlehem. 'Would you like to come speak at graduation?' Bishara said with a twinkle in his voice. 'I don't know when it will be, but we would love to have you!'

'I will plan to come as soon as you tell me,' I said, grateful that my friend was able to find a little humour in the midst of such chaos.

'Of course, if this lasts too long, we may have to cancel the semester.' Then he changed the subject. 'You know any day now, Salwa and I are going to be grandparents. Sami and Rana managed to escape a couple of days ago. They are staying with Alex and Brenda.'

'Congratulations. I hope this ends soon, so you can be with them.'

'My son was very brave getting out the way he did.' There was a sigh on the phone, then Bishara said, 'It's very tough here.

Several people we know have had their homes ransacked. The soldiers destroy everything, supposedly searching for terrorists. But it's so mean. They'll empty food supplies – sugar, flour, rice, wheat, everything – onto the floor so they cannot be used. Many buildings and homes have been completely destroyed. Ambulances are shot at, and people die because they cannot reach the hospital.'

'I wish I could be with you.'

'We have received many e-mails and phone calls. People are praying for us, and that keeps us going. Many Messianic Jews have sent food and medical aid. God is good and He will never forsake the people that have accepted His Son.'

'Hold onto that hope, my friend. And as soon as you let me know, I'll come to be with you.'

On 5 April Layaar Awad was born in a Jerusalem hospital. Sami and Rana rejoiced as the baby girl received wonderful care from the staff of doctors and nurses. But they couldn't help but think also of their friends in Bethlehem and other West Bank cities now under military control. As Sami held his wife's hand and gazed at their child, sleeping peacefully next to Rana, he said, 'I want to dedicate Layaar to the memory of all the children killed in both Palestine and Israel.' Rana squeezed his hand, tears forming in her eyes. Sami closed his eyes and prayed aloud: 'I pray that the message of the Prince of Peace will again be a light from Bethlehem to all corners of the world.'

THIRTY-TWO

MIRACLE IN HOLLAND

Voorthuizen, The Netherlands, April 2002

Salim Munayer looked around the room at the conference centre of Near-East Ministry (NEM). Pastors and church leaders with their families – ninety-four people – had been flown out of the war zone that was currently Israel and the West Bank, courtesy of NEM with help from Open Doors. Daily international news was reporting the Israeli army's incursions into West Bank after a spate of suicide bombings. Tanks patrolled Bethlehem. Curfews had been imposed on Hebron. Fierce resistance faced the Israeli army in the Jenin refugee camp.

Many considered it a miracle that this meeting was taking place. Because of the conditions in Israel, it was virtually impossible for Palestinians and Jews to meet inside the country. It took much prayer and negotiation to gain permission for these few men, with their wives and children, to leave the country and meet in a neutral location for five days. Now there was tension in the air. Palestinians sat on one side, Jewish believers on the other. Children were being led in a special programme elsewhere on the compound, allowing their parents to concentrate on the hard work ahead.

Lord, will You break down the barriers this week? Salim prayed. This conference could stimulate a process of reconciliation that could lead to healing and genuine peace for the war-torn region. Salim took a deep breath and stepped to the front of the room. After welcoming the group, he got right to the point: 'We are two nations living in one house. We share the living room, the kitchen, the corridor, the bathroom, the toilet, but not the bedroom. The fact is we do not like one another. Worse still, we hate one another.'

There was no sense avoiding the obvious, but he needed to establish the framework for their time together. Salim had prayed long and hard about the words that followed: 'Scholars engaged in studying and evaluating conflict between groups have observed certain phenomena that can help us understand hatred and prejudice. One is the division between *us* and *them*. Each side blames the other, saying that they have lost all moral and ethical standards. We are able to understand our own group and recognise its good qualities while overlooking our shortcomings, because it is important to distinguish between us (who are right and good and merciful) and them (who are evil and wrong).

'A second problem is the failure to see plurality within the other side. We generalise and stereotype the other, saying things like, "They all hate us and want to kill us." We are unable to see them as individuals with unique feelings and thoughts. Due to the language barrier, Israelis and Palestinians do not read each other's newspapers. Thus each side is dependent on very selective information given about the other side.

'Third is the problem of moral superiority. Thus we decide that *we* are more peace loving, trustworthy, and honest, and we view with contempt those who have different values.

'And last, there is the perception by each side that they are victims, and thus they are unable to see themselves as a threat to the other. If we are victims, then we cannot be the victimisers. The victims' mentality causes us to be blind to the others' pain, aspirations, and needs.

'These trends are obstacles in the process of reconciliation. However, this week, we have a wonderful opportunity to break through these barriers and recognise that each person, whether Jew or Palestinian, is created in the image of God and redeemed by the blood of the Messiah. Paul instructs us on how to treat one another: "Be devoted to one another in brotherly love. Honour one another above yourselves . . . Bless those who persecute you; bless and do not curse . . . Do not repay anyone evil for evil . . . Do not take revenge, my friends, but leave room for God's wrath . . . Do not be overcome by evil, but overcome evil with good." '[1]

The process of reconciliation began with worship. David Loden, the founding elder of Beit Asaf, a Messianic congregation in Netanya, played guitar and led the singing. Jack Sara, pastor of the Palestinian Jerusalem Alliance Church, assisted on the keyboard. There was a selection of hymns and praise songs in both Arabic and Hebrew, with phonetics provided for those who didn't speak the language. Some of the choruses were sung in English, which most of the participants understood.

David and Lisa Loden, originally from North America, had lived in Israel for nearly thirty years. In 1978 they had helped form a Messianic congregation in Netanya, a city on the Mediterranean coast twenty-one miles north of Tel Aviv. At that time they knew of only five such congregations in Israel worshipping in Hebrew. Five years later Evan Thomas from New Zealand joined them in the work, and the congregation became known as Beit Asaf. Today the body in Netanya was thriving, and there were between eighty and one hundred Messianic congregations throughout Israel.[2] David, a composer and teacher of music, along with Lisa had helped create indigenous music for this movement.

While the Netanya congregation was friendly with Arab believers, the idea of participating in a reconciliation effort like this had never occurred to the Lodens until David had what he calls a vision. 'It was in the form of a question,' he told his wife. 'The Lord asked me if I loved Him. Of course, my answer was "Yes, I love You." Then He began to go down a list. "Do you love My children?" "Yes, I love Your children." "Do you love all My children?" I thought of all the wonderful people we know around the world. "Yes, of course!" Then He said, "Do you love My Arab children?" I thought of the Arab brothers and sisters in Israel, in congregations in the north – they'd speak to our congregation; we'd speak to their congregations. "Yes, I do." Then He said, "How about My Palestinian children?" He specifically used the word *Palestinian*. I told Him, "Lord, that's different. They don't believe about the Bible as we do. They don't believe as we do about Israel or end-times prophecies. And besides, you know they are our enemies." Even as the words came out of my mouth, I was flooded with a feeling of shame and betrayal.'

Shortly after that dramatic encounter, David received a call from Salim Munayer of Bethlehem Bible College, asking him to come and resurrect the school choir and teach a music course. David considered it a strange request. 'Practically next door in Jerusalem, there are at least fifteen or twenty musically skilled people who could do this,' he explained. 'I live in Netanya, at least a two-hour drive to Bethlehem.'

'I've asked everyone I can think of,' Salim answered. 'No one is willing to come.'

At that moment David realised that God was testing him. Would he obey God's revelation? It was practically unheard of for an Israeli to stay overnight in the West Bank to serve a Palestinian institution. Yet shortly after that call, he began driving over to Bethlehem every Sunday afternoon, directing the choir on Sunday evenings, and teaching a class Monday mornings. It soon became the highlight of his week. Involvement in Musalaha logically followed soon after.

For Jack Sara, cooperating with David Loden was an even greater miracle. As he accompanied hymns and choruses on a keyboard, he couldn't help but recall his encounters with Israeli soldiers during the first intifada. He was only fourteen years old when he was picked up in the old city of Jerusalem, where he lived in the Christian quarter. The soldiers had questioned him roughly and beaten him for participation in a demonstration, which he had not attended. By the time he was released and limped back to his home, he'd decided, *If I'm going to get arrested and beaten, then I'm going to be darn sure it's for something I've done!*

Jack was part of the next demonstration – throwing rocks at soldiers, painting graffiti on walls, and waving the Palestinian flag. Shortly after that he joined the Communist party. He lost count of the number of times he went to prison over the next three years, but the last one was the longest – three months. Lying on a thin, lumpy mattress, he tried to make some sense of his life. What was he accomplishing with this cycle of protests and shouting insults at soldiers, arrests, and imprisonments, then release to repeat the process? Surely there was more to life than that!

As he thought about his life, he realised he'd become disgusted with the man lying on that mattress. Nominally he was a Catholic, but many of the Muslims he knew lived morally better lives than he did. He was smoking two packs of cigarettes a day and drinking every chance he could. If he was really going to help others, he needed to put his own life in order.

After his release, he heard about a man named Yohanna. One of his neighbours told him, 'Yohanna is a cultist.'

'What do you mean?' Jack asked.

'He doesn't believe like us Catholics.'

Two days later Jack ran into Yohanna and insisted boldly, 'I want to talk to you.' Yohanna and his roommate, Labib Madanat, met with the teenager in their apartment and told him the good news about Jesus Christ. Jack was ready for a new start. On the night of 10 August 1991, not far from where Nicodemus met Jesus in this same city, Jack Sara was born again.

'So now what?' he said to the two men. 'I want to study. I want to learn. And I want to help my people.'

Soon Jack became a student at Bethlehem Bible College. And what did Jack gain from the college? Years later he explained to Al that he had learned a 'Christian worldview'. 'You need to understand that 98 per cent of Palestinians are Muslim. When we go to school, our teachers are Muslim. The curriculum is written by Muslims. The majority of our classmates are Muslim. Our newspapers are oriented towards Muslims. So without realising it, Palestinian/Arab Christians are very much influenced by Islamic thinking and Palestinian movements, and church attendance isn't enough to overcome that. At Bethlehem Bible College, we are confronted with a biblical worldview. That was when I started really studying the Bible and understanding who God is and therefore how to view life.'

I FELT I WAS on holy ground. Johan Companjen and I were among the guests invited for an open meeting on the last night of this historic gathering. Our brothers and sisters had spent three days in private meetings, doing the hard work of getting to know each other, confessing their sins, and seeking to experience the oneness that Christ prayed for His Church. David Loden, who looked like a biblical patriarch with his bald pate and full, white beard, spoke to us from the Jewish perspective: 'We're here because we've made a mess of things in our country. I came to realise that I cannot love God and at the same time hate my brother. God showed me that I'm responsible for my brothers. Palestinians, just like Jews, are sons of Adam and Abraham. They're my brothers. However, in the last year, so much has happened in our country and we're all so wounded. We realise that we need healing and rest. We're getting that here. This is a time of healing for us and our children.'

Alex Awad, Bishara's younger brother and pastor of a multinational Baptist congregation in Jerusalem, addressed us from the Palestinian perspective. 'Jesus left the comfort and luxury of heaven and became a man, came down to earth. In order to achieve reconciliation, we too will have to be prepared to leave our "comfort zone" and find our brothers and sisters with whom we have difficulties, to discuss things and put them right. This is the commandment Jesus gives us in Matthew 5:23–24: "If you are offering your gift at the altar and there remember that your brother has something against you, leave your gift there in front of the altar. First go and be reconciled to your brother; then come and offer your gift." We are here this week to do that hard work of reconciliation with our brothers.'

There was a time of worship that concluded with all of us singing a new song, written by Lisa Loden several years before after a painful break in a relationship with a sister. The song was sung in English, Hebrew, and Arabic:

He is our peace; we shall be one.
He is our reconciliation.
The wall of partition He's broken down.
He is our peace; we shall be one.

Salim had asked me to say a few words to the crowd. I felt inadequate as he introduced me, telling them about witnessing one of my talks to Hamas nine years before, adding, 'Andrew certainly preached the gospel to them. And we pleaded with them to stop their terrorist activities.'

I knew what Hamas needed – they needed the Good News of Jesus Christ. What did this audience need? Not a sermon but certainly a word of encouragement.

'Today we are witnessing a foretaste of the real solution to the Middle East conflict,' I said. 'The wall that was built to keep people and nations apart has come down here in a mighty demonstration of the power of God. And as dedicated Christians, our reaction is: If God can do this to a few dozen people, He can do it to a million people.'

Yes, I really believed that. Why did this beautiful picture have to be limited to a few brave people? There had to be a way for people to see this picture and for it to grow to include hundreds, then thousands and more. 'Oh, that our hearts may be gripped by the potential power of Jesus to bring people together: Israelis and Palestinians, Christians in the West and in the East, starting where we should have been all the time – at the foot of the cross. There is only one Name given under heaven whereby we must be saved, and that includes saved from violence and terrorism, hatred and revenge. God has already taken the initiative and now calls all of us to follow. Yes, we've discovered the principle of God's solution. Now we must continue and work hard to see this Musalaha concept become a movement – like a mighty river, a flood not just a trickle!'

As I sat down, I realised that moments like this were what kept me going, even though I was pushing seventy-five and people were saying it was time to slow down. I wanted to shout 'Why resort to human resources and solutions when God offered Himself as the solution?'

Of course, a single meeting wasn't going to solve the problem, even with this group of leaders. A lot more work was needed and Salim said that there were plans for this group to continue meeting, whenever conditions in Israel and West Bank allowed. One of his hopes was that this group of pastors and Church leaders would study the Scriptures together, especially the difficult themes that separated them, such as passages dealing with prophecy and the land.

I prayed that these men and women would indeed continue to meet and demonstrate to Jews and Palestinians that real peace was found at the foot of the cross.

WHAT DO YOU PREACH
WHEN THERE IS SHELLING?

Bethlehem, April 2002

Every two or three days, curfew was lifted in Bethlehem for a few hours to allow people to get food and medical supplies. Unfortunately, that did not apply to 250 families living in the immediate vicinity of Manger Square. They were prisoners in their homes while the army surrounded the ancient church, shining bright lights at night, blaring loud announcements day or night, posting snipers above the walls ready to shoot anyone who moved. The streets leading to the square were littered with crushed cars, broken glass, and empty bullet shells. Broken pipes spewed water. Doors of shops were broken down and the shelves ransacked. Many buildings had been hit by artillery shells and left to burn, firefighters unable to get near enough to do their job. Bullets had damaged the walls of the church. Nerves were frayed, and no one knew when this nightmare would end.

Bishara tried to make contact with all of his students and staff. His secretary, Alison, and her husband and three daughters were typical of families who were going stir crazy in their homes. However, no one dared leave. 'Yesterday our neighbour was shot to death in his car as he returned from the market,' she told Bishara by mobile phone. Her husband, George, had made the same trip one day earlier. 'We thought the curfew was lifted. We don't always know because it's not always announced. Israeli snipers are positioned in a building above us.'

The family survived by watching television when power was available. There was twenty-four-hour news coverage, but when that became too much to endure, they switched to old movies or American sitcom reruns.

Alison's husband was nearing despair. He had been unable to go to work for a month and was recalling every humiliating experience he'd ever endured from the Israelis – the rude young soldiers who screamed at him at the checkpoint; the settlers who pointed their guns at him and his mother and siblings as they farmed their land; the military judge who had dismissed the legitimacy of their ownership of the farm; the soldier who had grabbed his younger brother by the neck; the captain who had refused to give him permission to go to Beer Sheva for his daughter's open-heart surgery. On and on it went. Memories of these humiliations seemed to make his worries more unbearable. Where would he get money for next month's food and water and electricity and rent and school fees?[1]

This was a Christian family simply trying to live a decent life while dealing with their constantly escalating frustration and anger. They wouldn't take desperate measures, like some in the militant Islamic groups, but somehow they had to manage their emotions. How much longer could they endure the pressure? Multiply that by hundreds and hundreds of families. Bishara knew he had to find a way to help people caught in this maelstrom. All he could do for the moment was send e-mails and make phone calls. Several organisations had committed to providing funds to help the Shepherd's Society, the relief arm of Bethlehem Bible College that Bishara had formed. It would aid families that were suffering the most, but right now they couldn't even reach those families.

As days turned into weeks, Bishara tried to keep busy. Because the garden was below street level, and cordoned off by a high wall, he was able to get out with Salwa and Doris and do some gardening. He wrote to his friends that there were a few 'good points' to being confined to one's home for weeks on end:

You have more time to pray and read the Word of God.

You sleep late.

You can enjoy your breakfast and you don't have to rush to work.

You can help your wife put away all the winter things and get ready for summer.

You can fix up things around the house – and I enjoyed that.

You can catch up on your letters.

Bethlehem, May 2002

The siege at the Church of the Nativity ended after thirty-nine days. The negotiated settlement sent thirteen men into deportation. Several more men were shipped to Gaza. The rest, who were simply caught trying to take shelter during the fighting, were allowed to return to their homes.

Two men from Open Doors went immediately to Bethlehem as soon as the army pulled out. Their written report touched me deeply. While the sights were appalling, the heartrending stories hurt much more. One family near the Church of the Nativity spent six weeks in their bedroom, not daring to move their heads above the level of the window for fear of being shot. Another couple had tanks parked next to their home for two weeks. 'We stayed inside for two weeks, eating what food we had once per day.'

One widow with two children to care for showed the men the ruins of her home just a few yards from Manger Square. She and her children had fled at the beginning of the fighting and, because of the siege, had not been able to go back. All the windows were broken and dust and dirt blew into the house. There wasn't a piece of furniture left intact. Her belongings were piled in one corner and the floor was filthy. On one wall there was a Syrian Orthodox Church calendar, the only picture not damaged. In the kitchen the sink and all the fittings had been torn out of the wall. 'Look at my refrigerator,' she said. 'It's new. I saved for months to buy it.' It stood in a corner, the doors bent open, the glass shelves broken, the inside stained by the food that had rotted during the weeks they were gone.

After walking through town and witnessing the devastation, the staff members met with several local pastors. While these men tried to minister to their flocks, they also were dealing with their own anger and frustration. 'Where is the Church worldwide?' said one. 'Where is the Christian world? How can they turn a blind eye?' Another said, 'While they were holding the main Christian population of Palestine hostage, what did the Church in the West do?'

What pastor has been trained to minister in such conditions? 'What do you preach when there is shelling and guns?' asked one, 'or when a member of my church rings me up on my mobile phone and says, "Please pray. There are Israelis in my house", or "My daughter is sick, and the ambulance won't come because of the fighting"?'

The report concluded, 'The last forty days have been a crushing blow to the Church – the worst in fifty years. It has been the culminating knockout punch to a Christian population reeling from twenty months of suffering during the most recent intifada. The continual fighting has frightened away the tourists, and many people have lost their jobs.' One person told our two staff workers: 'Twenty months without work is humiliating. I used to have some money, but now all is gone.' Said his pastor: 'Multiply that by thousands, and you have the story of Bethlehem.'

How indeed does one minister in such turmoil? These people were deeply scarred emotionally. According to the Open Doors staff, the first consequence would be many people leaving the country: 'The steady bleeding of emigration will turn into a haemorrhage. The consequence of lack of work and the continual insecurity means that people have no hope for the future. They see only one possibility – to leave and go to the United States or Australia or . . .'

But even in this darkness, there were glimmers of light. Through humanitarian aid, the door was open to reaching the local Muslim population. I read in the report: 'Late one evening some brothers from the Bible Society visited a Muslim family with a box of food. As they received the food, the people broke down and cried.'

As one Bethlehem pastor put it, 'We are trying to be the light in the midst of darkness, but you must keep the oil burning.'

How could we, the Church in the West, help our brothers in the Bethlehem area? Surely we had to respond quickly and substantially. 'We can start by helping to meet some of their physical needs,' said one of the staff when he returned from the trip. 'The Shepherd's Society wants to help seven thousand Christian families. There is an urgent need for medicines and food for those who have lost everything, and they need to hire local people to help distribute the relief.'

Within days Open Doors announced a project called Compass-ion Now. The goal was to raise $500,000 as quickly as possible to provide emergency relief in the form of food and medicine, plus subsidies to pay delinquent utility bills. Some of the funds would go to expanding a trauma-intervention counselling programme, particularly for children and youth who had been emotionally and psychologically traumatised.

I couldn't help but think of the words of Jesus in Matthew 25 about the judgment where the sheep were separated from the goats. I had preached on this passage at Islamic University in Gaza. To the sheep Jesus said, 'I was hungry and you gave me something to eat, I was thirsty and you gave me something to drink.' Jesus had said those recipients are His brothers and sisters; therefore, 'You did it for Me.' These Christians in Bethlehem were certainly more my brothers and sisters than the Hamas I visited in south Lebanon. How much more should we work to reach out to them in their time of need?

BISHARA'S INVITATION TO speak at graduation was fulfilled in mid-July, more than a month later than planned. Invitations were sent indicating that if there was a curfew on the designated day, the ceremony would occur on the next day when the curfew was lifted. I made a quick trip to Tel Aviv. One of Bishara's friends snuck me into Bethlehem where we waited three days for the curfew to lift. When the announcement came early one morning that there would be a six-hour reprieve, phone calls were quickly made and announcements scrolled along the bottom of local television screens. That day, fifteen new Christian leaders graduated, ready to begin their service in the Light Force.

THIRTY-FOUR

THE LIGHT IS A
LITTLE BRIGHTER

Gaza, December 2002

Frustrated trying to manoeuvre through crowded intersections with no traffic lights, our taxi driver took his chances on the winding, potholed, dirt back roads and alleys of Gaza City. But three blocks from our destination, he again faced the gridlocked main street. Horns blared with no effect. The driver shook his head and muttered, 'Ramadan'. Directly ahead women flocked to a large open-air market to buy food and gifts for Eid al-Fitr, the biggest Muslim holiday of the year, which celebrated the end of the month of fasting.

Seeing an open lane, the driver wound through the traffic and sped up a hill past the stalled lines. With horror we realised that this lane was for vehicles going in the opposite direction. Fortunately, we emerged at the top of the hill without meeting any oncoming cars. Then we turned in front of the three lines of cars onto a narrow side street, passed a large cemetery, and turned into the complex where our apartment building was located. Only later did we realise that this street was marked 'One Way', and we were going in the wrong direction.

The apartment building was part of the Baptist compound but

had seen little use since the start of the second intifada more than two years ago. Al and I were allowed to stay for just ten dollars a night. 'Remember, this is Ramadan,' the landlord said. 'If you go out before sundown, don't eat or drink anything in public. While we're not under their religious laws, such insensitivity would cause problems.'

Al and I went to our rooms to unpack. Suddenly, there was a loud explosion, and the concussion made our building shake. Two more explosions followed in rapid succession. Al hurried onto the balcony and saw several people, hands blocking their eyes from the sun, looking up at three Apache helicopters high in the sky, headed back to Israel. A woman from the apartment below us looked into the air, then up at Al and said, 'Welcome to Gaza!'

PASTOR HANNA PICKED us up at 4.00. Traffic had subsided by then. The women were home cooking, and most men had left work early for the much-anticipated feast. Al and I asked Hanna about the explosions. He explained that the gunships had attacked the Department of Health, killing one man and wounding five. 'Usually they don't bomb during the day,' Hanna said as he drove us to a downtown restaurant. 'They probably had intelligence that the man they wanted was in that office.' Then he added, 'Last night an Israeli helicopter flew just above our home all night. It was hard to sleep and very intimidating.' We were quickly beginning to experience the stress of daily life in Gaza.

Every table in the restaurant was set, each with an array of salads and stacks of pita bread. By 4.30 every seat was occupied. People talked quietly, but no one so much as touched any of the food or water. A television was on in the corner, and the proprietor watched for official notice that the sun had set and the final fast of Ramadan could be broken. The word came at 4.42, and immediately everyone began eating. A waiter came by, giving us a choice of whole chicken or kebabs of lamb or chicken. There were more than twenty people at our long table. Some were members of the Baptist church. Others worked either in a refugee camp or for a

Muslim relief agency. Together we were celebrating a partnership that had brought relief to 5,500 families in nearby refugee camps.

W E HAD DESSERT and coffee at Hanna's home. His wife, Suhad, welcomed us warmly when we entered the apartment. Shortly after we had seen them last year in Gaza, she had gone to Jordan to visit family. When it was time to return, she had been refused re-entry into Gaza. There followed ten agonising months seeking a visa. 'Even though they knew that she's married to a pastor, they still don't want to give her permission to come,' Hanna said. 'I think they were putting pressure on us to leave.'

'To leave Gaza?' I asked.

'That's what I believe.' Hanna had applied three times for the visa for his wife to return to Gaza. Three times it was rejected. Finally, he filed a petition with the Supreme Court of Israel. 'If the court had said no, I had my luggage ready to go and live in Jordan. We thought that we cannot live like this. It's been very painful, very difficult. My mother and two sisters have muscular dystrophy and need a lot of help. So you're torn between your wife and your mother, two sisters, and your church.'

'A terrible dilemma. Is there no compassion?' At that time Gaza was autonomous, under the control of the PA. Still, Israel restricted the citizens of Gaza from returning to their homes.

'Once I had a meeting with the Israeli ambassador in Jordan. There were a lot of people writing on our behalf to the ambassador. He said, "We're getting very tired of people writing to us about Suhad." Suhad hated going to the embassy because of the way they treated her. It was like you were begging.'

Fortunately, the Supreme Court ruled in Suhad's favour. 'How long can she stay now?' Al asked.

'Seven months. She can stay longer, but if she leaves to go see her family, then there is no assurance that she will be allowed back.'

I thought about the pressure this man was under. He relied heavily on his wife, and Suhad was an integral part of his ministry. As we enjoyed fruit and ice cream, I said, 'Please tell us how the church is doing now.'

'We minister to about 150 throughout the week.'

'They don't all come on Sunday?' Al asked for clarification.

'We have Sunday morning service at 10.30 and Sunday evening at 4.30. And through the week, almost every day, we have a meeting. Monday we have meetings for new believers and new leaders. We have a women's meeting on Tuesday, and youth ages twelve to eighteen on Thursday. Friday we have "Sunday school", ages five to twelve [Friday is the day off for most people in Gaza]. Saturday we work with university students. We also have several other meetings outside the church. We've held leadership training for PA leaders. We believe this is a good way to reach out to the community. We'll be starting another group soon.'

I thought of the church, barely breathing when I visited it six years earlier. Now it was thriving and reaching out into the community. The light was definitely a little brighter.

THE FIRST CALLS to prayer started shortly before 4.00 in the morning, and since this was a holiday, there were special services at all the mosques. Loudspeakers broadcast these services for all who were not dedicated enough to rise and attend. The noise made it impossible to sleep, so Al finally got up to make us coffee. The cacophony of preachers and chanters made it difficult to concentrate as we read our Bibles. We particularly noted when what sounded like a young boy took over chanting for a few minutes at one mosque. His high-pitched voice repeated, '*Allahu, Akbar; Allahu, Akbar*' or 'God is greater!' over and over, with particular emphasis on the next-to-last syllable.

From Psalm 80, Al read, 'O LORD God Almighty, how long will your anger smoulder against the prayers of your people? You have fed them with the bread of tears; you have made them drink tears by the bowlful. You have made us a source of contention to our neighbours, and our enemies mock us.'

As the last notes from the mosques died away at 7.30, we observed that the words of the psalm described many of the prayers of Muslims, Jews, and Christians. People call out in distress, 'Abba, Father.' The Muslims cannot know God as Father. They call out to Allah, 'the hearing one' but without knowing if He will answer their prayers. We wondered if that was the reason for the monotonous repetition we'd heard that morning – that they hoped perhaps to be answered because of their many words. But God has set us free and brought us into a personal relationship with Himself! That was the message the Church somehow needed to convey to Gaza.

After a light breakfast of apples and toast, we took a walk in the neighbourhood. Immediately outside the apartment compound, we noticed an empty lot filled with plastic chairs. At the gate stood a proud man dressed in a freshly pressed black suit with a red flower pinned on his lapel. Men from the neighbourhood were coming by to pay their respects. The two foreigners were conspicuous. 'Please, come in!' the man said, standing erect and proud at the entrance to the mourning tent. 'My son died on 28 Ramadan.' That was three days earlier. We couldn't determine how he died because as we took seats of honour, the man, a huge smile on his face, said, 'My son died as a martyr and is now in paradise. Please, become Muslims! It is so wonderful!'

For the next few minutes, he preached a sermon to us as passionate as that of any evangelist. The guests around him nodded their heads in agreement. Someone poured us a glass of juice, another offered us dates, and a third passed a dish of candy. As we accepted the refreshments, the man continued exhorting: 'Allah is the only answer. Not Bush, not Arafat, not Europe or the United States. Only Allah!'

When it was polite to leave, we warmly shook hands with the father, again offering our condolences. As we continued on our walk, we discussed whether we would be so proud and bold in our witness three days after one of our sons had died. This man told us that his son was in paradise because he had died as a 'martyr'. This man's faith was absolute. He had staked his life on that. How many Christians were just as certain of their faith? What about the local believers in Gaza? Without a similar faith and passion, how could they hope to be heard among the million-plus Muslims?

WE DROVE ALONG the Mediterranean Sea south towards one of the refugee camps. It was sad to see no one enjoying the beautiful beach. Numerous little beachside cafes, some with umbrellas up over their tables, were closed. Portions of the sand were disfigured by barbed-wire defences. This could be a wonderful tourist spot; instead it was a war zone. We parked at the headquarters of a Muslim NGO (non-governmental organisation) that was responsible for coordinating relief efforts in the area. The Baptist church was working with them to distribute food to the neediest families. The director, Khalid, explained that this was a small NGO. 'All who work here are volunteers,' he said. 'All of this is for God. Our friends at the Baptist church are a big help.'

'Do people come to you for help, or do you seek them out?' Al asked.

'Our volunteers seek them out.'

'They tell us who needs help,' Hanna added. 'Some NGOs discriminate. This one is honest and help is based on real need. We like to make a connection with the family and deliver the food and meat coupons ourselves.'

As we drove just a few minutes to Deir el Ballah (Camp of the Palm), Hanna showed us one of the coupons he would be giving to the families. On the top was a Scripture verse. The coupon stated that this was a gift from Gaza Baptist Church. We parked at the entrance to a dirt alleyway with a cement block wall on one side and ramshackle homes on the other. Green Arabic graffiti was prominent on the wall. Some of it was covered by a laundry line loaded with children's clothing. Several boys were playing next to a truck and they cheerfully said, 'Hello', and gathered around the foreign visitors.

Al pulled out his digital camera, and the boys drew around me for a photo. Then they eagerly looked at the picture on the little screen, talking excitedly. Later I saw in the picture that one of the boys had a toy pistol inadvertently pointed at my head. After that, everywhere we went throughout the camp, I noticed that most of the boys had toy pistols or machine guns. They were constantly dodging behind cars and playacting gun fights with their 'enemies'.

The first home we visited was actually a compound consisting of several rooms. Hanna explained that several brothers had combined their families and resources, living all together. There was a total of sixty-five people. Boys slept in one room, girls in another. Both dormitories were extremely neat, with sleeping pads piled high in one corner so the space could be used in other ways during the day.

The couple we visited invited us into their room, where the only furniture was a bed and a wooden cupboard. Cushions on the hard-packed dirt floor were used for sitting. On one wall there hung a carpet and a few hooks for coats. Two small family pictures and a digital clock stuck at 12.02 provided the only other decoration. The room was neat and extremely clean. 'Did they know we were coming?' Al asked Hanna.

'No, we never announce what families we will visit.'

The couple sat close to each other on the edge of their bed while we sat on the floor cushions. Hanna offered them the bag of groceries, plus a coupon that could be redeemed for two kilos of meat from a nearby butcher. The man was grateful. While his wife got up and left the room, he explained in Arabic, with Hanna translating for us, that he had two wives and eleven children. His oldest son was sixteen years old; his youngest was four. He'd been out of work for more than two years, and so his oldest child had to leave school.[1]

The man's wife returned with a bundle of very ripe bananas. She went around the room and gave one to each of us. These people were very poor but also proud – they felt bound to provide us hospitality, sharing whatever meagre provisions they had. I found myself deeply touched and as we ended our brief visit, I asked if I could pray for the family. They agreed, and we had a brief prayer. That was the least we could do, to leave the name of Jesus in that room.

As we left, we walked by the kitchen, which was open to the elements. A kettle over an open fire was in one corner, cooking the meal for the day. The women had just finished baking thin flatbread and offered us some. Surely a treat in every culture is the taste of freshly baked bread straight out of the oven! I noticed that the family was raising a few chickens and a goat and had two very skinny workhorses. Obviously they were doing everything possible to scratch out a living and provide for their children. Al commented that the primitiveness of the situation reminded him of the way pioneers probably lived in the American West 150 years ago. Only those pioneers had a much brighter future ahead of them.

As we walked back to our van, Al asked, 'Are there any Christians in this camp?'

'No, it is 100 per cent Muslim,' said Hanna. 'But we always offer to pray with them, and usually they appreciate it.'

'Where do you get the funds?'

'Some from the congregation. Some from friends of the church. And Samaritan's Purse is providing $15,000 a month for six months. That has allowed us to expand the programme.'

Driving back into the city, we couldn't help but reflect that our efforts seemed so little compared to the huge needs around us. However, light was shining, and who knew what God could do as a result of the efforts of this small but faithful congregation in downtown Gaza City?

THIRTY-FIVE

A DONKEY CRIES FOR GAZA

Gaza, December 2002

It was 4.00, the scheduled time for the programme to start, and the ballroom of the hotel on the Gaza beach had maybe one hundred people scattered among several hundred plastic outdoor chairs. Pastor Hanna didn't seem too concerned as he supervised the final details of the programme. Invitations for the event had been delivered over the previous three days. 'There is no point in sending out invitations earlier,' Pastor Hanna explained. 'People will forget. And besides, there aren't very many options available to people in Gaza right now.'

Hanna showed us the invitation. It was in an envelope with a CD-ROM that contained portions of the *Jesus* film, text of the book *More than a Carpenter* by Josh McDowell, a New Testament, and 'The Four Spiritual Laws'. I couldn't help but recall the three concerned men of this church six years earlier who had wanted to hold an evangelistic campaign. At that time they had no follow-up plan. Now Gaza Baptist Church was ready. There were books and other media resources, men and women who could handle follow-up meetings, and groups within the church so people could become part of a community.

Al and I walked outside the hotel onto the patio that bordered the beach along the Mediterranean Sea. Men in three boats were fishing about two hundred yards offshore. One man was throwing out a net to see what he could catch. Probably not much – the good fish were farther out, but Israeli patrols prevented boats from fishing out there. Many local fishermen had gone out of business, and the restaurants rarely served fresh fish anymore.

We prayed about the evangelistic meeting. This one was targeted particularly at people who called themselves Christian but who for whatever reason were inactive in any of the local churches. We had no idea how many people might fit into that category – perhaps one thousand, maybe more? Certainly, others could be attracted as well. 'Lord, may Your hand be over this event,' we prayed. 'May Your Spirit move hearts, and may there be much fruit harvested tonight.'

By the time the programme started at 4.35, the room was nearly full with some four hundred people. We laughed, realising that in Gaza we were operating on Arab time.

The first hour was devoted to music and testimonies. A group of children sang a special song that Labib Madanat, who had driven down from Jerusalem for the event, translated for us:

> Your peace passes understanding,
> abiding in us,
> and will never, never leave us.
> Whatever the enemy will say,
> Your peace will never leave us.

The chorus went:

> Peace, peace to God's people,
> wherever they are,
> wherever they are.

Labib explained that this song had become very popular at camps that Operation Palestinian Child conducted for Muslim children. This was a programme sponsored by the Palestinian Bible Society. The lyrics contrasted sharply with the songs glorifying martyrdom that Gaza children often sang.

Another song evoked a deep pathos:

Who feels my pain?
Who feels my weakness?
Only You, Jesus.

Our eyes were drawn to one of the singers, a young man who played guitar and whose singing seemed to come from deep within his soul. Yes, these people understood pain and weakness.

The main speaker was Kamal, an evangelist from Jordan. He was originally from Nazareth and joked about Nathanael, who had asked, 'Can anything good come out of Nazareth?'[1] 'People from there need a miracle to come to faith,' said Kamal. 'They're tough. Well, I'm one of those miracles.' Kamal told a little of his story, how he had worked in a nightclub and experimented with drugs, looking for happiness. When he didn't find it, he began a search for the truth instead. To illustrate that search, he walked us through the Scriptures, seeking advice from Moses, Daniel, Isaiah, Micah, John the Baptist, and Mary. He concluded with Jesus, who said, 'Come unto me.'

Kamal issued a powerful invitation, and more than one hundred people stood up to say they were committing their lives to Christ. *The light just got a little brighter*. The staff and leaders of Gaza Baptist Church would be busy for weeks following up with each of those who filled out response cards.

LATER THAT EVENING, we met the young man who had so captured our attention as he sang at the outreach event. Very quietly, speaking through an interpreter, Rami told how his childhood ended when he was nine years old, during the first intifada. 'We were a poor family, but it was a big family, a strong family. My brother Kader, who if he were still alive would now be thirty-two years old, was very smart. He was working selling gold.'

But Kader, Rami's hero, was killed at the age of eighteen. There was a demonstration near the market – young men and boys were throwing rocks at Israeli soldiers. On his way to buy groceries, Kader was caught up in the demonstration. He picked up a rock and heaved it, hitting the captain on his helmet. Immediately several soldiers chased after him. Kader tore down one of the dirt side streets, chose a house at random, and hid under a bed – there was no other place to hide.

The soldiers had no problem finding the boy. Rami could picture the horror as they began to beat his brother with sticks. 'Stop!' said one of the commanders. He handed them a large empty sack. 'Put this over him so we don't get splattered with blood.' Then they continued the beating.

Rami had heard that the prime minister of Israel, Yitzhak Rabin, had told the soldiers to 'break the bones' of every Palestinian young man they hit. *How many of your bones did they break?* he wanted to ask his brother.

While beating him, the soldiers demanded to know his religion. When he replied, 'Christian', they hauled him outside to a jeep and tied him cruciform on the hood, then paraded him through the streets of Gaza. When they finally arrived at the military headquarters, he was dumped on the cement floor. 'He needs medical attention,' someone said. But no doctor was allowed to look at him. The boy died on that floor.[2]

'A blackness entered my heart,' Rami said of that incident. Within months, his mother became ill and died. Then another brother started attacking soldiers with Molotov cocktails. He was arrested and imprisoned for five-and-a-half years. 'I had a huge anger in me. I needed someone bigger than me to help me contain this kind of anger. No one cared for me after this time. I became lonely. My father became very weak. I had to stay with him. I cleaned him, fed him, took care of him. But I was very angry, because my father wasn't with me to encourage me and because I wasn't with my friends.'

Rami determined he would find a way to get even with those who had murdered his brother and were responsible, in his mind, for the death of his mother. He was finishing high school when his father died. He failed the compulsory tests that are required if one wants to attend college. He started drinking alcohol. 'I was born into a worldly lifestyle out of a womb of sadness,' he said.

What a profound statement! I thought.

Rami knew he needed help and took the first steps when a Catholic priest encouraged him to study and retake the tests, then helped him learn to be a secretary, and found him a job at the Ministry of Antiquities.

'I know you weren't a Muslim, but were you ever drawn to groups like Hamas or Islamic Jihad?' Al asked.

'I wanted to kill Jews. I thought about becoming a Muslim.'

'What prevented you?'

'I didn't know anything about my [Christian] religion.' He admitted there was a huge spiritual gap in his life. In the summer of 2001 he attended a conference called Summerland, 'Just because I was bored.' It was sponsored by Gaza Baptist Church. 'I went each day. On the third day, the Lord was speaking to me through the Holy Spirit. That was when I accepted the Lord Jesus, and my life changed.'

'Please, tell us how your life changed,' Al prompted.

'Even though I accepted the Lord, there was still some of that blackness in my heart towards the Jews. There were inner battles. I began to study the Word of God. I started going to church. My life began to change little by little. Then I read in the Bible, "Love your enemies. Pray for them and bless those who persecute you." I got angry. I closed the book. It was very hard, very hard.'

That was when he met Abu Yahya, the manager of The Teacher's Bookshop who worked closely with Pastor Hanna and was a member of Gaza Baptist Church. 'He's the one who helped me grow in my relationship with the Lord. He taught me how to love people. He told me, "You have to pray." I prayed many long nights that I would be able to accept the Jews. One day (less than a year ago) I wanted to go visit my sister in Jerusalem. I had to get permission from the Israeli government. I went. I was very upset, uptight. But I was praying. Then I saw the soldiers with their big weapons. The first soldier, I saw his face, and there was light. I knew I loved him. He searched me strongly. But I was happy. In my heart there was peace. They sat me on a chair. Strongly. I was looking at all of them. I wanted to tell them that I want to kiss you, to all of them.'

Al grinned. 'Arabic style, on the cheek!' he said. Rami smiled and nodded. This was the power of the gospel. This was the hope for the Middle East. One man's heart, filled with hate, was replaced with a new heart, one filled with the love of God.

'Where do you go from here? Has God showed you what you are to do with your life?'

'I want to be a man of God. I'm knocking on doors. Maybe a

pastor – no, a minister, not a pastor. I want to be a great Christian. The Lord wants to shape me so that I could preach the Word of God to all the world, to the Muslims, Jews, Christians.'

'Your testimony is a picture of what I believe is the only solution for this area,' I said to Rami. 'It's a picture of what God can do, but each individual needs to allow God to do it.'

Later, after Rami left, Al and I reflected again on how the light had almost gone out in the Baptist church a few years ago. Now, with the evangelistic outreach and young converts like Rami, there was hope that the light would grow brighter. Then there would be less darkness, less despair, less violence.

WHAT WAS THE truth about Gaza? Listening to terrorist group leaders and Israeli spokesmen, it seemed like no one ever really heard the other side. What we did know was that people were dying from the fighting every day – thirteen just in the four days we'd been in Gaza.

The sun had set, leaving only a thin orange strip in the west. High above us we could hear the whine of F-16s. Then they flew south, and we heard several explosions, like the ones we'd heard our first day in Gaza, though farther away. This was the fourth attack in five days. Al seemed agitated. I tried to assure him that this was nothing like what I'd experienced in Beirut, but he didn't find that comforting.

About twenty minutes later we heard sirens. Two speeding cars tore into the Al Ahli Hospital compound next door, stopping at the emergency room door. An ambulance followed. It was dark and hard to see. It appeared that one child, his legs dangling lifelessly, was being wheeled into the emergency room. Another older man was supported as he limped into the building. We couldn't tell who the third patient was that was rolled inside on a trolley, but we could see a man – perhaps husband to the patient or father – who was greatly agitated. He kicked the car he'd ridden in and shouted. A crowd quickly gathered and loud voices rang through the compound.

More cars drove up, and another ambulance, all delivering injured patients. Then someone came out and spoke to the agitated man. All was quiet for a moment. Then a scream of agony erupted from the man. He ran into the courtyard, emitting howls of such anguish that our souls cringed. A trolley emerged, with a sheet covering the body. The ambulance accepted the body and drove off, we assumed to the morgue.

We wondered if tomorrow this man would be dressed up in a suit, wearing a flower, inviting us to become Muslims.

As we packed our suitcases the next morning, preparing to leave Gaza, a donkey started madly braying outside. Al glanced out the window and saw it standing in the middle of the street, refusing to move, blocking traffic as it stood and bawled. How symbolic. All of Gaza, even the donkeys, seemed to be crying.

The night before, we had heard the agonising, bloodcurdling howl of anguish of a man who had lost a loved one. His cry was like that of thousands of Palestinians and Israelis. Thousands had died in this intifada, and for each one, mothers and fathers, brothers and sisters, husbands and wives had wept. For what purpose was all of this suffering? A piece of land? Was that all? No, it was for much more. It was about dignity, fairness, ambition, resistance, human rights, and religion.

Psalm 88 seemed like an appropriate prayer this morning: 'O LORD, . . . day and night I cry out before you. May my prayer come before you; turn your ear to my cry.' Surely that was the cry of thousands here. 'You have put me in the lowest pit, in the darkest depths. Your wrath lies heavily upon me.' That must be what they feel here, both Palestinians and Jews.

In just a few days Christians would celebrate Christmas. I thought of another verse often read at Christmas services: 'The light shines in the darkness, but the darkness has not understood it' (John 1:5). God will shine His light through His people, but the darkness may not understand it. We had tried to do our little part, to shine a light into Hamas and Islamic Jihad. The Gaza Baptist Church was doing its part, shining a light by visiting destitute Muslim families in refugee camps and putting on evangelistic campaigns. The Bible bookshop in Gaza City was doing its part – many were walking in and seeing the light. Al Ahli

Hospital, operated by the Anglican Church, was shining a light to thousands who were sick and injured.

The light, however faint, was shining in Gaza, but the darkness didn't seem to understand it. Didn't they realise that this light was their only hope?

SNEAKING INTO
BETHLEHEM

Bethlehem, December 2002

Al and I very much wanted to visit our friends at Bethlehem Bible College, but Bethlehem was under curfew. If we went to the only official entrance, soldiers would turn us away.

'There is a way to get in,' said Bishara over the phone. He told me how to instruct the driver, who was picking us up outside Gaza. He gave me a location on the edge of Beit Jala. 'Call me on Al's mobile phone just before you arrive, and I'll have our van pick you up.'

Later that day we drove through the bypass tunnel from Jerusalem, took the first exit, and doubled back onto the road that led to Hope School, just outside the border of Beit Jala. A huge pile of dirt and rocks blocked the road into the old town. On top of the rubble several taxi cab drivers, brave enough to defy the military authorities, were competing vigorously for fares. Several of them hurried down the hill to help us with our suitcases.

'Someone is meeting us,' I said as one of the men tried to wrest a suitcase from my hand. I could see a homemade white flag displaying a black cross on a pole attached to the college van parked on the other side of the dirt and rock pile. Two more men grabbed several of our bags and began hauling them over the rocks and dirt. Then they demanded a tip – five dollars, even one dollar. They pleaded – they were hungry; there were kids to feed; this was the only way they could earn money. After loading the cases into the van, we were blocked by several taxis. Al had given one of the drivers five American dollars for hauling his two suitcases. The grateful driver directed traffic to make sure we escaped the taxi jam before sundown.

One block away the streets were empty. It felt like we were driving through a ghost town. Five minutes later, having taken the back streets and alleys to avoid the main Jerusalem-Hebron Road, we were hauling suitcases up the stairs to the college's guest rooms on the fourth floor.

Outside, the wind was howling. From my window I could see trees swaying and laundry looking like it might blow off the lines of several homes behind the school. Two children were playing in a courtyard that couldn't be seen from the main roads. There were no other signs of life. I half expected to see some tumbleweed rolling down the streets. This scene gave new meaning to the popular Christmas carol, 'O little town of Bethlehem, how still we see thee lie'.

The college was deserted. Doris welcomed us and started heating the kettle for tea. Bishara joined us. There was another volunteer couple there. They came from the United States and lived in an apartment in the basement. Al and I now brought the total population of the school to seven.

AFTER A LIGHT supper, we walked over to Bishara's office in the administration building. The main road in front of the school was pitch-black. Power to all of the traffic signals and streetlights had been cut off months before. By daylight we had seen the damage that tanks had caused. The metal awning of a storefront across the street was torn and left dangling. Several street lamps were bent. The prints of tank treads were imbedded in the street and sidewalks. With no cars on the streets, there was an ominous feel to the town.

In front of Bishara's desk are two couches where – when the

school is open – people from the college and community frequently drop by for coffee and conversation. 'We have many nights like this,' Bishara said as he prepared coffee. 'It's so quiet and sad to walk past all of the dark, unused rooms. We're falling further and further behind in our studies. If we lose too many more weeks, we may not be able to hold a graduation ceremony this school year.'

'How are people handling the curfew?' Al asked.

'Many Christians cannot take it anymore. They just pack up and leave, sell everything and go to North America, South America, Australia – anywhere they have relatives. It's easy to get out, if you plan to leave for good. But if Christians continue to leave . . . the problem is that the Church is dying. This is where the Church is really suffering, because it loses members all the time. They are seeking a better future for their children. Right now, under curfew, all the children are denied schooling.'

'How have your students been affected by the occupation?'

'One of our students, Michel, barely missed being hit by a missile. He went to answer the telephone just seconds before the missile hit the place where he had been standing. The family rushed outside, and another missile hit their home, destroying it. That's the closest any of our students have come.'

'That's too close!' I said.

The college had set up the Shepherd's Society to provide relief to local families that needed food or medical attention. 'Every time curfew is lifted, we have people coming to the school looking for help,' Bishara said. 'We give what we can. For those who need immediate help, I have parcels of food and coupons that can be redeemed for food at three different stores. They're worth 200 shekels and allow them to obtain enough food for two to three weeks. Last month we helped 170 families in this way. For ongoing help, we use the Shepherd's Society.' The Open Doors' project Compassion Now was providing some of the money for this assistance.

Bishara told us about George, a father of seven children. The family lived in a single-room apartment near the Church of the Nativity and was confined there for forty consecutive days during the siege. Several times soldiers searched the premises. 'The family belongs to Immanuel Church and participates in many of the church's weekly activities. But both husband and wife lost their jobs. We provided them with $100 a month through their church, which they used to pay small instalments towards accumulated utility bills and tuition fees for their children's education.'

More stories poured out. Julia, a seventy-year-old widow, living alone, had an accumulation of utility bills and couldn't afford needed medical treatments. Shepherd's Society helped, but what meant most to Julia was the social worker who spent time just listening to her. 'She is scheduled to receive regular follow-up home visitations to ensure that her circumstances do not deteriorate.'

What many of the local people wanted more than anything was employment. 'Many families feel a sense of acute shame when asking for assistance of any kind,' Bishara explained. 'For example, Victor and his wife, they have three small children. He's been out of work for nearly two years and his level of desperation was high. Still, he expressed genuine preference for paid employment as opposed to receiving a handout. He's been recommended for a work programme, which will put hundreds of people to work in organisations throughout the Bethlehem area cleaning, repairing, and restoring the town.' Of course, that programme couldn't really get underway until the curfew was lifted.

CLOUDS HUNG LOW over the Bethlehem region, obscuring the buildings of Gilo as well as the hills surrounding us. The minarets of two mosques seemed to touch the bottom of the clouds, and their light shimmered through the mist. During the night, we had heard rain battering the shutters. The wind was still strong, threatening to bring more rain, but the mood was upbeat at Bethlehem Bible College with the news that curfew would be lifted for six hours, beginning at 10.00 that morning.

There was a bustle of activity. Charles, the American volunteer, had taken the van, flying the homemade Christian flag, to collect employees from their homes. Several professors were preparing classrooms for lectures. The cook was getting ready in the kitchen to prepare a hot lunch for faculty and students. Several support staff were answering phones and making photocopies in the administration building, while in the basement Shepherd's Society staff prepared for the inevitable influx of people looking for help.

Word that school was open spread via television messages scrolled along the bottom of the screen of the local station. By 10.30 about half of the fifty-five students had managed to arrive. With the professors, they gathered in a basement meeting room to hear Academic Dean Salim Munayer, who had travelled to Bethlehem from his home in Jerusalem, announce which classes would be meeting. Before they were dismissed, Bishara read from Romans 8.31: 'If God is for us, who can be against us?' Then he encouraged the assembly: 'These are such comforting words to us. God came to us and lived in our midst. One of the names of Jesus is "God with us". Let's remember that He is with us today.'

He reminded the students of a citywide party planned for two thousand people on 21 December at a local hotel – an annual event the college held to celebrate Christmas in the community. 'Nothing can stop us from celebrating Jesus' birthday,' he said. Bishara had told us that they were proceeding with plans for the party, less than two weeks away, even though there was considerable doubt whether the political situation would improve and the curfew would lift.[1]

'We need to fill our lives with prayer,' Salim said, 'and to glorify God in this situation.' And so, before classes began, the students and faculty spent about ten minutes in corporate prayer. One of the professors, also a local pastor, closed with a passionate plea in Arabic. Though I couldn't understand the words, I could feel the longings that expressed what all of us were feeling.

As the students headed to class, Al and I decided to take advantage of the opportunity to walk freely through the town. We headed south on the Jerusalem-Hebron Road. At the intersection with El Murida Street, just a block from the school, there was a traffic jam of taxis and cars trying to turn or drive through the crossing. With the useless traffic lights swinging above him in the wind, a volunteer traffic cop tried to direct cars while a Muslim woman, covered in black *jilbab*, looked on in amusement.

It was obvious why the traffic lights didn't work. There was a large electrical box by the green wrought-iron fence in front of the building that housed the Latin Patriarchate. The box was charred black. Around the corner was parked the burned skeleton of a car.

We wound our way through the traffic and continued down the road to view the remains of the local PA government office. It was impossible to tell how tall the building had once been – its floors were pancaked on top of each other. Eight months earlier, F-16s had destroyed it. Scrawled on the cinder block wall in front of the compound were these English words: 'Occupation Kills'.

We turned down Al-Mukata'ah Street and walked through the narrow alleyways where about half of the shopkeepers were open for business. For the most part, shopping was limited to food and other necessities. The streets were crowded with men and women hustling to make the most of six hours of freedom. No one knew when the residents would again be released from their house prisons. Over the past three weeks, Bishara said, curfew had, on average, been lifted only once every four days.

Johnny's Gift Shop, which was next door to the Alexander Hotel, was the only one of a row of curio shops open along Manger Street, so Al decided to do some Christmas shopping, picking out olive wood souvenirs for family and friends. Since Al had met Johnny on his previous visit, he inquired about how business was going. This prompted Johnny to serve us tea with a sprig of mint he'd grown in his backyard. He told us he was eager to move away, to take his son, who was sitting in a corner reading, to America. 'I bought the hotel and this shop because business was going to grow before the year 2000. I added forty rooms to the hotel. Now it's closed. No one wants to come to Bethlehem.'

Al bought several ornaments and a mother-of-pearl inlaid box for his wife. As Johnny gave him change, he thanked us, saying that this was his first sale in seventeen days.

It started raining again as we hurried back to the college to join the students and staff for lunch. During a simple but warm meal, we talked with several students. Louiza, a fourth-year student who spoke excellent English, lived in the old city of Jerusalem. That morning she was refused admittance at the checkpoint into Bethlehem, even though curfew was lifted. 'It's only for them [meaning residents of Bethlehem], not for you,' the soldier gruffly explained. So she had climbed over the stone wall at the Catholic compound of Tantour and walked through a muddy field to reach the school. 'This is my last year,' she explained. 'I want to finish school and get my degree.'

Two young men were with her, and she translated for us. Walid was in his fourth year. He lived with four brothers and three sisters in Beit Sahour. 'I hope to work with the youth in my church,' he said when we asked him about his plans after graduation. 'For now I want to study God's Word, so I can teach the Bible.'

Fahdi told us that he believed the trials that he and all the residents of Bethlehem were enduring were like a fire that purified them and would eventually produce good. 'Our suffering is discipline from God, because we have left Him and gone our own way.'

'How has the military occupation affected you and your family?' Al asked.

'The soldiers came and searched our house for weapons,' he said. 'They asked me, "Do you have any weapons?" I said, "Yes, I have the Bible, Jesus Christ, and the power of the Holy Spirit." They didn't like my answer. One soldier threw my Bible away, like trash. But then they left. Another soldier smashed our car and my cousin's car.'

'What will you do when you graduate?'

'I hope that God will use me to draw my people as near to Christ as he's drawn me.'

At 1.00 the students headed upstairs for more classes. But shortly after that, an Israeli army jeep, an orange light revolving ominously on its roof, drove slowly by, blaring an announcement over loudspeakers. 'Curfew is back on,' said Bishara.

'I thought it was lifted until 4.00,' Al said.

Bishara shrugged. This was simply the way life was. Classes immediately ceased, and students and faculty scrambled to get back to their homes. By 2.15 the streets were empty.

A heavy rain descended on Bethlehem and beat against the abandoned school building. It would have been depressing if we had not remembered the words of the students. We commented on Fahdi's spirit. He said he was armed with the Bible and the power of the Holy Spirit. There was hope for the West Bank as long as Christian students were brave and prepared to stand firmly and proclaim their hope in Christ.

THIRTY-SEVEN

A DANGEROUS GAME

Bethlehem, December 2002

'You need to meet Nawal,' said Bishara. Al and I were talking with him in his office about the impact of some of the graduates of Bethlehem Bible College. Among others, we had met men like Hanna Massad, pastor of Gaza Baptist Church, and Jack Sara, pastor of Jerusalem Alliance Church, but we wanted to see other types of ministry, particularly one among the women.

So during another lifting of the curfew, Al went to Beit Sahour and the home of Nawal Qumsieh and her husband. They lived on the second floor of a two-storey building. He sat in a spacious living room that opened into a dining area as Nawal told about attending Bethlehem Bible College and how for ten years she had tried, with little success, to reach out to neighbours. Then, after the miraculous healing and birth of Jacob, Nawal's phone started ringing constantly. Eagerly she explained how callers would ask: 'Would you pray for my son? Please pray for my daughter. Pray for my husband. I was amazed; miracles happened. God did it! So now, during the uprising, I have many phone calls.'

'Please, tell me about them,' Al said.

'A mother called from Beit Jala. They were bombing near her house and her daughter was breaking down and crying because of fear. I had her put the girl on the phone and prayed with her. I asked her to pray for Jesus to protect her and the family. The next morning, the girl called me. She said, "I saw Jesus last night. I was afraid, but He came near me and said, 'Don't be afraid anymore because I'm protecting you. I'm watching over you and your family.' The fear is gone!" And then she started encouraging the other girls and boys and telling them that Jesus is watching over Beit Jala. Many, many miracles are happening like this.'

Because Nawal insisted that women tell their husbands before she would meet with them, some doors were closed to her. But many more were opened. Nawal gave an example: 'One husband, he was an atheist. His wife wanted me to pray for her about a problem, and he said, "I don't mind if you try." He went to work. I came to her house, and we opened the Word of God and I started to read to her. Suddenly her husband came in the house. She was surprised – she said her husband never came back to the house after he left for work. He wanted to hear what I was saying. He sat in the next room and listened to our conversation. He was more hungry spiritually than his wife.'

The primary need of these people was a universal issue. 'They need love! I went to pray for one woman who had severe headaches. After we prayed, she asked, "Did God show you anything about me?" Yes, I said. He showed me how much He loves you. She broke down and cried in a very bad way. "God loves me?" she asked. "Why? Nobody loves me." That's what so many people here believe – that nobody loves them. That nobody wants them.

'Jesus ministered to people through their needs. He went to sick people not to the healthy people – people sick in spirit, sick emotionally. That's mostly what we have here in Beit Sahour. We have people with broken hearts. Most believe that God doesn't love them. They think God loves the Jewish people, but He doesn't love the Arabic people. They are not the chosen people, so they don't deserve God's love. All Arabic people feel that way, especially Muslims.'

'How do you address that?'

'I read the Bible to them, the verses about how God loves the world. I explain the work of the cross, how He loves you and me so much that He went to the cross – for everybody, even criminals. So everybody is loved by God, but it's up to you if you accept His love or not. Most of the people I talk to accept His love, because that's what they seek, that's what they need. Some people have asked me why I don't tell about judgment. These people already know judgment. They're already in hell with this situation. What they need to understand is God's love. One person told me she never heard about this word *love*, that she only knew about sexual love. Everybody wants to know that Jesus loves him, even with his condition, with his situation, with his circumstances.'

And what does Nawal do after people respond to the love of Christ? 'I give them Bibles, and we used to have neighbourhood meetings.' Because of curfew, such meetings were now infrequent. When the time comes that restrictions are lifted, Nawal won't do the typical Western-style meeting where a general invitation is issued for a Bible study. 'If I minister to a woman in her home, she doesn't want anybody outside to know what's happening there. I don't want to force her to come to meetings and share this with other women, so I say to her, "I will come to you next Wednesday. Okay?" And she is free to invite any women – neighbours, aunts, nieces, anybody who needs help. Sometimes two or three people come. Sometimes six. Sometimes ten or twelve. I minister to all who come.'

During curfew when Nawal couldn't meet with women in her neighbourhood, she spent much of her time in prayer. 'I'm praying for a financial breakthrough for the people,' she explained. 'This area used to live from tourism, but for two years there is nothing. Most of the men don't have jobs. [Her husband had been without work for two years.] It's good on one side that we are made to look to God. But it's very hard – if you see your child is hungry and you can't feed him, you feel bad. My husband and I, we have a chance to go to America and live with our children and have a nice life. But I just stay here because of God's work. God wants me to be here.'

This woman's faith, expressed in total dependence on the leadership of the Holy Spirit, was allowing God's love to spread throughout her community. We wanted to know if she had anything to say to the Church in the West.

'I've said to God, 'These people outside have to hear our cry.' We are crying because we feel that we are alone. Because we are Arabic people, we feel we are not welcome anywhere. But the

Israeli people, oh, they are welcome. We feel we are totally rejected, even the Christians. It's like we are not human beings.'

Nawal soberly expressed sadness that part of the body is being ignored. 'Let's say we are the finger of that body. We are hurt. Why doesn't the body help? They don't do anything or even say, "We love you." So many times I cry to Jesus hard from my heart. Women tell me they need help for medicine or food, and all I can say is to pray to Jesus, and I will pray with them and we cry out together. But somebody has to bring food, so they will know that Jesus loves them. That's the work of the Church, of the body of Christ. I believe with all my heart that Jesus loves the Palestinian people. Jesus hurts for them. Jesus cries for them and wants to help them. But He can't do it without the Church – they are His hands, His legs, His eyes.'

Later, when Al told me about his visit with Nawal, I told him how deeply saddened I was to hear those words. We agreed that Nawal was right, that God loves His Church, *every* part of His body, whether it is in the West or Middle East, whether Palestinian or Jew. Nawal was doing exactly what the Church needed to do in this region, but she was only one person. We needed a thousand more Nawals. Maybe then there would be hope for peace. But if the rest of the body didn't help, how could it happen?

R IZEK SLEIBI SEEMED stressed, and understandably, for curfew had started ten minutes earlier and he was worried about getting home safely without encountering a patrol. He was a psychological counsellor and directed the Al-Aman centre at Bethlehem Bible College – a counselling centre the school had helped set up to assist Palestinian families traumatised by the conflict.

We were discussing with him the emotional health of the children of Bethlehem, which was of particular concern among community leaders. Al and I had talked briefly with Solomon Nour, since 1992 the principal at Hope School, about how kids were responding there. 'We're having major behaviour problems,' he admitted. 'I've had to ask the teachers to be extra patient with the students and understand that they are suffering from terrible emotional trauma.'

Dr Sleibi agreed with Solomon. 'The circumstances in Bethlehem have pressured the normal life of children and students and left them with little or no sense of personal security,' he explained, adding that they are exhibiting classic symptoms of post-traumatic stress disorder. Speaking clinically, he added, 'The stressor criterion involves a threat to life, intense fear, helplessness, and horror.' He handed me a paper he'd prepared on child trauma and bolted out the door.

We sat on the hard wooden bench of the foyer of the administration building and read over the assessment. Primary school children were losing bowel and bladder control, crying frequently, sucking their thumbs. They were often re-enacting traumatic events they had witnessed or experienced. Older children were complaining of headaches and visual and hearing problems. They were fighting with or withdrawing from peers, and suffering from sleep disturbances.

'Pretty sobering report, isn't it?' Bishara had stepped out of his office and saw us reading Dr Sleibi's paper. 'We're seeing a whole generation of dysfunctional children developing.'

With a shudder I observed, 'They will be the next generation of suicide bombers. What can we possibly do to reverse this trend?'

'That's why we've developed this programme of training workshops for counsellors, social workers, and school teachers. And we're doing some other programmes.' For example, they had started Operation Blessing, which brought doctors from the West for a few days to perform operations; they distributed shoebox packages from Samaritan's Purse, though the most recent shipment was tied up at the port in Tel Aviv; Bethlehem Bible College students conducted a Bible school programme in the summer, sometimes with the help of volunteers from a church in California. 'But it's not enough,' Bishara admitted, shaking his head.

I knew the Palestinian Bible Society, under Labib Madanat's leadership, had a project called Operation Palestinian Child, which had put on inspirational programmes in more than fifty communities for some fifteen thousand children – Muslim and Christian. It included a puppet programme, group singing, and a clown doing magic tricks. At the end of the programme each child received sweets. For one hour the children could escape their difficult circumstances, but in the process, they also got a glimpse of the love of Christ.

There were a hundred times more children who couldn't enjoy even that one-hour programme. These kids had learned to chant Yasser Arafat's well-known quote: 'We will come to Jerusalem if it takes millions of martyrs.' But a few of them were seeing an alternative. Labib showed me a report in which a worker said, 'The kids are literally dry sponges. Whatever comes along can fill them. If we don't do anything, the devil will, and the devil is.'

U NDER THE DARK clouds, threatening more rain, the kids came out to play a dangerous game. On both ends of the street in front of Bethlehem Bible College, packs of children rolled trash barrels and gathered other debris to build a feeble barricade against the jeeps and armoured personnel carriers that would inevitably come down the street. Bishara watched with us and explained that the army had to be careful when they approached such barriers. Perhaps there was a bomb hidden in one of the pipes or barrels. So the army vehicles would have to stop and investigate, and in some cases call for reinforcements to remove potentially deadly materials. Of course, this day they'd find only an empty barrel. How embarrassing! The kids would laugh in their hiding places, pleased that – at least in their imaginations – they had 'defeated' the Israeli army.

This afternoon no soldiers interrupted their play. The kids lit a small bonfire at the intersection to the south and kept peering down the street towards the bunker at Rachel's Tomb, ready to scamper away and hide in the narrow alleyways of their refugee camp if soldiers came after them. I could only imagine their boredom and anger. They spent most of their time caged in crowded apartments with no release for their frustration. What hope could anyone offer them? *Lord, there must be an answer.*

A MODEL OTHERS
CAN FOLLOW

Petach Tikva, Israel, December 2002
I thought often of those children. What was their hope? It was a terribly disturbing question, but there were people who encouraged us to see another picture.

Karen Alan, a young, recently-married woman, had witnessed a particularly gruesome triple suicide bombing in 1997, while employed by King of Kings College. She was now one of the employees in the Musalaha office, responsible for helping coordinate desert encounters, conferences, retreats, and other events that brought together Arab Palestinian Christians and Jewish believers in Jesus.

The possibility of an attack was never far from the thoughts of Israelis. 'Recently I found myself again only a minute away from a bus bombing and headed in exactly that direction,' she told us. 'Also my husband has been extremely close to a car bomb and a gunman.'

'How do you keep functioning with the threat of violence all around?' Al asked.

'These sort of tragedies are so common here, and you find many people traumatised by the mere fact that they "heard the bomb". Since I've met brothers and sisters on both sides who have suffered and continue to suffer from the situations in ways much worse than my own experience, I've allowed myself to see pain other than my own. So many people are wrapped up in their own pain, thinking that they have been wronged the most. Thus we are stuck. I'm called to be a bridge builder, and I know that my identity first and foremost is as a citizen of heaven.'

'So Musalaha is the perfect place for you to work!'

'What Musalaha does is essential. There is such separation and segregation between the believers in Israel and those in the Palestinian areas. There is plenty of misunderstanding and there's friction among the leaders of both believing communities, due to such little personal interaction, and, of course, opposing theologies. If we were able to get the two sides together, this would be truly the best testimony for Christ anyone could offer here.'

Of all the ministries in Israel, I found myself drawn most to this one. It seemed the most ambitious but also the riskiest. It wasn't an idea promoted by foreign missionaries but was birthed in the local Christian community. It didn't just talk about the problem between Palestinians and Jews. It brought the two sides together and provided a means for them to reconcile. The stories were dramatic. Who wouldn't be moved by the experience of men like Yitzhak and Wa'el who bridge the chasms of language and culture in a desert encounter!

Yet it seemed so idealistic. Even among Christians, there were challenging realities that divided them. I was aware that there were believers on both sides who would have no contact with brothers or sisters on the other side, who perhaps even questioned the validity of their faith. If Christians couldn't experience unity, what hope was there for the massive divide between Muslims and Jews?

To try and answer that question, Salim Munayer invited us to a rustic campground lodge with about twenty families. I was curious to learn what had happened since pastors and elders from both sides had met in Holland eight months earlier. 'We've met once since April,' Salim had told us. Tonight would be the second gathering. 'These follow-up meetings are very important. You have to really work on that because if you don't, people go back to the old way of thinking.'

Most of what happened in Holland occurred behind closed doors. 'On the second day, we agreed that we needed to repent,' Salim said. 'Everyone participated, repenting of anger, of hatred, of polluting their hearts. Everybody was crying. It was a very cleansing time.'

The campground in Petach Tikva, near Tel Aviv, was rather rustic, except for the sports facilities. The focal point was a complex of four baseball fields, the only such sports venue in Israel, complete with light standards. Somehow it was hard to picture America's national pastime being enjoyed in the Holy Land.

Families arrived throughout the afternoon, toting children and diaper bags. There were hugs and traditional kisses on the cheeks. Many of the participants, both Jewish and Arab, came from within Israel proper. We wondered if any Palestinian church leaders would come from within the West Bank, particularly from Bethlehem, which remained under curfew.

Howard, an elder of Beersheba Messianic Congregation, recognised Botrus, a lawyer and elder of the Arabic Baptist Church in Nazareth. The two men embraced and immediately started catching up on news. Howard told Al that the meetings in Holland had been a 'release for all of us, to get out of the tension and just be together'. For Botrus, the Holland trip marked the first time he'd interacted with Jewish brothers since college. 'This encounter helps you see the other side,' he said as we entered the lodge. 'There is something more important than just the national barriers. We're brothers and sisters in Christ. That's what's most important.'

As some forty children were herded into a large room, where staff of Youth With A Mission had volunteered to lead a special programme, the parents relaxed as a fire burned in the stone fireplace, cutting the chill of the meeting room. It was an hour past the scheduled starting time of 3.00, but no one seemed anxious. As they had in Holland, the group began with worship, with David Loden and Jack Sara leading. They concluded the worship time by singing, 'He is our peace. We shall be one. He is our reconciliation'.

There was no need to break the ice. Each couple eagerly took their turn updating the group on family and ministry concerns. Lisa Loden reported that one of the elders in their church was suffering from a kidney disease. A pastor asked for prayer for healing of an eighteen-year-old church worker who had just been diagnosed with cancer. Several churches were planning outreaches for Christmas. A pastor from Nazareth reported that his church, after years of decline, was showing signs of life and growth. An elder praised God for healing his son: 'After four years of prayer, the answer came when we prayed for him in Holland!'

For a few moments, the tortuous intifada seemed to disappear from the minds of all in the room. They were united by common concerns shared by all Christians – for health and safety of family members, for outreach efforts, for growth of their congregations. Of course, they couldn't escape the reality of life outside those walls. Nihad, a pastor from Bethlehem, reminded them as he reported: 'Yesterday, I didn't think I could be here. Under curfew, the military turns most requests away. But miracles still happen. They let me and my family out for this meeting!'

Then he asked for prayer for his family and for the believers in Bethlehem. 'It's very depressing. We're now in our fourth week of curfew. That's hard, especially for a person like me who is always in action.' There were several knowing nods around the room – most of these leaders felt the same desire to be active in Christian service. There was also impact on the family: 'My children are missing school. They missed three months last spring. For now, my wife is homeschooling.'

He went on to report about the condition of the Church in Bethlehem. 'Five hundred Christian families have left this year. Many more have applied for emigration. Within the next year, one third of the Christians will be gone. The ministry is hard. I wonder what sermon I should preach to the people. I hesitate to make calls. What will I tell people? And yet it is more important to prepare the people than the sermon. I need wisdom to know what to say to these people. May God have mercy on us and shorten these days.'

It was a moment of humble honesty, one that touched every heart in the room. One of the Messianic pastors rose and put his arm around his brother. 'I want to pray for you.' Fervently, all of the people entered into prayer, for Nihad and his family and congregation, for Christians in Bethlehem, for peace in the nation, and for all the needs and concerns that had been raised. Time seemed to stand still. No one noticed that dinner was half an hour late being served.

It was sundown, the start of Shabbat, and befitting the family feel of this meeting, David and Lisa Loden led the traditional ritual that starts the day of rest in Jewish homes. Lisa lit two candles, then waved her hands over them to welcome in the Shabbat. Then she covered her eyes and in Hebrew recited: 'Blessed are You, Lord our God, King of the universe, who sanctifies us by the blood of Yeshua and commands us to be a light to the nations.'

David then held up a cup of wine and recited Kiddush, taken from Genesis 1–2: 'And there was evening, and there was morning, a sixth day. The heavens and the earth were finished, the whole host of them. And on the seventh day God ended His work which He had made and He rested on the seventh day from all His work which He had made. And God blessed the seventh day, and sanctified it because in it He had rested from all his work which God had created and done. Blessed are You, Lord, our God, King of the universe, Who creates the fruit of the vine.'

A ceremonial washing of hands followed and then David blessed two loaves of bread, sprinkling salt over them as a reminder that we as believers in Yeshua are to be the salt of the earth: 'Blessed are You, Lord, our God, King of the universe, Who brings forth bread from the earth.' He then broke apart the loaves and gave a portion to each table. Each of us took a piece, then poured wine from the bottles on each table. Then it was time to participate in a sumptuous buffet of chicken, rice, spaghetti, and pastries.

DAVID AND LISA Loden provide a glimpse into the conditions under which Messianic believers live in Israel. David said that while he doesn't like to use the word *persecution,* every Messianic believer experiences some form of harassment. 'I've been accused of everything from theft and deception to paying people to go through the waters of baptism – all sorts of nonsense.'

Some congregations have suffered more than others. A Messianic synagogue in Haifa was firebombed in 1997. Orthodox Jewish protestors taunted Messianic believers in northern Galilee as they were gathering to baptise thirteen adults. The homes of several Messianic leaders were attacked with petrol bombs. Fortunately, no one was killed. There were also incidents of Messianic believers being evicted from their apartments or losing their jobs, usually under pressure from Orthodox Jews.[1]

But David assured us that things were improving. 'Officially we do have what is known as freedom of religion and freedom of expression. Harassment in any form does not happen on an official level. We do get a lot of pressure from the religious authorities, particularly from the rabbinate and religious Jewish orthodox establishment. Recently there has been a higher degree of tolerance, because there is more of an awareness in the populace generally that Messianic Jews do exist, and many people are quite tired of all the religious coercion.'

Of course, Messianic believers suffer with the rest of the Israeli population. Several suicide bombers have struck in crowded areas of Netanya. 'Four or five of our people have been right in the vicinity of these attacks,' David explained. 'You cannot imagine the sights, the sounds, the smells. It is not for us to go into detail. However, I want to tell you one story.

'There was a young woman, not a believer, who while serving in the army met and fell in love with a young man from our church. He prayed much for her, and we prayed also for her. She was on vacation from the army for a few days and went into a large shopping mall in Netanya. A suicide bomber blew himself up in front of the mall, killing twenty-two people. Of course, she heard and saw it all. She was in deep shock. She found another way out of the mall and went back to her apartment. Locking herself in, she sat down in tears, opened the Bible, and read the New Testament from beginning to end. On that very day she gave her life to the Lord. We've had the privilege and blessing of marrying this couple, baptising them, and also seeing their first child born. Even in the most horrible of circumstances, God is working. That's why our congregations are growing so quickly. That's why the congregations of the Arab churches in the West Bank and in Israel are full to overflowing.'

Many members of the congregation of Beit Asaf have participated in Musalaha events. David's wife, Lisa, and one of his co-pastors, Evan Thomas, are on the board of the ministry. Lisa participated in the first Musalaha women's conference in 1995 and has been organising the women's side of this movement ever since. What the Arab and Jewish women discovered were the similarities in their faith. 'Our expressions might be quite different,' said Lisa, 'but our personal experience with God is so similar. I've been in other frameworks where Arab women had never met a Jewish believer, so it was a shocking thought to them that you could be Jewish and be a believer in Jesus. They think if you're a believer in Jesus, then you have to be a Christian and no longer identify yourself as Jewish. We also can identify with one another on common ground as women – we are mothers; we are daughters; we are women struggling for our place in society. These are common issues. Meeting together on this ground is essential, because in other spheres of our lives, the forces seek to divide, separate, and cause dissension, suspicion, and fear.'

A BIBLE STUDY WAS planned for the last two hours of the evening. But this study would be unusual because of the topic being discussed. 'Part of the process of reconciliation is learning together about certain biblical themes on which we may agree or disagree,' Salim said by way of introduction. 'Our task is to deal with the issues in a way that builds unity. That's why we've first spent time building relationships. We've built trust; we have experienced brotherly love. This provides us with a platform for presenting different perspectives and dealing with different opinions. So tonight we will have the first of what I hope will be a number of Bible studies. We want to explore topics like prophecy, land issues, governmental authority, and justice.'

As a one-page, double-sided list of questions was passed to each person in the room, Salim said, 'In our last meeting, most participants expressed a desire to study the word *Israel* and address the question, Who are the people of God? It's not possible to cover the entire issue tonight – the word *Israel* occurs around 2,300 times in English Bibles; 2,267 in Hebrew. We have chosen several points that relate to the theme. I am not proposing a position but giving some guidelines for a study together. Let us encourage and build up each other in the spirit of truth and love.'

We glanced over the handout and instantly realised that this would be a volatile discussion in any setting, but especially now in the Holy Land, between Palestinian and Jewish pastors, with the second intifada raging. The questions would produce strong responses on both sides:

Who are Abraham's offspring? What was their identity and what was the sign of the covenant? What was the relationship of the non-Jew to Abraham's covenant with God?

Who are the heirs of the covenant? Could the covenant be redirected? If so, what happens with the promises to the 'people of God'?

How does God identify His people? Who is the 'Israel of God' today? Who is included? Who is excluded?

Scripture passages were listed under each question, and I knew many more could be included. For centuries scholars had debated them in 'safe' settings. Doctoral dissertations had been written about these issues. But here the stakes were much higher. I already knew that some of my Palestinian friends felt they were second-class citizens in God's kingdom. And some of the Messianic believers were convinced that the Old Testament promises about the land were for them alone, not for the whole Church. Certainly not for the Palestinians!

The spirit of the meeting had already been established during the times of worship, sharing, and prayer. For the most part, the women were quiet while the men debated in the Middle Eastern tradition. Sometimes the statements were intense, but never did any of the participants lose control.

The first question was simple: 'Who was Abraham?'

'Obviously, he was not a Jew!' said one pastor.

'He is identified, most importantly, as a man of faith,' said another.

Salim, as moderator, then asked about Abraham's seed. One pastor noted it was always singular. Another that it was always connected to the land.

'And what is the definition of seed?' asked Salim.

Here things got a little more interesting. A Palestinian: 'People who have the faith of Abraham. See Genesis 17. In the covenant of circumcision, all males in his household were circumcised.' A Messianic leader: 'The children of Abraham – that's what Abraham understood. He was thinking only of an heir.'

The comments came fast and intense and I couldn't tell who was speaking. Yet no one interrupted any speaker – the spirit in the room was sweet, but with intellectual intensity. Salim had intended to break into smaller groups for a more systematic study, but the men and women wouldn't hear of it. Even though there was some jumping around from issue to issue, everyone wanted to hear all of the opinions and weigh all of the evidence.

Someone mentioned Romans 4: 'How did Paul define the children of Abraham? He is the father of Jews and non-Jews – of all who believe.'

One side said faith superseded circumcision. The other said it was an issue of identity based on physical birth and circumcision. 'The promise to the seed cannot be cancelled,' said one pastor, 'but it can be added to.'

David Loden rose to speak: 'The issue is obedience. We've been cast out of the land twice because we've lived in disobedience to God. Jeremiah 3:14 says, "Return, you faithless children." I think that word "faithless" is so bland. Literally, it should read, "Return, you *naughty* children." '

Botrus understood the implications and asked, 'Then where is the prophetic voice of Messianic Jews calling the nation to repent and be righteous?'

A Messianic pastor replied, 'If we were not Christians, we could have a very long discussion about injustice on both sides and reach no conclusion.'

That led to a tense discussion about terrorism and issues of righteousness and justice. One Palestinian pastor wondered why the strongest advocates for Palestinians were leftists and atheists, not believers. A Messianic pastor wanted to know why he didn't hear Palestinian believers speaking out against terrorism and suicide bombers.

The tension was rising. Salim calmed the audience, saying, 'We don't have enough communication between the two sides, but we're also having a hard time within our communities.'

Botrus said, 'I believe we here, Jews and Arabs, are the hope of the land. My heart is that I understand you and you understand me. Every time there is a suicide bomber, we pray as a church for the families.'

Salim agreed: 'We are immersed in the suffering of our people. Both are suffering. We don't need to decide who is suffering more.'

Nihad, fighting back tears, stood and announced, 'I am not a citizen of this world.' There was a stillness in the room as he gained his composure. 'So I can speak without politics. The moment you say, "I am Palestinian", or "I am Jew", you are talking politics. I hurt when I hear believers justify why Israel is in Bethlehem. I preach against bombing. I do not justify it. I am not a Palestinian.'

'You are a citizen of heaven!' David Loden said.

The entire room burst into applause, and Nihad grinned as he said, 'That's it! You and I, we belong to another kingdom, and that is the basis of our unity!'

As the group gathered in a circle for prayer, Salim reminded them, 'For now let's keep confidentiality. Be careful what you say about this meeting, because of the context in which we've talked.'

AL AND I REFLECTED on a remarkable six hours. Certainly there had been an airing out of issues, but it was done in a spirit of love and care built on two earlier meetings where trust was established. There was warmth as the families dispersed and a sense that this was a historic occasion. The rest of the region may not pay much attention, but I felt God was pleased with what had happened this evening.

Later, in the cramped offices of Musalaha in Jerusalem, we asked Salim, 'So what is the future for this work of reconciliation?'

'At first, we mostly had only evangelicals involved from both sides. Now we have people from the traditional churches participating. Orthodox, Catholic, Lutheran are involved with us. We are having our first camp next summer for Palestinian and Jewish youth ages ten to fourteen.[2] The next step is to involve nonbelievers. Every one of us in both communities is in touch with nonbelievers. So every time we meet, our friends and neighbours and co-workers know we are meeting people from the other side. These people ask us how we impact the other society. So we would like, maybe next year, to do a conference only for nonbelievers.'

'Can that really work? Your approach is so distinctively Christian.'

'Our thinking is that we want to be a model. We want to bring more people into the process until we reach a critical mass where it becomes a movement. We've already made some impact. Ten years ago reconciliation was not an issue. Now there is awareness, and other groups are beginning to try this.'

'I agree with you. We have often discussed that we need models that others can replicate. Musalaha needs to become a movement. That is something the Church is indeed uniquely positioned to do.'

There was something else on my mind, and I thought this would be the right place to ask the question: 'What can the Church in the West do to help?'

Salim sighed and then said, 'I wish the Church would understand the struggles Palestinians have. We have to deal with Judaism. We have to deal with Islam. And we have to deal with who we are, with our nationalism. Plus we have to deal with Western Christianity.'

I asked him to explain.

'Here's the problem. What is the vehicle of Westernisation here in the Middle East? It's mainly in Israel. It's the Jews. So that puts a question mark on the Palestinian Christians, because their beliefs and lifestyle can indicate that they like the Israeli side more than the Palestinian side, so that they are perceived as betraying their community. Then add to that other Christian groups that express dislike for Palestinians. That's hard to deal with.'

Salim didn't go into detail, but I knew he was talking about organisations that automatically approved of any actions by Israel above any claims made by Palestinians, Christian or otherwise.

So was there hope for those children violating curfew in Bethlehem, building barriers in the streets to taunt Israeli soldiers? And what about the children of Israel, who lived in fear of being on the wrong bus when a suicide bomber boarded and who faced the certain prospect of military service and having to confront fellow dwellers of the land? The politicians weren't solving the problems. The nations of the world were issuing resolutions that were ignored.

Could anyone do any better? The Musalaha meeting showed us the answer. The Church was the only hope for the Middle East, not because she had a better programme or more political insight. She didn't. What she had was a way to bring people from both sides together based on the work of one Man whose birth two thousand years ago would be celebrated in a few days. His light still shone through believers here in the Holy Land. Many didn't understand the light. Many covered their eyes and refused to acknowledge the light. Others attacked the light and tried to put it out. But surely there were those who realised the bankruptcy of a peace process that had brought no peace for fifty years. For those who were willing, they could see the answer – Palestinians and Jews meeting at the foot of the cross.

THIRTY-NINE

NOW WHAT?

Gaza City, October 2003

A crowd gathered around a television monitor to watch as the film reached its climax. As Roman soldiers nailed Jesus to a cross, a hush fell over the group. Most of these curious Palestinians had been taught as Muslims that Jesus wasn't really crucified but was taken to heaven and replaced on the cross by Judas Iscariot.

The Palestinian Ministry of Culture had organised a book fair at a Gaza shopping mall, and fifteen local bookshops displayed a varied assortment of resources on Palestinian nationalism, English instruction, technology, computer software, and especially Islam. Among them was an exhibit by The Teacher's Bookshop, displaying and selling Christian materials. For five shekels (about one US dollar) people could buy a package containing the book *More than a Carpenter* by Josh McDowell, a New Testament, and a videocassette version of the movie *Jesus.* More than one hundred packages were sold, but it was the visual depiction of Jesus crucified, dead, and risen again that drew the crowds. After each showing of the movie, people lingered to talk with the staff of the Palestinian Bible

Society and to thumb through Bibles and other Christian books.

One young man kept returning each day. 'I cannot take any of these books home,' he said apologetically. 'My family would destroy them.' Instead, after each discussion he'd go home and scour the Internet to learn more about Jesus, returning the next day with new questions.

Since this was a Muslim-dominated society, a few visitors were agitated by the Bible bookshop display, but most were curious. Mall employees even brought people to the booth and urged staff to tell them about the Bible. Numerous school groups visited and learned how the Quran recognises that the Torah (Old Testament) and *Injil* (New Testament) are from heaven. Then the staff would teach that the Bible is God's Word and present the gospel. One elementary schoolgirl listened, then said, 'If I stay a bit longer in your place, I will get a brainwash; this is something that is too attractive to hear.'

Over ten days, 6,200 people saw the exhibit. On the final day, a man who had visited the display several times came to help the staff pack up books and clean the shelves. 'I'm going to miss seeing you every day,' he said. The staff told him to come and visit them anytime at The Teacher's Bookshop. It was obvious that he had experienced the love of Jesus. Long after the books and theological discussions are forgotten, the love he experienced would be remembered.

Colorado Springs, November 2003

How does one end this story? There is no 'happily ever after' conclusion. The conflict in the Middle East isn't resolved. There has been no signed peace accord. 'Just what have you accomplished?' Al asked me. 'What are the results of your work?'

I know what many readers want. Their unspoken demands are: Show us the terrorists who repented! Where is the peace plan you negotiated, Andrew? What impact have you had on Yasser Arafat and Hamas leaders as a result of your conversations with them?

But I can't produce measurable results. I can only ask this question: What if I had *not* gone? Let's take the report we just read from Gaza. Over ten days approximately 6,200 people were exposed to the Good News. Only God knows what happened in those hearts.

What if there had not been a bookshop in Gaza? There would have been no display at the book fair, and those 6,200 people would have missed the chance to see the light. And why did this shop exist? Because one man, Labib Madanat, had a vision. How did he get that vision? By seeing that you could speak to Muslim fundamentalists about Christianity and they would listen. And why did those Hamas leaders listen? Because I went to see them in their time of need.

Suppose I hadn't gone to Marj al-Zohour? Perhaps God would have sent someone else. But that's the point: Each of us needs to respond to God's call. Is it God's heart to reach Palestinians with the Good News of Christ? Then we must go. More important, we must strengthen the Church there so it can spread the gospel.

Here's another scenario. Suppose there wasn't a Bible college in Bethlehem? Who would be pastor of Jerusalem Alliance Church if Jack Sara, trained at Bethlehem Bible College, were not the pastor? Who would be taking phone calls from distraught Christian and Muslim women who need a friend like Nawal Qumsieh to point them to the grace of Christ? Without Bethlehem Bible College, she wouldn't be in ministry. And who would have trained Pastor Hanna Massad? Without Pastor Hanna, would Gaza Baptist Church still exist? And if not, how would Rami have found peace for his tormented soul?

That school was the result of a dream and the incredible hard work of Bishara Awad. But someone needed to encourage him, pray with him and for him, and tell his story so others could get involved and help him in many practical ways including financial support. Any Christian can do that, and fortunately many now do that for Bishara.

Couldn't foreign workers have done what these men and women did? At this moment (November 2003) Israel wasn't giving visas to Christian workers. It was likely that without trained local leadership, the Church would have scattered and become ineffective. The light would be a lot dimmer. Perhaps it would have gone out altogether.

Look at Salim Munayer – no outsider could have organised the reconciliation efforts of Musalaha.

Look at Doron Even-Ari, director of Bible Society of Israel, and Labib Madanat, his counterpart in the West Bank and Gaza – they have far more opportunities for ministry in Israel and Palestine than any foreign worker would have.

Hanna, Bishara, Salim, David and Lisa Loden, Nawal, Jack, Labib, Doron, and too many more to name – they are the Light Force in Israel, West Bank, and Gaza. They are the only hope for the Middle East because they are the light of Jesus.

But they can't make it alone. They need the rest of the body of Christ. The parts that are strong need to help the weaker members.

Al thought about my passionate statements. Finally he asked, 'So what should Christians in the West do?'

Our brothers and sisters have told us what they need. First, and most important, they have begged us to pray! It's been the same throughout my fifty years of ministry; wherever I've gone to encourage my brethren, they have always requested prayer.

Let me reiterate the point I just made. In relation to our work in Communist countries, the point is the same: What if we had not done it? I have never attached much value to our work except spiritual value. But who knows what would have happened to the Church in the Soviet Union and Eastern Europe if we had not gone and if we had not prayed. Because of our prayers and our actions, incredibly much did happen, for which nobody, certainly not us, can take any credit.

Prayer is a critical part of the work of Open Doors, and thousands are praying for the Middle East. Prayer connects us with the body. It helps us identify with those who suffer and struggle as Christians in difficult situations. Prayer brings these problems to the one source that can really make a difference, but it must be intelligent prayer, not 'God bless the missions wherever they are in the world today'. Intelligent prayer is where you open your heart and your ears. One way to start is to pray every time you see news from the Middle East. Pray for families that suffer because of the casualties on both sides. Pray for the gospel to be spread among Jews and Palestinians. Pray for the men and women you've read about in this book – that their ministries will bear fruit. Maybe you could also pray for that frightened young Muslim fundamentalist who may be preparing to go and blow himself up – that God would speak to his soul, perhaps through a local Christian who is brave enough to tell him the Good News that Jesus Christ died for him.

Palestinian believers aren't asking for much – just a little room in our hearts. Bishara and Labib have both said to me, 'Don't stop loving Israel, but love us as well.' Isn't there room in our hearts for both? This leads to my next point. Prayer should draw us to the place and the people that we pray for. When you pray, you may find that God wants you to answer your own prayer by doing something. All of us can give. The missions mentioned in the book can always use our help: The Bible societies of Lebanon, Israel, and Palestine; the work of Naji Abi-Hashem, via Venture International; Arab Baptist Seminary in Lebanon; Hope School in Beit Jala; Bethlehem Bible College; Shepherd's Society; Beit Asaf congregation in Netanya; Musalaha; Hanna Massad and Gaza Baptist Church, via Mission to Gaza. (See the appendix for contact information for these ministries.)

You can also help through the ministry of Open Doors. We are committed to strengthening the Church in the Middle East through projects that support many of these ministries. This year, at the request of Messianic congregations, we will begin providing discipleship training for young people, primarily those who have just finished their military service.

Finally, you can go! I'm not excited about tourism, but if you are planning to go to the Holy Land to see the biblical sites, why not also plan to visit some of the living stones? Seek out your brothers and sisters. I want to emphasise this point – what I have done you can do as well. There is no special skill involved. Attend a Saturday or Sunday service with local believers, whether in a Messianic congregation or at a Palestinian church. It would be a huge encouragement to them and to you!

I WISH I KNEW where I first heard this story. To me, it captures the essence of the conflict in the Middle East and points powerfully to the solution. I close our book by sharing it as I have received it:

A certain man had two sons. One was rich and the other was

poor. The rich son had no children, while the poor son was blessed with many sons and many daughters. In time the father fell ill. He was sure he would not live through the week, so on Saturday he called his sons to his side and gave each of them half of his land as their inheritance. Then he died. Before sundown the sons buried their father with respect.

That night the rich son could not sleep. He said to himself, *What my father did was not just. I am rich; my brother is poor. I have plenty of bread, while my brother's children eat one day and trust God for the next. I must move the landmark that our father has set in the middle of the land so that my brother will have the greater share. Ah, but he must not see me; if he sees me, he will be shamed. I must arise early in the morning before it is dawn and move the landmark!* With this he fell asleep and his sleep was secure and peaceful.

Meanwhile the poor brother could not sleep. As he lay restless on his bed, he said to himself, *What my father did was not just. Here I am surrounded by the joy of many sons and many daughters, while my brother daily faces the shame of having no sons to carry on his name and no daughters to comfort him in his old age. He should have the land of our fathers. Perhaps this will in part compensate him for his indescribable poverty. Ah, but if I give it to him he will be shamed; I must awake early in the morning before it is dawn and move the landmark that our father has set!* With this he went to sleep and his sleep was secure and peaceful.

On the first day of the week, very early in the morning, a long time before it was day, the two brothers met at the ancient landmark. They fell with tears into each other's arms, and on that spot was built the *new Jerusalem.*

ORGANISATIONS

The following ministries are mentioned in this book. If you wish to learn more about them, you may contact them as follows:

Arab Baptist Seminary: www.abtslebanon.org
Bible societies:
Lebanon, www.biblesociety.org.lb
Israel, www.biblesocietyinisrael.org
West Bank and Gaza, www.pbsociety.org
Bethlehem Bible College, including volunteer opportunities: www.bethlehembiblecollege.edu
Beit Asaf Messianic Congregation in Netanya: www.beit-asaph. org.il
Musalaha: www.musalaha.org
Hope School in Beit Jala: www.hope-school.8k.com
Hanna Massad and Gaza Baptist Church, contact Christian Mission to Gaza, 3433 Ellesmere Dr., Corona, CA 92882, USA
Naji Abi-Hashem and Venture International, contact Venture International, P.O. Box 7396, Tempe, AZ 85281-0014, USA
Open Doors: www.opendoors.org for information on the international work and links to national bases.

NOTES

Chapter 1 The Horror

1. In 1999 the school was renamed Israel College of the Bible.
2. See Brother Andrew with Vern Becker, *God's Call* (1996; reprint, Grand Rapids: Revell, 2002), 13–17.
3. Jews who believe in Jesus (called Yeshua) as Messiah.

Chapter 2 Not a Mindless Terrorist

1. An Arabic word that means 'shaking off' or 'an abrupt and sudden waking up from sleep'. The first intifada started in 1987 and lasted nearly six years.
2. *Injil* is the Arab word for 'Gospel', used by Muslims for the New Testament.
3. The next day when he picked us up for our meeting with Sheikh Al-Shami, Abdul told us that he had already read half of *God's Smuggler*, and he asked if we could get him any more books about Christianity. Eighteen months later, we met him again and gave him three more Christian books in Arabic, plus an Arabic Bible. He said both he and his oldest son had read *God's Smuggler* and he had visited the Bible bookshop in Gaza City.

Chapter 3 Where Was the Church?

1. Kibbutzim are communes in Israel where multiple families live together and combine resources in agricultural and other business enterprises.
2. D. H. Vogel, ed., *Paul Schneider, der Prediger von Buchenwald* (Berlin: Evangelische Verlagsansalt, 1961).

Chapter 4 Weeping for Lebanon

1. For one of the best accounts of the war in Lebanon, see Robert Fisk, *Pity the Nation: The Abduction of Lebanon* (New York: Simon and Schuster, 1990); see also Thomas L. Friedman, *From Beirut to Jerusalem* (New York: Random House, 1989, 1990, and 1995).

Chapter 6 The Need for Wisdom with Zeal

1. *Marhaba* means 'hello' in Arabic.

Chapter 7 A Plan for Peace

1. After Naji earned his doctorate, he settled in Seattle, Washington, where he is involved in counselling and teaching. He spends about four months each year in active ministry in Lebanon and the Middle East. Among other activities, he teaches at Arab Baptist Seminary and provides counselling to struggling individuals and families.

Chapter 8 It's Just a Mess

1. See Fisk, *Pity the Nation*, 437.

Chapter 10 I Have No Power

1. See William Dalrymple, *From the Holy Mountain* (New York: Henry Holt, 1997), 217.

Chapter 11 Meeting with an Ayatollah

1. This scene was inspired by stories of various hostages. Sources include Terry Anderson, *Den of Lions* (Ballantine Books, 1993); Brian Keenan, *An Evil Cradling* (Vintage, 1992); Sis Levin, *Beirut Diary* (InterVarsity Press, 1989); John McCarthy and Jill Morrell, *Some Other Rainbow* (Bantam, 1993); and Terry Waite, *Taken on Trust* (Harcourt Brace, 1993).

2. The title Sayyid indicated Fadlallah was a descendant of the Prophet Muhammad through the Imam Husayn. An ayatollah (from the Arabic meaning 'sign of God') is a Shi'ite leader recognised as teacher, judge and administrator. The title is the highest rank among Shi'ite Muslims and is bestowed by informal acclamation.

3. Shi'ites are a smaller but more radical element of Muslims than the Sunnis, who form the majority. Sunnis simply follow the model behaviour and teaching of Muhammad. See Don McCurry, *Healing the Broken Family of Abraham: New Life for Muslims* (Colorado Springs: Ministries to Muslims, 2001), 85–88.

4. Quote and background information about Fadlallah taken from R. Scott Appleby, ed., *Spokesmen for the Despised* (Chicago: University of Chicago Press, 1997), 83–181.

5. Arabic for 'Thank you.'

Part 3 West Bank and Gaza

1. See Benny Morris, *Righteous Victims* (New York: Knopf, 1999), 189–258.

2. For more information about the Christian population in Israel, West Bank, and Gaza, see Betty Jane Bailey and J. Martin Bailey, *Who Are the Christians in the Middle East* (Grand Rapids, MI: Eerdmans, 2003). The authors write: 'Within the 1948 borders of Israel, there are today about 105,000 Christians, approximately 2 percent of the total population. . . . The largest Christian communities in Israel are Greek Catholics (Melkites) and Greek Orthodox. . . . In Palestine (including Gaza, the West Bank, and occupied East Jerusalem) there are an estimated 76,000 Christians who represent 3 percent of the total population. More than half of these Christians belong to Greek Orthodox parishes. . . . In Gaza, where Christianity dates to the preaching of the Apostle Philip . . . there are today only about 2,000 Christians' (152–53).

Chapter 13 A Well-Aimed Stone

1. Bishara and his wife, Salwa, obtained permanent resident status in Israel after Salwa applied for and was granted a family reunion.

Chapter 14 I Want to See Living Stones

1. For more information about this defining event in Palestinian history, see Benny Morris, *The Birth of the Palestinian Refugee Problem, 1947–1949* (Cambridge University Press, 1987), 113–15; see also Morris, *Righteous Victims*, 207–9. Benny Morris is professor of history at Ben-Gurion University in Beersheba, Israel.

Chapter 15 What Are We Supposed to Do?

1. One dunam equals 1,000 square metres, approximately one-quarter acre.
2. A thorough overview on the first intifada can be found in Morris, *Righteous Victims*, 561–610.
3. See ibid., 565.
4. Ibid. See also Amira Hass, *Drinking the Sea at Gaza* (New York: Henry Holt, 1996), 145–48. Her figures vary from those of Morris, but she makes the same point. As a reporter on Palestinian affairs for the Israeli newspaper *Ha'aretz,* Hass writes: 'Palestinians in the occupied territories receive an average of 93 litres per day per capita (101 litres in Gaza and 85 in the West Bank); Israelis living in the territories receive 280 litres per day' (145).
5. For details about these two wars, see Morris, *Righteous Victims*, 259–346.

Chapter 16 Bringing the Two Sides Together

1. This story is a dramatic reconstruction. Yitzhak and Wa'el are characters created for this book, but their story is based on those of actual participants in Musalaha and interviews conducted by Barbara Baker for Compass Direct News Service.
2. A large cloth used by Arabs as a head covering.

Chapter 17 What Will This Suffering Accomplish?

1. For example, see Beverly Milton-Edwards, *Islamic Politics in Palestine* (London: I. B. Tauris, 1996), 103–4, 123.
2. See Morris, *Righteous Victims*, 577.
3. For excerpts of the Hamas charter, see Walter Laqueur and Barry Rubin, eds., *The Israel-Arab Reader,* 6th ed. (New York:

Penguin, 2001), 341–48. The complete text of the charter can be found at www.palestinecenter.org/cpap/documents/charter.html.

Chapter 18 Every Tent Is a Mosque
1. An imam leads prayers in a mosque. The title is also used for Muslim leaders.

Chapter 20 A Meal with Terrorists
1. In July 2003 Yossi Beilin, former Israeli Minister of Justice and architect of the Oslo Accords and Geneva Plan, told me personally that 'the deportation of the Hamas to Lebanon was a big mistake'.

Chapter 21 How Far Do I Go?
1. See Anton LaGuardia, *War without End* (New York: Thomas Dunne Books, 2001), 290–95. LaGuardia was Middle East correspondent based in Jerusalem for the *Daily Telegraph* and went to Hebron to cover the story. He writes, 'Nearly as many people were killed outside the mosque as inside it. One bloody clash took place outside the hospital itself where, for some reason, a squad of soldiers had decided to make a provocative appearance' (292).

Chapter 22 What I Saw Today Are God Seekers
1. It's been suggested that Goldstein intended just such a reaction. In *From Beirut to Jerusalem,* Thomas Friedman writes: 'Baruch Goldstein, I am convinced, understood that the only way to break that silence was not with some garden-variety act of terrorism, not just by killing a few Palestinian children or pregnant women. No, it required something so outrageous, so unspeakable, that it would move masses of Palestinians to react, which he hoped would trigger a massive Israeli counter-reaction and suddenly the silent majorities, instead of being passive and inert, would be mobilised, angry, and at each other's throats. So he shot up one of the holiest sites of Islam' (New York: Anchor Books, 1995), 559.

Chapter 24 What Kind of People Does the Book Produce?

1. Traditionally the road Jesus took to the cross.

Chapter 25 Hamas Would Like a Cease-Fire

1. See Friedman, *From Beirut to Jerusalem*, 106–25.
2. *Abu Amar* means 'Father of the Builder' and would be used by people Arafat considers friends.
3. See the Balfour Declaration in Laqueur and Rubin, eds., *The Israel-Arab Reader*, 16. See also Morris, *Righteous Victims*, 73–76.
4. Quoted in Hanna Massad, 'The Theological Foundation for Reconciliation between the Palestinian Christians and the Messianic Jews' (PhD diss., Fuller Theological Seminary, 1999), 158–59.

Chapter 26 Called to a Higher Statecraft

1. Matthew 26:1–2 NKJV.
2. Sheikh Yassin was killed by an Israeli missile on 22 March 2004. Dr Abdulaziz Rantisi was immediately named Yassin's successor as leader of Hamas. Rantisi was assassinated by an Israeli missile on 17 April 2004. No successor to Rantisi was officially named, but several Israeli media sources reported that the new Hamas leader was Mahmoud Zahar (see Haretz, 26 April 2004). Zahar was the last of the original founders of Hamas still living.

Chapter 27 The Teacher's Bookshop

1. Indeed, later, Mahmoud Zahar told me that he had visited the shop.

Part 4 The Second Intifada

1. The figures were taken from the Middle East Policy Council web site at www.mepc.org/public_asp/resources/mrates.asp.
2. Over nearly six years of the first intifada, there were a total of 80 Israelis and 1,070 Palestinians killed. In just the first year of the second intifada (December 2000 through December 2001), 232 Israelis and 904 Palestinians were killed. See B'TSELEM, the Israeli Information Centre for Human Rights in the Occupied Territories, at www.btselem.org.

3. It appears that a local Muslim tribe known for its violence did much of the shooting at Gilo. See David Neff, 'Thugs in Jesus' Hometown', *Christianity Today* (Dec. 2003), 60–61. Neff was reviewing the book *A Season in Bethlehem: Unholy War in a Sacred Place* by Joshua Hammer.

Chapter 30 It Is Not Suicide – It Is Religious

1. Amanda Ripley, 'Why Suicide Bombing Is Now All the Rage', *Time* (15 April 2002).

Chapter 32 Miracle in Holland

1. Romans 12:10–21.
2. See *Facts and Myths about the Messianic Congregations in Israel*, a survey conducted by Kai Kjaer-Hansen and Bodil F. Skjott (Jerusalem: United Christian Council in Israel, 1999).

Chapter 33 What Do You Preach When There Is Shelling?

1. Alison captured her experiences in a journal. See Alison Jones Nassar and Fred Strickert, *Imm Mathilda: A Bethlehem Mother's Diary* (Minneapolis: Kirk House, 2003).

Chapter 34 The Light Is a Little Brighter

1. School is not free. Even though it costs only a few dollars, it is more than many families can afford.

Chapter 35 A Donkey Cries for Gaza

1. See John 1:46.
2. See www.lebnet/~bcome/palestine/xian.html, which reported on the deaths of three men in Gaza on 2 February 1988; see also www.en.falastiny.net/books/massacres.

Chapter 36 Sneaking into Bethlehem

1. A week later the Christmas party was cancelled because of continuing curfew and travel restrictions.

Chapter 38 A Model Others Can Follow

1. See Compass Direct News Service articles at www.compass direct.org.
2. Musalaha sponsors an annual meeting for youth leaders. One

of the leaders suggested they conduct a youth camp. It was held from 28 July to 1 August 2003, and twenty Israelis and twenty Palestinians participated.

SELECTED BIBLIOGRAPHY

Anderson, Terry. *Den of Lions*. New York: Ballantine Books, 1993.

Appleby, R. Scott, ed. *Spokesmen for the Despised: Fundamentalist Leaders of the Middle East*. Chicago: University of Chicago Press, 1997.

Armstrong, Karen. *Jerusalem: One City, Three Faiths*. New York: Ballantine Books, 1996.

Avnery, Uri. *My Friend, the Enemy*. London: Zed Books, 1986.

Awad, Alex. *Through the Eyes of the Victims: The Story of the Arab-Israeli Conflict*. Bethlehem: Bethlehem Bible College, 2001.

Bailey, Betty Jane, and J. Martin. *Who Are the Christians in the Middle East?* Grand Rapids, MI: Eerdmans, 2003.

Barghouti, Mourid. *I Saw Ramallah*. Trans. Adaf Soueif. New York: Anchor Books, 2000.

Bentley, David. *Persian Princess @ magi.com*. Belleville, Ontario, Canada: Guardian Books, 2002.

Bishara, Marwan. *Palestine/Israel: Peace or Apartheid*. London: Zed Books, 2001.

Blumenfeld, Laura. *Revenge: A Story of Hope*. New York: Washington Square Press, 2002.

Carey, Roane, ed. *The New Intifada: Resisting Israel's Apartheid*. New York: Verso, 2001.

Chacour, Elias. *Blood Brothers*. New York: Chosen Books, 1984.

____, with Mary E. Jensen. *We Belong to the Land: The Story of a*

Palestinian Who Lives for Peace and Reconciliation. San Francisco: HarperSanFrancisco, 1990.

Chapman, Colin. *Whose Promised Land? The Continuing Crisis over Israel and Palestine.* Grand Rapids, MI: Baker, 2002.

Dalrymple, William. *From the Holy Mountain: A Journey among the Christians of the Middle East.* New York: Henry Holt, 1997.

Diamant, Anita, and Howard Cooper. *Living a Jewish Life: Jewish Traditions, Customs, and Values for Today's Families.* New York: HarperPerennial, 1991.

Dolan, David. *Israel at the Crossroads: Fifty Years and Counting.* Grand Rapids, MI: Revell, 1998.

Ellisen, Stanley A. *Who Owns the Land?* Portland, OR: Multnomah, 1991.

Fisk, Robert. *Pity the Nation: The Abduction of Lebanon.* New York: Touchstone Books, 1990.

Friedman, Thomas L. *From Beirut to Jerusalem.* New York: Anchor Books, 1995.

——. *Longitudes and Attitudes: Exploring the World after September 11.* New York: Farrar Straus Giroux, 2002.

Gordis, Daniel. *If a Place Can Make You Cry: Dispatches from an Anxious State.* New York: Crown, 2002.

Hass, Amira. *Drinking the Sea at Gaza: Days and Nights in a Land under Siege.* Trans. Elana Wesley and Maxine Kaufman-Lacusta. New York: Henry Holt, 1999.

Hiro, Dilip. *Sharing the Promised Land: A Tale of Israelis and Palestinians.* New York: Olive Branch Press, 1999.

Holliday, Laurel. *Children of Israel, Children of Palestine: Our Own True Stories.* New York: Pocket Books, 1998.

Hourani, Albert. *A History of the Arab Peoples.* New York: Warner Books, 1991.

La Guardia, Anton. *War without End: Israelis, Palestinians, and the Struggle for a Promised Land.* New York: Thomas Dunne Books, 2003.

Levin, Sis. *Beirut Diary.* Downers Grove, IL: InterVarsity, 1989.

Lewis, Bernard. *The Middle East: A Brief History of the Last 2,000 Years.* New York: Scribner, 1995.

——. *What Went Wrong? The Clash Between Islam and Modernity in the Middle East.* New York: Oxford University Press, 2002.

Loden, Lisa, Peter Walker, and Michael Wood, eds. *The Bible and the Land: An Encounter.* Jerusalem: Musalaha, 2000.

Miller, Judith. *God Has Ninety-Nine Names: Reporting from a Militant Middle East.* New York: Simon and Schuster, 1996.

Milton-Edwards, Beverly. *Islamic Politics in Palestine.* London: I. B. Tauris, 1999.

Morris, Benny. *The Birth of the Palestinian Refugee Problem, 1947–1949.* Cambridge: Cambridge University Press, 1987.

——. *Righteous Victims: A History of the Zionist-Arab Conflict, 1881–1999.* New York: Knopf, 1999.

Munayer, Salim J. *In the Footsteps of Our Father Abraham.* Jerusalem: Musalaha, 2002.

——, ed. *Seeking and Pursuing Peace: The Process, the Pain, and the Product.* Jerusalem: Musalaha, 1998.

Patai, Raphael. *The Arab Mind.* New York: Hatherleigh Press, 2002.

Philpott, Ellie. *My Enemy, My Friend.* Tonbridge, Kent, England: Sovereign World, 2002.

——. *Travellers on the Narrow Road.* Tonbridge, Kent, England: Sovereign World, 1999.

Raheb, Mitri. *I Am a Palestinian Christian.* Minneapolis: Augsburg, 1995.

Reuters. *The Israeli-Palestinian Conflict: Crisis in the Middle East.* Upper Saddle River, NJ: Prentice Hall, 2002.

Rittner, Carol, Stephen D. Smith, and Irena Steinfeld, eds. *The Holocaust and the Christian World.* London: Kuperard, 2000.

Schiff, Ze'ev, and Ehud Ya-ari. *Israel's Lebanon War.* Ed. and trans. Ina Friedman. New York: Simon and Schuster, 1984.

Sennott, Charles M. *The Body and the Blood: The Middle East's Vanishing Christians and the Possibility for Peace.* New York: Public Affairs, 2001.

Shipler, David K. *Arab and Jew: Wounded Spirits in a Promised Land.* New York: Penguin Books, 2002.

Shlaim, Avi. *War and Peace in the Middle East: A Concise History.* New York: Penguin Books, 1995.

Stern, Jessica. *Terror in the Name of God: Why Religious Militants Kill.* New York: HarperCollins, 2003.

Waite, Terry. *Taken on Trust.* New York: Harcourt Brace, 1993.

Wallach, John and Janet. *Arafat: In the Eyes of the Beholder.* London: Mandarin, 1990.

Yad Vashem. *The Holocaust.* Jerusalem: The Holocaust Martyrs' and Heroes' Remembrance Authority.

Fiction

Stone, Robert. *Damascus Gate.* New York: Scribner, 1998.

Uris, Leon. *Exodus.* New York: Bantam, 1959.

——. *The Haj.* New York: Bantam, 1985.

——. *QB VII.* New York: Bantam, 1972.

Wilentz, Amy. *Martyrs' Crossing.* New York: Ballantine Books, 2001.

THE AUTHORS

Brother Andrew began his work in 1955 as a one-man mission – visiting, teaching, and taking Bibles to Christians behind the Iron Curtain. That work has since developed into Open Doors International, a nondenominational organisation with bases around the world. When not travelling, Brother Andrew makes his home in the Netherlands.

Al Janssen has co-written or authored more than twenty-five books, including Focus on the Family's *The Marriage Masterpiece*. He is chairman of the board for Open Doors (USA) with Brother Andrew and is writer-in-residence for Open Doors International. Janssen lives in Colorado Springs, Colorado.

Other books about the Persecuted Church

Tortured for Christ

'Neither prison nor torture can frighten the Christians of the Underground Church.'

Richard Wurmbrand endured months of solitary confinement, years of periodic physical torture, constant suffering from hunger and cold, the anguish of brainwashing and mental cruelty. His captors lied to his wife, saying he was dead. Yet he went on to tell the West the truth about Christianity behind the Iron Curtain.

Updated new edition published October 2004: ISBN 0 340 86368 4

God's Smuggler

A new edition of this all-time Christian classic, with recently written material bringing Brother Andrew's story up to date.

Since its publication in the late sixties, *God's Smuggler* has been read by more than ten million people. The adventure-packed, inspirational true story tells of Brother Andrew's journey from humble beginnings to a worldwide mission to bring Bibles to Christians cut off from the Church.

New edition published March 2005: ISBN 0 340 86294 7

Hidden Sorrow, Lasting Joy

Anneke Companjen, wife of the President of Open Doors International, tells the true stories of twenty contemporary Christian women from all around the world. Some suffer direct persecution for what they believe. Others are the wives, mothers and daughters of the men who are imprisoned, tortured and murdered. Every story is unique: challenging, shocking and an inspiring witness to God's provision.

Updated new edition published February 2005: ISBN 0 340 75675 6

The Hiding Place

As the Nazi madness swept across Europe, a quiet watchmaker's family in Holland risked everything for the sake of others, and for the love of Christ. Despite the danger and threat of discovery, they courageously offered shelter to persecuted Jews. Then a trap brought about the arrest of Corrie ten Boom and her family. Could God's love shine through, even in Ravensbrück?

Long-awaited new edition published November 2004: ISBN 0 340 86353 6

"Each of us needs to respond to God's call."

"The Light Force in Israel, West Bank and Gaza...can't make it alone. They need the rest of the body of Christ. The parts that are strong need to help the weaker members. You can help through the ministry of Open Doors." - Brother Andrew

Founded by Brother Andrew in 1955, Open Doors serves the body of Christ worldwide by providing persecuted Christians with Bibles and Christian literature, leadership and pastoral training, community development schemes, prayer and personal encouragement. Open Doors works in nearly 50 countries with Christians who are most at risk.

Visit our websites to find out how you can respond to God's call. You will find the latest information and details of how you can help through prayer, action and giving.

If you are in the UK:
www.opendoorsuk.org

If you are elsewhere in the world:
www.od.org

Open *Doors*
Serving persecuted **Christians** worldwide

UK Registered Charity No. 260600

For more information
on Open Doors

For updated prayer points, or to learn about additional resources and involvement opportunities with the Persecuted Church, please contact your national Open Doors office.

Open Doors
PO Box 53
Seaforth
New South Wales 2092
AUSTRALIA

www.opendoors.org.au

Missao Portas Abertas
Rua do Estilo Barroco, 633
Chacara Santo Antonio
04709-011 - Sao Paulo, SP
BRAZIL

www.portasabertas.org.br

Open Doors
30–5155 Spectrum Way
Mississauga,ON
L4W 5A1
CANADA

www.opendoorsca.org

Åbne Døre
PO Box 1062
DK-7500 Holstebro
DENMARK

www.opendoors.nu

Portes Ouvertes
BP 139
F-67833 Tanneries
Cedex (Strasbourg)
FRANCE

www.portesouvertes.fr

Offene Grenzen Deutschland
Postfach 1142
DE-65761 Kelkheim
Bundesrepublik
GERMANY

www.offene-grenzen.de

Porte Aperte
CP45
37063 Isola Della Scala, VR
ITALY

www.porteaperteitalia.org

Open Doors
Hyerim Presbyterian Church
Street No. 403
Sungne 3-dong
Kandong-gu #134-033
Seoul
KOREA

www.opendoors.or.kr

Open Doors
PO Box 47
3850 AA Ermelo
THE NETHERLANDS

www.opendoors.nl

Open Doors
PO Box 27-630
Mt Roskill
Auckland 1030
NEW ZEALAND

www.opendoors.org.nz

Åpne Dører
Barstolveien 50 F
4636 Kristiansand
NORWAY

www.opendoors.no

Open Doors
PO Box 1573-1155
QCCPO Main
1100 Quezon City
PHILIPPINES

Open Doors
Raffles City Post Office
PO Box 150
Singapore 911705
Republic of Singapore

www.opendoors.org/ODS/
index.htm

Open Doors
Box 990099
Kibler Park 2053
Johannesburg
SOUTH AFRICA

www.opendoors.org.za

Puertas Abiertas
Apartado 578
28850 Torrejon de Ardoz
Madrid
SPAIN

www.puertasabiertas.org

Open Doors
PO Box 27001
Santa Ana, CA 92799
USA

www.opendoorsusa.org

Portes Ouvertes
Case Postale 267
CH-1008 Prilly
Lausanne
SWITZERLAND

www.portesouvertes.ch/en

International website:
www.opendoors.org

Open Doors
PO Box 6
Witney
Oxon 0X29 6WG
UNITED KINGDOM

www.opendoorsuk.org

A VERY BRIEF HISTORY

LESS THAN FORTY YEARS after Christ ascended into Heaven the Romans put down a Jewish revolt and destroyed the second temple in Jerusalem. A second revolt in 135 AD resulted in the banishment of Jews from Jerusalem. Many Jews scattered to various parts of the world. But the land was not empty. Arabs, many of them Christians, were already living there and more migrated to Judea, Samaria, and Galilee.

In 638, Jerusalem was conquered by Muslim warriors and in 692 the Dome of the Rock was completed over the spot where Abraham was said to have offered up Isaac, where the Holy of Holies was located in two Jewish temples, and where Mohammad supposedly ascended into Heaven on his night journey. During the Middle Ages the land and particularly Jerusalem saw many conflicts between armies of Arab Muslims and Christian crusaders.

In 1882 the first wave of Jews, fleeing from persecution, returned to the land from Russia. As the nineteenth century drew to a close the Zionist movement under the inspiration of Theodor Herzl was born. It argued that Jews could only be safe by having their own country in Palestine or elsewhere. In 1917 the Balfour Declaration stated Britain's support for a Jewish national homeland in Palestine. Great Britain assumed control of Palestine after World War I.

Over the years Arab and Jewish groups often battled for control of the region. Meanwhile pressure built on Jews in Germany and spread throughout Europe following Nazi conquests. The result was the Holocaust in which 6,000,000 Jews died. After World War II many Jewish survivors headed for British-controlled Palestine and pressure grew for a Jewish state. In 1947 the United Nations voted to partition Palestine into two states, one for Jews, the other for Arabs, with Jerusalem as a neutral city. Fighting between the two sides broke out immediately, and where Jewish forces prevailed, Palestinians fled, becoming refugees in Lebanon, Jordan, and Gaza.

Israel declared itself a state on 14 May 1948. Armies from surrounding Arab states immediately attacked but Israel repelled the invasion. When fighting ceased, Jordan occupied the West Bank, Egypt the Gaza Strip, and Israel controlled the rest of the land. A form of peace lasted until 1956 when Israel attacked Egypt and conquered much of the Sinai Peninsula. Israel later withdrew under world pressure. At an Arab summit in Cairo in 1964, the Palestinian Liberation Organization was formed. War erupted again in June 1967 and in six spectacular days Israel overwhelmingly defeated forces from Egypt, Jordan, and Syria, and in the process conquered East Jerusalem, West Bank, Golan Heights, Gaza, and Sinai.

Since 1967, these are a few key events:

1969 Yasser Arafat is elected Chairman of the PLO
1970 Jordan's army defeats PLO guerrillas in a civil war. Yasser Arafat moves his operation to Beirut.
1973 Egypt and Syria attack Israel on Yom Kippur. Though taken by surprise, Israel rallies to repel the invasion.
1975 Civil war erupts in Lebanon.
1979 Peace treaty signed between Egypt and Israel.
1982 Israel invades Lebanon and drives the PLO into exile in Tunis.
1987 The first Palestinian uprising or intifada erupts in West Bank and Gaza.
1993 After secret negotiations between Israel and PLO, the Oslo Accords are signed in Washington. The agreement includes a plan to transfer Gaza, Jericho, and portions of the West

Bank to Palestinian control. This marks the end of the first intifada.

1995   Yitzhak Rabin, who signed the Oslo Accords with Yasser Arafat, is assassinated by an extremist religious Jew.

1996   Yasser Arafat elected president of Palestinian Authority.

2000   Camp David summit fails. Ariel Sharon visits the Temple Mount, igniting the Al-Aqsa Intifada.